D0213908

THE SOCIOLOGY OF ART

Also by the editors

David Inglis, *Culture and Everyday Life*
David Inglis and John Hughson, *Confronting Culture: Sociological Vistas*

The Sociology of Art
Ways of Seeing

Edited by David Inglis and John Hughson

© Selection, editorial matter and Introduction © David Inglis and John Hughson 2005;
Ch 1 © David Inglis 2005; Ch 2 © Jeremy F. Lane 2005; Ch 3 © Alexandra Howson 2005;
Ch 4 © Robert W. Witkin 2005; Ch 5 © Paul Willis 2005; Ch 6 © Janet Wolff 2005;
Ch 7 © David Inglis 2005; Ch 8 © Mike Hepworth 2005; Ch 9 © Andrew Tudor 2005;
Ch 10 © Alan Swingewood 2005; Ch 11 © David Inglis and Roland Robertson 2005;
Ch 12 © Helena Wulff 2005; Ch 13 © Janet Stewart 2005

All rights reserved. No reproduction, copy or transmission of this
publication may be made without written permission.

No paragraph of this publication may be reproduced, copied or transmitted
save with written permission or in accordance with the provisions of the
Copyright, Designs and Patents Act 1988, or under the terms of any licence
permitting limited copying issued by the Copyright Licensing Agency,
90 Tottenham Court Road, London W1T 4LP.

Any person who does any unauthorised act in relation to this publication
may be liable to criminal prosecution and civil claims for damages.

The authors have asserted their rights to be identified
as the authors of this work in accordance with the Copyright,
Designs and Patents Act 1988.

First published 2005 by
PALGRAVE MACMILLAN
Houndmills, Basingstoke, Hampshire RG21 6XS and
175 Fifth Avenue, New York, N.Y. 10010
Companies and representatives throughout the world

PALGRAVE MACMILLAN is the global academic imprint of the Palgrave
Macmillan division of St. Martin's Press, LLC and of Palgrave Macmillan Ltd.
Macmillan® is a registered trademark in the United States, United Kingdom
and other countries. Palgrave is a registered trademark in the European
Union and other countries.

ISBN-13: 978-0-333-96266-4 hardback
ISBN-10: 0-333-96266-4 hardback
ISBN-13: 978-0-333-96267-1 paperback
ISBN-10: 0-333-96267-2 paperback

This book is printed on paper suitable for recycling and made from fully
managed and sustained forest sources.

A catalogue record for this book is available from the British Library.

Library of Congress Cataloging-in-Publication Data
The sociology of art : ways of seeing / edited by David Inglis and John Hughson.
        p.   cm.
    Includes bibliographical references and index.
    ISBN 0-333-96266-4 — ISBN 0-333-96267-2 (pbk.)
    1. Arts and society.   I. Inglis, David.   II. Hughson, John, 1958–
NX180.S6S618 2005
    306.4′7—dc22   2005051275

10   9   8   7   6   5   4   3   2   1
14   13   12   11   10   09   08   07   06   05

Printed in China

Ars non gratia artis?

Contents

List of Figures

Acknowledgements

The editors would like to thank colleagues at the Universities of Aberdeen, Durham and Wolverhampton for their help in putting this book together.

Very sincere thanks are due to Catherine Gray and Sheree Keep at Palgrave for their help and support during the extended birth process of this book.

Many many thanks are also due to the contributors, who not only kindly agreed to our requests to write pieces for us, but who also treated with great patience the extended production process of the present text. Your forbearance has been gratefully appreciated.

We gratefully acknowledge the permission of the editors of the journal *In[]visible Culture: An Electronic Journal for Visual Studies* to reproduce Janet Wolff's chapter, which first appeared as 'Cultural Studies and the Sociology of Culture', in Issue Number 1, Winter 1998.

Notes on Contributors

Mike Hepworth is Reader Emeritus in Sociology, University of Aberdeen. His publications in the sociology of ageing and the sociology of culture include *Surviving Middle Age* (Blackwell, 1982, with Mike Featherstone), *Confession: Studies in Deviance and Religion* (Routledge, 1982, with Bryan S. Turner) and *Stories of Ageing* (Open University Press, 2000).

Alexandra Howson has lectured at the Universities of Edinburgh, Aberdeen and Abertay, Dundee, and is currently a Visiting Fellow in Women's Studies, University of California, Berkeley. Her publications in the sociology of the body, the sociology of culture, the sociology of health and illness, and feminist theory include *The Body in Society: An Introduction* (Polity, 2003) and *Embodying Gender* (Sage, 2005).

John Hughson is Senior Lecturer in Sports Studies, University of Otago. His publications in the sociology of culture, art, leisure and sport include *Confronting Culture: Sociological Vistas* (Polity, 2003, with David Inglis) and *The Uses of Sport: A Critical Study* (Routledge, 2004, with David Inglis and Marcus Free).

David Inglis is Senior Lecturer in Sociology, University of Aberdeen. His publications in social theory and the sociology of art and culture include *Confronting Culture: Sociological Vistas* (Polity, 2003, with John Hughson), *Culture and Everyday Life* (Routledge, 2005) and *Globalization and Social Theory* (Open University Press, 2005, with Roland Robertson).

Jeremy F. Lane is Lecturer in French, University of Nottingham. His publications in the areas of contemporary French social theory, and post-war French society, culture and politics, include *Pierre Bourdieu: A Critical Introduction* (Pluto, 2000) and 'The French Contribution to Contemporary Cultural Analysis', in W. Kidd and S. Reynolds (eds) *Contemporary French Cultural Studies* (Arnold, 2000).

Roland Robertson is Professor of Sociology, University of Aberdeen. His many publications in social theory, the sociology of religion, the sociology of culture and the study of globalization and global social change, include *Talcott Parsons: Theorist of Modernity* (Sage, 1991, edited with Bryan S. Turner) *Globalization: Social Theory and Global Culture* (Sage, 1992), *Global Modernities* (Sage, 1995, edited with Mike Featherstone and Scott Lash), *Globalization: Critical Concepts in Sociology* (Routledge, 2002, edited with Kathleen White), and *Globalization and Social Theory* (Open University Press, 2005, with David Inglis).

Janet Stewart is Lecturer in German, University of Aberdeen. Her publications in the sociology and philosophy of space, architecture and communication, with a particular geographic focus on Berlin and Vienna, include *Fashioning Vienna: Adolf Loos's Cultural Criticism* (Routledge, 2000) and *Blueprints for No-Man's Land: Connections in Contemporary Austrian Culture* (Peter Lang, 2004, edited with Simon Ward).

Alan Swingewood is retired from Sociology, London School of Economics. His publications in social theory and the sociology of art and culture include *The Myth of Mass Culture* (Macmillan, 1977), *A Short History of Sociological Thought* (Macmillan, 1984), *Sociological Poetics and Aesthetic Theory* (Macmillan, 1986), and *Cultural Theory and the Problem of Modernity* (Palgrave, 1998).

Andrew Tudor is Professor of Sociology, University of York. His publications in social theory, the sociology of culture and the sociology of cinema include *Beyond Empiricism: Philosophy of Science in Sociology* (Routledge, 1982), *Monsters and Mad Scientists: Cultural History of the Horror Movie* (Blackwell, 1989) and *Decoding Culture: Theory and Method in Cultural Studies* (Sage, 1999).

Paul Willis is Professor of Social/Cultural Ethnography, Keele University. His publications focus mainly but not exclusively on the ethnographic study of lived cultural forms, 'informal cultural production' and the construction of cultural worlds 'from below'. His books include *Learning to Labour* (Gower, 1977, reprinted several times), *Profane Culture* (Routledge, 1978), *Common Culture* (Open University Press, 1990, with S. Jones, J. Canaan and G. Hurd), *The Ethnographic Imagination* (Polity, 2000) and *Learning to Labour in New Times* (Routledge, 2004, edited with Nadine Dolby & Greg Dimitriadis).

Robert W. Witkin is Professor of Sociology, University of Exeter. His publications in the sociology of art and aesthetics include *The Intelligence of Feeling* (Heinemann Educational Books, 1974), *Art and Social Structure* (Polity, 1995), *Adorno on Music* (Routledge, 1998) and *Adorno on Popular Culture* (Routledge, 2002).

Janet Wolff is Associate Dean for Academic Affairs in the School of the Arts, Columbia University. Among her many publications in the sociology of art and culture are *Hermeneutic Philosophy and the Sociology of Art* (Routledge, 1975), *The Social Production of Art* (Macmillan, 1981, repr. 1993), *Feminine Sentences* (Polity, 1990), *The Culture of Capital: Art, Power and the Nineteenth Century Middle Class* (Manchester University Press, 1990, edited with John Seed), *Aesthetics and the Sociology of Art* (Macmillan, 1993), *Feminine Sentences* (Polity, 1990), *Resident Alien: Feminist Cultural Criticism* (Polity, 1995), *AngloModern: Painting and Modernity in Britain and the United States* (Cornell University Press, 2003).

Helena Wulff is Associate Professor of Social Anthropology, University of Stockholm. Her publications include *Twenty Girls: Growing Up, Ethnicity and Excitement in a South London Microculture* (Almqvist & Wiksell International, 1988), *Youth Cultures: A Cross-Cultural Perspective* (Routledge, 1995, edited with Vered Amit-Talai), *Ballet across Borders: Career and Culture in the World of Dancers* (Berg, 1998), and *New Technologies at Work: People, Screens and Social Virtuality* (Berg, 2003, edited with Christina Garsten).

Introduction: 'Art' and Sociology

David Inglis and John Hughson

What does the word 'art' mean to you? Does it conjure up images of paintings and sculptures in galleries, or orchestras playing Beethoven and Mozart? Does it express works by great geniuses or pretentious bores? Does it suggest to you pictures by John Constable and Claude Monet, or 'installations' by Tracey Emin and Damien Hirst? Does it make you think of enjoyable evenings out, or nights of interminable boredom? Does art excite you or turn you off? Do you prefer Schwarzenegger films to ballet performances, or Bridget Jones to Jane Austen? Does the word 'art' connote things you feel you could not live without, or things you have no interest in at all?

Your answers to those questions and others like them reveal a lot about you, not just about your personal tastes and dispositions, but also about your position in society. As we will see throughout this book, the ways in which each of us thinks about 'art' are expressive of some of the most important aspects of our social existence. Even those who have no interest in art, or actively dislike it, inadvertently reveal a lot about themselves when they make their opinions known.

In the same vein, a whole society's attitudes towards art can tell us a lot about that society. We can begin to get a handle on how a society 'works' if we consider the role played by art within it. Are the arts accorded important roles in a particular society, or do they operate merely at the sidelines? Do a wide variety of people in that society actively participate in making art or not? Are the audiences for particular arts drawn from a wide range of social backgrounds or do they come from particular groups? Are the arts open to all or are they the preserve of privileged elites? Answering questions like that allows us to get to grips with important aspects of the nature of a particular society as a whole. In other words, looking at art is an excellent way of looking at society.

By the same token, we can understand a lot about art by looking at society. To be more precise, we can come to understand art in more interesting and sophisticated ways than otherwise we might, if we consider the relations between art and society. This is the central contention of the sociological study of art. Its claim is to provide ways of thinking about art that other academic disciplines downplay or ignore altogether. By examining the social contexts in which art is produced by certain people (artists), managed by certain people (e.g. concert hall managers, art gallery owners), and engaged with by other people (audiences), we can begin to see what 'art' really is, how it functions in our society, and what implications it has for how we live.

Given this, the sociological study of art is emphatically *not* just a specialised academic exercise, which studies esoteric things that are of interest only to a special few. It is *not* just of interest to those people who are 'art lovers'. In fact, the sociology of art often has some uncomfortable lessons in store for people whose lives revolve around the arts, either by making a career out of them or by spending their leisure time in artistic pursuits. Instead, the sociology of art is for anyone who is curious about the society and culture in which they live. It gives us novel, and often provocative, insights into many aspects of the way we live. The implications of these insights stretch far beyond the specific world in which the arts are located, for they reveal important things about other aspects of society, such as politics and education.

The sociological study of art often produces analyses that are deeply controversial, and which upset received wisdoms and widely accepted ideas. Above all, the sociology of art comprises a series of challenges to commonsense notions, common both in the university, in the world of art, and in everyday life. As a result, the sociology of art should be seen not as a peripheral part of the discipline of sociology but as one of its key areas. Without a focus on the arts and how they operate in society, sociology's critical capacities would be impoverished indeed.

Key questions

Throughout this book, the central questions the sociology of art addresses will be apparent. These include:

- What is 'art'? What counts as 'art' and what does not? Who decides what is 'art' and what is not?
- In what ways are 'art' and 'society' related? How does the nature of society impact upon the nature of art? How does art influence social relations?
- In what ways are the arts and forms of social power connected?
- How are the arts dealt with in different types of society?
- How are artworks made? What is an 'artist'?
- How are artworks distributed to audiences?
- What are the ways in which audiences make sense of artworks?
- Why do some people like certain types of art and not others? What does a person's taste tell us about them?

The various contributions to this book illustrate the different sorts of answers that have been put forward by sociologists and others in their attempts to understand the social significance of art.

Structure and purposes

This book has both a dual structure and purpose. In terms of structure, it is split into two sections. The first section deals with the theoretical ideas that inform the sociology of art. The second shows how various theoretical positions in the sociology of art can be utilised to analyse particular artistic contexts. The chapters in this section comprise empirical case studies of particular forms of artistic practice.

In terms of the purposes of the book, it has two main aims. First, it seeks to introduce those with little or no prior knowledge of the sociology of art to the main themes, issues and problems developed and encountered by sociologists – and cognate others – when they deal with 'artistic' matters. In particular, Chapter 1 by David Inglis, provides an outline of the major parameters of sociological understandings of art, illustrating the various key theoretical orientations and empirical analyses that together make up the sociology of art's special take on its subject matter. He particularly emphasises the *critical* nature of the sociology of art, showing that important strands within it refuse to take at face value many of the ideas about art that are current in our society.

The second aim of the book is to consider both, where the sociological study of art stands in the present day, and where it might go in the future. In this regard, all the other chapters in this book, in both the 'theoretical' and 'empirical' sections, make contributions to answering the question 'where might the sociology of art go from here?' It would be rash to claim that this book, written by a specific collection of authors, has within its capacities fully to 'take the pulse' of the sociology of art in the present day, and thus to make confident prognoses as to its future on the basis of that diagnosis. Nonetheless, what we offer here are a set of suggestions – which we believe are both productive and profitable – as to some of the challenges the sociology of art faces today, some of the problems it has to overcome, and some of the ways out of its present difficulties. No pretence is made here at total comprehensiveness or utter exhaustiveness in identification, diagnosis or remedy; after all, another set of authors may have focussed upon a somewhat different set of problems and issues. Yet as editors we do feel that many of the issues raised by the contributors, and a number of their proposed ways of further developing the sociology of art, will chime with many readers of this book who know the field and who discern its various strengths and weaknesses. Taking all the chapters together, we believe the reader already cognisant of the issues at stake will find many fruitful avenues for further thought and reflection as to how the sociological study of art could be taken further in the years to come.

Ways of seeing

What, then, are the issues raised by the various contributors to this book as to the current and possible future states of the sociology of art? In this section, we will briefly delineate the key themes we feel that emerge from the contributions taken together as a whole. In the first place, it is striking the degree to which the work on the sociology of art by Pierre Bourdieu is central to a number of the chapters here. Despite the inevitable problems as to representativeness of the wider field any book like this encounters, this state of affairs may indeed reflect the important role the work of Bourdieu plays in the present day, both in the sociology of art and in the sociology of culture, more generally. In Chapter 2, Jeremy Lane provides a critical delineation of Bourdieu's analysis of the 'field of cultural production'. This chapter provides a notably lucid summary of Bourdieu's account of the social structuring of relations of artistic production.

Bourdieu's notion of the 'art world' as a 'field', structured around and by opposed forces of artistic orthodoxy and rebellion, has proven to be a very useful tool for many sociologists, for the purposes of thinking through the socially mediated nature of artistic endeavours. This is evidenced in the present context by its utilisation for the understanding of artistic forms and practices as diverse as 'art house' cinema (Andrew Tudor – Chapter 9), opera (Alan Swingewood – Chapter 10) and international ballet (Helena Wulff – Chapter 12). Each of these authors have used Bourdieu's notion of 'field' in somewhat different ways. Swingewood utilises it as means of developing a novel account of the genesis of opera as a distinct 'artistic' entity and enterprise, increasingly freed over time from the direct dictates of aristocratic governance. Tudor not only draws upon it to show how a distinctive sphere of 'art' cinema was erected in Britain throughout the twentieth century, but he also uses it to describe the dissolution and fall of this sphere under an array of forces such as the rise of home video. Tudor's use of the 'field' terminology is innovative, precisely insofar as both Bourdieu himself and those following him have tended to analyse the historical genesis of artistic fields, rather than their decline and disappearance. Wulff utilises Bourdieusian ideas to structure her ethnographic account of a number of major ballet companies, and the problems both management and performers must negotiate in a field increasingly dominated by the forces of advertising, marketing and corporate sponsorship. Her ethnographic approach reveals some of the subtleties and nuances of the field as it actually operates, important details that might be overlooked by less empirically attuned accounts of artistic fields.

As an aside here, we may remark that the sociology of art in the present day seems notably well-equipped to meet Bourdieu's general desiderata for sociology, that studies of particular subjects should be based around an arsenal of methods, rather than be mono-methodological in nature. Represented in this book are a wide array of ways in which sociologists can seek to grasp artistic matters, not just ethnography as advocated by Wulff (and also Paul Willis – Chapter 5), but also analysis of historical documents (Tudor), sociologically informed 'close readings' of particular texts (Swingewood, Mike Hepworth – Chapter 8) and the empirical analysis of the responses to specific texts by critics and lay audience members in specific socio-historical circumstances (Hepworth, Willis). The diversity of research methods available today to sociologists generally is a boon to the sociologist of art; the sheer range of ways in which one can investigate one's area of interest is surely a major feature of this particular set of approaches to artistic matters.

Whether the influence of Bourdieu (who sadly died in 2002) on the sociology of art will continue for a long time to come is a moot point. What we can say at this juncture is that while the benefits of a Bourdieu-inspired approach to matters of artistic production and consumption are amply attested by these chapters, it remains the case that there are certain problems thrown up by them too. In some senses, this may not be the fault of Bourdieu himself. As Janet Wolff (Chapter 6) notes, his work can be appropriated in a number of ways, even as a 'tool for empiricism' of a rather naïve sort. In Chapter 7, David Inglis suggests that the Bourdieusian attitude towards matters artistic, despite all its protestations of being constantly 'critical' of all fixed ideas, can itself threaten to turn into a dogma, one in which all the claims of those other than sociologists (other sorts of academic, practitioners in the artistic field, etc.) are derogated in favour of an all-encompassing 'sociological imperialism' in explanation and analysis. This paper argues for a Bourdieusian account of why this sort of orthodoxy has come to be so prominent in the sociology of art in the present day. Both Wolff and Inglis advocate in their own ways more reflexive awareness among sociologists of art as to the often tacit assumptions that underpin their attitudes and working practices. Given that sociologists are professionally trained to lay bare the discursive practices of others, it is unfortunate that they sometimes seem rather less keen to hold up to the light their own, often subterranean, notions and (using the word in Gadamer's sense) 'prejudices'.

This point takes us to another key issue raised by many of the contributions here, namely the sociology of art's relations – sometimes friendly, sometimes fraught – with other academic disciplines. In Chapter 7, Inglis argues that sociologists should not fall into the trap of having rather derogatory attitudes towards the apparently 'sociologically unenlightened', such as aestheticians and art historians. Both Hepworth and Swingewood go some way in their papers to outlining what sociologically inflected modes of aesthetic inquiry might look like, such that sociologists and aestheticians might work with, rather than against, each other. In Chapter 4, Robert Witkin not only sets out his highly stimulating theory of relations between social relations and modes of representation, he also indicates, in his drawing upon the work of the sociologically minded art historian Arnold Hauser – an unjustly neglected figure today in certain ways – that the divide between 'sociology' and (certain types of) 'art history' is both false and unproductive. Witkin's contribution also indicates how ambitious theorising about large-scale artistic–historical processes can – and indeed should – make a comeback after the waters of postmodernism, with its suspicion of 'grand narratives', have receded.

The often 'interesting' relations that pertain between sociology and the discipline of cultural studies are dealt with here in a number of ways. Janet Wolff argues that sociology could learn a number of valuable lessons from the latter, not least a more flexible approach to issues of subjectivity. In Chapter 3, in the context of discussing the relations between 'feminist art' and multidisciplinary 'feminist theory' (including feminist cultural studies), Alexandra Howson concurs with such sentiments, but adds that cultural studies also has much to learn from sociology. While postmodern and poststructuralist perspectives, within feminist theory and without, have provided valuable means of conceptualising certain issues of representation, she notes that they lack crucial 'sociological' dimensions. Howson argues for the development of a feminist sociology of art that is able to deal effectively with 'social' factors as well as issues of textual representation, a paradigm she argues is currently underdeveloped.

In a somewhat converse manner, Paul Willis develops a cultural studies critique of the sociology of art, arguing that it, paradoxically enough, remains too wedded to common sense views that 'aesthetic' matters are part of the isolated universe of the 'high arts' alone. Instead, Willis argues for a reorientation of the sociology of art's analytic dispositions, such that aesthetic phenomena are seen as part and parcel of the materials of everyday culture and thus as constitutive elements of the social process as a whole. This raises interesting methodological and epistemological issues of how to represent 'aesthetic' matters that are not institutionalized or open to easy scrutiny. The need for sociology to think through new modes of verbal – and other – forms of representation of particular subject matters is raised by Janet Stewart's strikingly original chapter. In the context of discussion of architectural forms in Berlin, Stewart not only poses some difficult questions as to the 'artistic' status of architecture, but also notes that since architectural discourse can draw on social theoretical ideas, and because the latter can also appropriate ways of thinking and representing from the former, a standard 'sociology of architecture' approach is insufficient to grasp such interplays of meaning and concepts; instead, a way of talking and writing must be developed which combines sociological thought and the conceptual and aesthetic dimensions of architectural discourse. Her paper raises a series of questions that will have to be addressed in other areas of substantive inquiry beyond that of the architectural.

Stewart's paper also touches upon a key thematic that has come to occupy centre stage in sociology, generally, in the last decade or so. This is the theme of globalisation, which in many ways is currently effecting a conceptual revolution in the discipline, moving analysis away from processes contained within nation states towards the comprehension of cross-border movements, activities and phenomena. Precisely because artistic developments in a 'world city' like Berlin can have global implications, so in the present day must the sociology of art seek to refine its conceptual and methodological tools such that 'globalizing' tendencies in artistic production, distribution and consumption be identified and held up to the light. This is a task that Helena Wulff's chapter on international ballet engages with from an ethnographic perspective. Likewise, in Chapter 11, Inglis and Robertson (the latter being one of the pioneers of the sociological and multi-disciplinary analysis of globalization) set out some theoretical and methodological precepts for the study of 'global' cultural forms, through a case study of the fascinating contemporary phenomenon of 'world music'. Controversies over what this phenomenon is, what it entails and how it should be interpreted, illustrate that developing the tools of a global sociology of art is not an easy accomplishment. But a lack of focus on the 'global' dimension in artistic and cultural affairs is something that the sociology of art cannot afford in the twenty-first century.

Overall, this book indicates that, among other things, globalization, reflexivity, the lasting (or otherwise) impact of Bourdieu, and continuing debates with other disciplinary perspectives, are issues of profound importance for the sociology of art at the start of a new century. We hope that this book gives the reader a good idea of what the sociological study of art involves, what issues are at stake in it, and why the questions sociology asks about art are relevant and important. We also hope to have shown how the sociology of art has developed, how it is flourishing in the present day, and how various new challenges – and new ways of dealing with them – are now opening up for it. By the end of the book, we hope that the reader will have come to see that without a sociological perspective, our understandings of art, society and ourselves would be much diminished.

Part I
Theory Past, Present and Future

Thinking 'Art' Sociologically

David Inglis

Introduction

The sociology of art encompasses many different themes and issues, from micro-level analyses, such as studies of how the people called 'artists' actually carry out their work, to macro-level considerations, such as thinking about the place of 'art' in the general structure of modern societies. Sociologists, and others who draw upon sociological ideas, have turned their attention to a great many issues connected with artistic matters.

In this chapter we will set out the main themes that have guided, and have arisen as a result of, these investigations. Like any other branch of sociology, the sociology of art is made up of different theoretical perspectives and empirical foci. Despite this, there is much broad agreement on many key issues amongst scholars of many different persuasions. This chapter does not pretend to provide totally comprehensive coverage of all aspects of the 'sociology of art'. Nonetheless, in what follows we will emphasise points of convergence between different scholars and different perspectives to illustrate the set of generally shared ideas that together make up the sociological analysis of art.

We will first look at how sociologists have gone beyond commonsense views of what 'art' is and what it means. We will then examine how sociologists have also carried out similar operations for the notion of 'artist'. After that we shall consider how 'art' and 'society' might be related to each other. Finally we will show how one might sociologically analyse how 'art worlds' operate and how they are related to wider social forces.

Taking issue with 'art'

One of the key ideas that sociology has contributed to the understanding of artistic matters is the notion that we should not take the word 'art' at face value and accept it uncritically. In the contemporary Western world the word 'art' is commonly taken to refer to a set of things that contains certain types of painting, sculptures, books, theatrical and musical performances and suchlike. In everyday commonsense understandings, certain objects are regarded as being clearly and identifiably 'artistic' in nature. The idea that a sonnet by Shakespeare, a painting by Van Gogh or a play by Goethe is indeed an artwork, almost goes without saying, so obviously 'artistic' in nature are such things. There is apparently an 'essence' of art, such that some things are clearly 'artistic' and others not.

Most forms of the sociology of art, however, break with such commonsense understandings of what is 'art' (Duvignaud, 1972: 23). Instead, sociologists argue that no object has intrinsically 'artistic' qualities. Instead, sociologists tend to see the 'artistic' nature of an 'artwork' not as an intrinsic and inalienable property of the object, but rather as a label put onto it by certain interested parties, members of social groups whose interests are augmented by the object being defined as 'art' (Becker, 1984). This labelling process might be quite unintentional and unconscious. Nonetheless, it is a central idea of most forms of sociology of art that the label 'art' is never neutral. Some social group always stands to gain in some way or another by a particular object being labelled as 'art', or conversely, another object being denied that label (Wolff, 1981: 40). In other words, the sociological view tends to see 'art' as always thoroughly bound up with *politics*, the latter term is meant in its widest sense, where it refers to conflicts and struggles between different social groups.

From this perspective, the things called 'artworks' are always part of the social world, even if some interested parties claim that they exist somehow 'above' and 'beyond' society in an elevated realm of their own. This is the root of sociology's opposition to the academic discipline of aesthetics (Bourdieu, 1992 [1979]). This branch of philosophy, sociology alleges, has classically seen artworks as existing only in and of themselves. But the ways in which aestheticians try to understand the 'pure' nature of 'art' is only made possible by ignoring to all intents and purposes the ways in which these 'artworks' are always embedded in social and political contexts. Without analysis of such contexts, sociologists claim, the analysis of art will remain far too idealised and abstract. One must always realise that something only counts as 'art' because a particular powerful person or group has defined it to be so.

If 'art' is a label put on certain things by certain people, where did this label come from? Sociologists stress that the term 'art' – and its sister terms 'artwork' and 'artist' – are *historical inventions*, that first appeared in the West several hundred years ago. Before that time, the term 'art' in the modern sense did not exist. Instead, people in the medieval world produced certain cultural items for use in particular ways. For example, religious icons were made in order to decorate churches and to give a sense of the presence of God (Williams, 1981: 96). It is only at a much later date, primarily from the nineteenth century onwards, that such icons are redefined as 'art' by groups of people who have an interest in classifying them in that way – groups such as museum curators and art historians. From a sociological perspective, when such groups label medieval religious artifacts as 'art'; they unwittingly are reinterpreting the past in the light of their own interests. It is in the interests of such groups, who act as the professional custodians of 'art', to appropriate the past and claim professional expertise and control over it. But in so doing, they take the specifically modern notion of 'art' and anachronistically apply it to ages when such an idea did not exist.

The same issue applies when we realise that the idea of 'art' is not just a *modern* invention but a *Western* invention too. Societies outside the West do not possess the modern Western categories 'art', 'artist' and 'artistic', and thus, strictly speaking, do not have 'art' at all (Shiner, 2001). Only modern Western societies have 'art', because only this type of society operates with the very category 'art' itself. When today cultural objects from a non-Western society, such as drawings by Australian Aboriginals or the headdresses of Native Americans, are displayed in Western museums as 'art', these objects have undergone a systematic reinterpretation as to their value and function from the way they were understood in their original social context. Whilst originally such objects would have been seen by the people that made and used them to have religious or ceremonial significance, once the Western label 'art' has been put on them in the context of a museum, they lose their initial cultural meanings and are redefined in Eurocentric ways. This shows that what appears in museums of 'art', and the ways in which they are displayed and represented are never, and can never, be neutral (Meyer, 1979; Price, 1989; Dubin, 1999).

It has often been remarked that the term 'art' does not exist on its own but exists along with terms that are its opposites. Since the time of the Romantics the categories 'popular culture' and 'mass culture' have fulfilled the role of being 'art's' opposites (Gans, 1974). Whilst 'art' connotes things that are thoughtfully made and which resist easy understanding, these other categories connote quite the opposite, indicating things that are shallow, easily compre-hended and made without thought through means of factory-like mass production. One can find literally hundreds of authors who over the last century and a half have argued that 'art' is superior to 'popular culture', their writings being reflective of wider public attitudes as to the exalted position of 'art' over other cultural forms. We will cite one particularly famous example of this sort of writing. In an article of 1939, the American art critic Clement Greenberg (1986 [1939]) divided the world of cultural objects up into two categories, both of which were seen to be 'objective' and indisputable classifi-cations. On the one side was 'avant-garde art' which was made by individuals possessed of vision and thoughtfulness; such art could be comprehended only by those who made the necessary intellectual efforts to do so. On the other side there was 'kitsch', a term which for Greenberg describes the world of mass culture – of comic strips, Hollywood movies and lurid newspapers and novels. For Greenberg 'kitsch is mechanical and operates by formulas. Kitsch is vicarious experience and faked sensations. Kitsch changes according to style, but remains always the same. Kitsch is the epitome of all that is spurious in the life of our times' (Greenberg, 1986 [1939]: 12). For Greenberg and for many other intellectuals of his period and later, there was no question that 'art' (in this case, of an avant-garde form like abstract expressionism in painting) was just 'naturally' superior to all other forms of culture.

Sociologists are deeply sceptical of claims abut the 'naturalness' of anything, especially categories used to rank cultural forms on a scale from 'high' to 'low'. For sociologists, *all* categories and ways of classifying things are social fabrications, reflective or expressive of the social conditions of a particular society or a specific social group within it (Durkheim and Mauss, 1969 [1903]). No classification or selection of what is 'art' or 'popular culture', 'good' or 'bad', 'refined' or 'crude' and so on, is 'neutral' or 'objective'. Someone might claim that a particular piece was 'good art', but someone else might have a quite different opinion if he or she was a member of another social group and was using other ways of classifying things. For sociologists, what counts at any one time as 'art' in general, let alone as 'good' art, is historically contingent, and rooted in the life conditions of the group to which the people making the classifications belong. As the sociologist of knowledge Karl Mannheim (1985 [1936]: 22) put it, 'every concept...every concrete meaning...[contains] a crystallization of the experiences of a certain group'. Thus definitions of what is 'art' and what is not are thoroughly bound up in processes of struggle and conflict between different social groups, with each group more or less unintentionally trying to define cultural reality in such a way as to suit its best interests. When a person defines a particular object as 'great art', to the sociological eye this tells 'us' less abut the 'artwork' itself and more about the tastes and preferences of the social group that person hails from. From this perspective, when authors like Greenberg assert the superiority of certain types of culture over others, they are failing to realise that their judgments are not 'objective' but are in fact expressive of the tastes of a particular social group, in this case a highly educated intellectual elite (Gans, 1978 [1966]). In this way, these authors are guilty not only of a certain type of cultural snobbery, but also of naïveté and a lack of self-reflection.

It is not just that the ideas as to 'art' particular people have are expressive of the preferences of the group to which they belong. According to many sociologists, especially those influenced by Marxist ideas, the *dominant* ideas about 'art' in a particular society will be expressive of the preferences of the dominant social groups in that society. Mannheim (1956: 184) argues that in societies where 'the political and social order basically rests upon the distinction between "higher" and "lower" human types, an analogous distinction is also made between "higher" and "lower" objects of knowledge or aesthetic enjoyment'. In other words, where there is a class division between rulers and ruled, 'upper classes' and 'lower classes', culture will be divided upon those lines. There will be a culture of the ruling classes that is defined as 'high', and a culture of the lower classes that will be defined as 'low'. The value of a particular object (like a work of 'art') involves how it is perceived by members of a given society, and in turn this perception is determined by the characteristics of who produces or possesses the object. Thus cultural objects produced or used by lower class persons will be perceived by society at large as having relatively little value. But those cultural objects produced or used by higher class persons will have relatively high value attached to them. Quite simply, then, views dominant in a particular society as to what things are 'artistic' and what things are not will be closely connected to the tastes and preferences of dominant social groups. These dominant groups could be classes or they could take some other form, such as ethnic groups. Some Afro-American intellectuals allege that the 'canon' of 'great works' of literature (Jane Austen, Joseph Conrad, Henry James, etc.) taught until recently without question in American schools and universities is a Eurocentric fabrication, rather than a neutral reflection of what constitutes important literature (Corse and Griffin, 1997). White people (or rather, white intellectual elites) have defined their own culture as 'superior' when in fact other cultural forms, such as writing by black authors, could be quite as worthy of interest and study. Because classifications of what counts as 'art' are never immutably fixed, certain cultural forms such as cinema, jazz and photography, can be at one point in time regarded as 'popular culture', and at other times (certain elements of them) can be defined as 'art' or something approaching it (Peterson, 1972; Christopherson, 1974; Lopes, 2002). Once again, a sociological perspective stresses that 'art' is always part of wider social life, and cannot be treated as if it were a realm wholly cut off from all sorts of social influences, both manifest and latent.

Not only the reputation of a particular 'artwork' or a specific cultural genre but also the standing of a particular artist, shifts over time. The 'share price' of an artist can be very low at one point in time and very high at another, these shifts resulting from struggles between different social groups, each seeking to label their own preferred forms of 'art' as being superior to the forms preferred by others (Lang and Lang, 1988). A historically informed sociological approach tends to suggest that the 'canon' of 'great works of art' is a social fabrication, dependent on what particular people – especially powerful people – at a particular time think is 'great art', rather than merely being a reflection of works that are intrinsically 'great'. One way in which a particular 'artist' can be given 'everlasting fame' – at least for a time – is for him or her to be defined as a 'classic' by those who construct school and university curricula. In this way, the artist is defined as someone whose works are worth attending to, even hundreds of years after their death. But from a sociological perspective, given other circumstances, they might never have been defined in that way at all, and another otherwise neglected or forgotten figure would have taken their place. Shakespeare might in the present day have been totally forgotten if his works had not had people over the last few centuries evangelising on his behalf, attesting to his 'greatness' and defining his plays as 'crucial' cultural forms that must appear on the curricula taken by schoolchildren and university students.

Taking issue with the 'artist'

Just as 'art' is a modern, Western label put by certain individuals or social groups onto certain objects, so too is the term 'artist' a label that can be conferred – or not – on certain people. To be labelled as an artist brings, in our society, certain advantages with it, such as a certain type of power, status and, possibly, wealth. Thus there is a lot to be gained, and a lot to be lost, depending on whether a person gets defined as an 'artist' and whether a large number of people accept the label.

Sociologists argue that it is not appropriate to generalise the idea of the 'artist' – a single person engaged in creative activity towards making a particular 'artistic' artefact – to all societies. This is because this idea of an isolated individual artist is a fairly recent Western notion that first appears in the early modern period (Williams, 1981: 112). Before this period in the West, and in other societies at all times, there has been no corresponding category. This is because such creative work has often been done in groups rather than by individuals, so the individualism of the modern Western notion of 'artist' means the term could not be applied directly to other societies or the pre-modern West. The idea of the artist as 'genius' is an invention of the Renaissance and early modern periods (Wolff, 1981: 27; DeNora, 1995). The hot-headed, temperamental artist begins to become a cultural type in the late eighteenth century; for example, one of the earliest dramatisations of such a figure is contained in Goethe's (1985 [1790]) play *Torquato Tasso*, dating from 1790.

The early modern period also witnessed the splitting of the ideas of 'artisan', which came to mean a skilled manual worker, and 'artist', which takes on the meaning of a highly gifted, idiosyncratic person possessed of a singular 'artistic' vision (Gimpel, 1969: 5). The stereotypical image of the 'artist' as a lonely and isolated figure, set against the constrictions of polite society, is an invention of the nineteenth century (Wolff, 1981: 11). Why did such a view of the artist come to prominence at this time? First, such a view was in part a function of the self-understanding of artists of the period, who developed a way of representing themselves in a more glamorous – and indeed rather self-serving – way than hitherto was possible. Second, it was also a representation of the 'artist's' new and more precarious position in the division of labour. As the institution of patronage, where the artist was directly commissioned by a buyer to produce a particular piece, went into decline, artists were compelled to produce works for an art market in which their wares might or might not be bought (Zolberg, 1983). The view of the lonely artist is thus connected to the relatively insecure conditions of employment faced by many artists from the early nineteenth century onwards. Third, the idea of the 'artist' as a unique individual 'genius' was also developed by the broad group of early nineteenth-century thinkers called the Romantics, who sought to protest against what they saw as the increasingly dreary and prosaic nature of life in a burgeoning industrial capitalist society based around the search for profits rather than morals or values (Hauser, 1982: 14). Romantic thinkers set up the new figure of the 'artistic genius' as the hero who would struggle against this dehumanising society (Weiskel, 1976; Berlin, 2000). The Romantics are also responsible in large part for developing the idea of 'Art' with a capital 'A', that is, as a special, almost holy realm, that stands outside and above of ordinary society because of its great spirituality and moral transcendence. This type of Art was seen to be made only by Artists, unique and highly gifted, if not to say deeply neurotic and uncontrollable, persons (DeNora, 1995). The activity of such people, due to its completely unique characteristics, was not and could not be 'compared to the humdrum production of ordinary objects' (Coser, 1978: 225). On this view, the artist is a great individual wholly unlike, and superior to, the common herd, and his products – Art – are seen to be unique individual expressions of his temperament and personality.

We can see from these views that in many ways 'Art' had come to function as a substitute for religion in a society that was becoming in certain ways ever more secular, for Art was seen to be almost 'holy' in nature and 'above' ordinary social considerations. In certain ways, 'Art' came increasingly to replace God, at least among the upper classes, and especially the intelligentsia, as the repository of moral values that were seen to be higher than the mere pursuit of money (Horkheimer, 1972). Likewise, the artist replaced religious figures such as prophets as the figure whom one should venerate because of his privileged insights into 'spiritual' and extra-mundane matters.

These views, which developed particularly from the early nineteenth century in large part still inform contemporary understandings of art and artists. The sociology of art seeks to challenge the hold these views have on contemporary understandings of 'art', arguing that we cannot remain beholden to the ideas of the Romantics and their predecessors because their ideas are in some ways mystificatory and have the effect of hiding some of the ways in which what we call 'art' is made, distributed and consumed. Sociologists therefore are interested in demystifying the idea of 'artist'. For example, the notion of 'genius' is seen more as a label attached to particular persons by other people, than an indication of any intrinsic mental or intellectual qualities they may possess (Becker, 1978). Seeing the issue of artistic talent in this way helps explain why in the course of Western history there have been so few 'great' women artists. This is not because women are any less talented than men. It is in part because women were not given the same opportunities to express their creative capacities as men were. It is also because the people labelling certain cultural producers as 'geniuses' tended themselves to be men, and the idea of genius was defined to be a masculine quality. Moreover, the kinds of cultural production that pre-twentieth-century women were channeled into, such as needlework, were not defined as worthy of the honorific title 'art'. In these various ways, a patriarchal bias can be revealed in ideas about 'great artists' (Nochlin, 1973; Martindale, 1978; Parker and Pollock, 1981; Sydie, 1989; Tuchman, 1989; Battersby, 1994).

Another way of challenging the Romantic notion of 'artist' is to emphasise the fact that no 'artist' ever makes their 'art' wholly on their own. They are reliant, directly or indirectly, on a whole series of other people in order to do what they are doing, whether painting a picture or even writing a poem. In other words, we should get away from the myth of the unique and singular 'artist' to examine how particular people who have been labelled as 'artists' are 'artistically' educated and trained (at institutions called 'art schools'), how they seek to make their livings (e.g. by seeking to get their works published or displayed for sale), and how even in their most 'private' and 'creative' moments they are reliant in one way or another on other people and are enmeshed in a whole series of social relationships. For example, Norbert Elias's (1993) study of Mozart stresses the intricate social networks of power and influence that the composer was wrapped up in, such that he often had to produce music that was pleasing to the people who had commissioned music from him, rather than composing what he himself wanted. Seeing the 'artist's' position within complex social networks need not just stress the limitations placed on artists, but can also identify the enabling aspects of the social relationships artists find themselves within. This entails examining how a particular 'artist' is involved within a particular *division of cultural labour*. Becker (1974: 767) puts this point in this way:

> Think, with respect to any work of art, of all the activities that must be carried on for that work to appear as it finally does. For a symphony orchestra to give a concert, for instance, instruments must have been invented, manufactured and maintained, a notation must have been devised and music composed using that notation, people must have learned to play the notated notes on the instruments, times and places for rehearsal must have been provided, ads for the concert must have been placed, publicity arranged and tickets sold.

The effect of this sociological 'de-centring' of the 'artist' is to show that 'art' is always collectively rather than individually produced. Even the poet toiling away in isolation is dependent on many other people, each carrying out their own particular roles in a cultural division of labour, such as his or teachers who initially nurtured his or her talent, and those who distribute it such that other people can have access to it.

According to many sociologists, the study of what our society calls 'art' can only really progress if we ditch the highly specific and ideologically loaded terminology of 'art', 'artworks' and 'artists', and replace these with the more neutral and less historically specific terms 'cultural forms', 'cultural products' and 'cultural producers' (Williams, 1977: 138; Wolff, 1981: 138; Bourdieu, 1993a). These cultural products – be they paintings, sculptures, forms of music or whatever – should be regarded as being made by certain types of cultural producer, and as being used by particular groups of people in particular ways in specific social contexts. By using the more neutral term 'cultural products' for particular objects, and 'cultural producers' for the people who make those objects, the sociologist seeks to break with a view that she/he sees as having dominated the study of cultural forms for too long, namely trying to understand everything in terms of the category 'art'. This is a category that is too limited and context-specific to encompass all the different cultural products that people in different societies make and use. It is a term that is also too loaded to take at face value and to use naively in study of our own society. Since it is in the interests of certain social groups to define some things as 'art' and others as not, the very term 'art' itself cannot be uncritically used by the sociologist who wishes to understand how and why such labelling processes occur. Quite simply, then, in order to study cultural matters, many sociologists believe one has to reject the terms 'art', 'artwork' and 'artist' as the basis for our analysis. Instead, these terms become important *objects* of analysis themselves.

'Art' and 'society'

At the most basic level, the sociological study of art involves examining the relations between 'art' on the one hand and 'society' on the other, although this is a very simplified description of what the sociology of art seeks to do (Clark, 1970). More specifically, sociology poses the question: in what ways do social relations and institutions impact upon the creation, distribution and appreciation of artworks? In this section we will look at ways in which we might tease out the relations between the creation of 'artworks' and 'society' (social relations, structures and institutions).

Seeing art 'in its social context' has a long pedigree in studies of art, by both sociologists proper, the 'proto-sociologists' who lived before an identifiable discipline called 'sociology' appeared in the later nineteenth century, and certain types of art historian. If we look at the history of endeavours of this sort, we see that the earliest attempts to relate the creation of 'artworks' to social factors actually related artworks to the *cultural*, rather than explicitly *social*, contexts in which they were produced. Perhaps the very first proto-sociologist of art was the early eighteenth-century Neapolitan scholar Giambattista Vico. In Vico's view, every particular culture has its own *style*, a particular unifying principle, such that all of the parts of the culture, no matter how apparently diverse – its language, religious beliefs, everyday habits and its art – are all informed by the same underlying ideas and attitudes (Berlin, 1976: xvii). For Vico, therefore, the culture is like the 'soul' of the society, its animating spirit, and the art of a society is highly expressive of that soul. From this perspective it is possible to see artistic production more as the expression of the mores and attitudes of the group than of the personal dispositions of the individual maker. The actual person (or persons) who makes the artefact can be seen more as manifesting the mentality of the group in their productions, rather than expressing any kind of 'individual' vision. This is how Vico understood the particular case of the ancient Greek poet Homer. Vico alleged there was actually no such person as 'Homer' at all. The tales associated with that name were the anonymous productions of the oral culture of the early Greeks, produced by many different minstrels and troubadours over a long period of time. Since the 'Greek peoples were themselves Homer', literary works that were seemingly the products of a single 'genius' were in fact artefacts expressive of the folk culture of the time (Vico, 1999 [1744]: 382).

Ideas of this type were subsequently taken up by thinkers in both France and Germany. In the former, figures such as Madame de Stael (1803) carried out studies of literature and the influences upon it of such factors as the religion, legal system and customs of particular cultures. Later in the nineteenth century, Hippolyte Taine, often acknowledged as the foundational figure in the modern sociology of literature, attempted to study the literary artwork not as the 'mere individual play of imagination, the isolated caprice of an excited brain, but a transcript of contemporary manners, a manifestation of a certain kind of mind' (Laurenson and Swingewood, 1972: 32). The same sort of approach to artworks was also influential in Germany. The philosopher J.G. Herder (1800), one of the foundational figures in the Romantic movement mentioned earlier, developed the theme of culturally contextualising art by attempting to explain why certain forms of art flourish in particular cultural contexts but not in others. In a similar vein and at around the same time, G.W.F. Hegel (1975a,b) provided an analysis of how the 'spirit' of a given culture, especially its ideas of what values are the most noble and praiseworthy, expresses itself most fully and comprehensively in the artworks produced in that culture.

This type of Hegelian analysis has had certain twentieth-century followers in sociology. For example, the work of the sociologist of literature Leo Lowenthal (1957) analyses the development of plays and novels from the sixteenth century onwards, as expressions of the most profound aspirations towards human freedom characteristic of particular periods within European modernity. On this view, works by figures such as Shakespeare or Cervantes contain privileged insights into how people in a particular time and place understood themselves and the world in which they lived (Lowenthal, 1961: xii). One of the founders of modern sociology, namely Max Weber, also sought to locate particular 'artworks' in wider cultural contexts. On Weber's (1958) account of the development of styles of music in the West, he argues that Western music developed in much more rational forms than the music of other civilizations, and is thus reflective of the particularly pronounced rationalistic nature of Western culture. From the Middle Ages onwards, Western music involved a 12-tone scale, unlike in places such as India and China which had a different set of scales and chords. Western composers developed their music on the basis of rational experimentation with the permutations possible within the 12-tone scale. As a result, Western music developed in ways that derived logically from the initial scale patterns. In addition, Weber notes that the 'orchestra' is a cultural phenomenon unique to the modern West. Its characteristics are a somewhat 'bureaucratic' and rational organization of the different sections (wind, strings, etc.). The ways of composing for this type of musical organisation are inevitably more about rule-following and procedures for attaining harmony than are other types of music-making. Weber argues that the rationalization of Western music is an expression and symptom of rationalization processes that were part of the creation of modern Western culture more generally. The 'rational' character of Western art, at least in its musical forms, is expressive of a wider, pervasive culture of high degrees of rationality characteristic of the West (Feher, 1987).

Ways of approaching art that insist on locating it in its cultural context were not just influential in later sociology, but also in particular sectors of the discipline of art history, illustrating the fact that certain forms of thinking in both disciplines have much in common with each other. An important strain of art historical research in German-speaking countries developed out of Hegel's version of the need to see art in cultural context. Heinrich Wolfflin was concerned to develop an 'art history without names', that is, to see the works of particular artists as the expression of stylistic patterns that were themselves products of wider cultural forces (Hauser, 1985 [1958]: 120, 124). Later exponents of this style of art history, which comes close to sociological concerns about art and artists, include such twentieth-century figures as Erwin Panofsky and Arnold Hauser (1991). Echoing Vico's ideas on Homer, Panofsky (1951) argued that the anonymous artisans who designed and constructed the Gothic cathedrals of the European middle ages operated inside an overall cultural mentality that was expressed both in architecture and in scholastic philosophy. The very structural form of the cathedrals mirrored the configurative principles of scholastic thought, the dominant intellectual paradigm of medieval Europe, where each part of an argument is logically deducible from the previous part. In this way Panofsky asserted that architecture as a form of 'artistic' practice was wholly bound up with the patterns of thought dominant in wider medieval European culture. Once again, artworks were seen in a contextualising way as expressions of wider cultural forms.

A classic modern example of this sort of thinking is Ian Watt's (1985 [1957]) study of early eighteenth-century English novels by figures such as Defoe and Richardson. Watt traces the nature of the novel form to changes in wider social and cultural life of the period. For example, earlier authors such as Aphra Behn had named their characters in archetypal ways – e.g. Mr Badman – to demonstrate explicitly the qualities of that person. But an increasing sense of individualism and an increasing awareness of the unique nature of every person that was developing in the wider culture of early eighteenth-century England, was reflected in the new breed of novelists naming their characters 'in such a way as to suggest that they were to be regarded as particular individuals in the contemporary social environment' (ibid.: 20). Moreover, Watt sees the novel's new emphasis on past actions being seen to cause present ones as reflective of innovations in natural science, which pioneered new and more minute descriptions of causation in nature (ibid.: 26). The ways in which the story is told, and the form in which it is presented, are therefore seen as being made possible by wider cultural changes.

Clearly it makes good sense to understand artworks in relation to the culture in which they were made. But one of the problems with analysing artworks in this matter is that the term 'culture' is very vague. In addition, claiming that wider cultural factors are 'reflected' in the form or content of certain artworks does not show precisely by what means this happened; it is as if the surrounding 'culture' always and automatically somehow makes its presence felt in the artwork (Barbu, 1970). On this sort of view, the artist is merely a kind of 'midwife', giving voice to the cultural trends of the time. Thus the key problem with these sorts of analysis is that they tend to see a direct and unmediated connection between the wider cultural context out of which artworks have 'sprung', and the artefacts themselves.

Another important way of thinking about the relation of the creation of 'artworks' and wider 'society' comes from the Marxist tradition. Marxian analysis replaces the rather vague focus on 'culture' described above, with the more precise claim that artworks are both produced within, and expressive of, the 'material conditions' of a society at a given period in time. By 'material conditions', Marx primarily meant the social relationships that govern the economic realm of a given society. For Marx (1977 [1859]: 21), it is the socio-economic 'base' of a society which shapes the nature of that society's 'cultural superstructure'. The latter is in part comprised of *dominant ideologies* which disguise the nature of the power held by dominant, elite groups by representing the social order as operating in the interests of all groups in that society. This outlook encouraged Marxist analysts to see artworks as thoroughly 'ideological' in nature. What artworks do is embody the ideologies dominant in a given society at a certain period in time. These ideologies are the products of the thinking of particular social classes. For example, Lucien Goldmann's (1964) famous study of the plays of Racine sought to show that the playwright's works embodied the tragic vision of life held by the *noblesse de robe*, a fraction of the French aristocracy whose power was in decline at the period in the seventeenth century when Racine wrote.

The Marxist analysis of 'material factors' effecting the nature of artistic production brings with it its own problems. Can artworks really be seen just as automatic expressions of socio-economic relations? After all, this would be to ignore how actual artists go about their labours, making them seem as if they are mere mouthpieces for particular ideologies (Williams, 1977: 97). The specificities and subtleties of particular works of art are lost in what is now generally accepted as too crude a form of Marxist analysis. This way of thinking also ignores the possibility that the world of art exists in ways that are in some senses 'autonomous' of, or at least not directly determined by, socio-economic relations. Most twentieth-century thinkers operating within the Marxist tradition have rejected the idea that artworks are direct expressions of the 'economic base' of a society or of 'dominant ideologies' in the 'cultural superstructure'. Instead, they have sought to find ways of identifying the relatively *indirect* and *mediated* relations between 'material', 'ideological' and 'artistic' factors.

One of the most influential thinkers in this direction was the Hungarian philosopher and art analyst Gyorgy Lukacs. For Lukacs (1971 [1923]) the economic 'base' does not directly produce the 'cultural superstructure'. Instead, there is a series of complex relations between each part of a society, which is regarded as a totality. Lukacs used the term 'mediation' to refer to this state of affairs. Each element of a given society should be seen as part of the whole of that society, that is the *social totality*. It is the totality that shapes the nature of each of its constituent parts. Therefore each part is not directly shaped by another part, but by the nature of the totality. Consequently, 'culture' is not directly shaped by the 'base', but by the particular arrangement of other parts of the totality, such as the economic and political systems. They in turn are indirectly effected by the nature of 'culture'. In other words, there is a series of *mediations* – indirect relationships – between each part, rather than direct cause-and-effect relations between them. To understand artworks and how they are made, therefore, we must situate their production as one element in a particular social totality, and examine the relations that pertain between the various spheres such as politics, the economy, the education system and the sphere of 'artistic' production. What people situated in the latter sphere do at a particular time is dependent on the nature of the overall social totality. As another major Marxist theorist, Theodor Adorno (1967: 30), put it, instead of trying to locate particular 'artworks' as being expressive of particular 'material conditions' or 'ideologies', instead one must 'decipher the general social tendencies which are expressed in [them]'. In other words, artworks express the nature of the social totality, and not of a particular element – e.g. a social class, the economic base – within it. While the views of both Lukacs and Adorno are open to question, nonetheless they are expressive of wider Marxist attempts in the twentieth century to produce more refined and nuanced accounts of artistic production than that offered by a rigid application of Marx's original 'base' and 'superstructure' model.

Most contemporary versions of the sociology of art recognise that in Western modernity there has come to develop a particular social institution called the 'art world'. This way of thinking draws upon the theme of *social structural differentiation*, a central idea in macro-sociology, developing out of the work of a range of figures, including Herbert Spencer (1961 [1897]) and Emile Durkheim (1984 [1893]). This is the notion that as modernity evolves, ever more specialised subsystems develop, each of which is an institution oriented around a core activity. This is a movement away from a medieval social structure, where the same institutions carried out more than one form of activity (Sztompka, 1993). In the medieval world, there was no separate institution called 'art'. Instead, cultural production was bound up with other social spheres, especially that of religion: hence the fact that the overwhelming number of artifacts from this period that modern people call 'art' were in fact produced for religious purposes (Williams, 1981: 96). It is only in modernity, and especially from the middle of the nineteenth century onwards, that a separate social institution defined by people of the time as the 'art world' comes to be established (Luhmann, 2000). Given this, instead of looking in a very general way at the relations between 'art' and 'society', modern sociology tends to see the problem as involving looking at the relations and connections between the 'art world' and other social institutions. Most sociologists also are of the view that in modernity the institution called 'art' has become partly, but not wholly, autonomous of other social institutions. The task is to identify a way of thinking about 'art' that simultaneously gasps that it has a history of its own, but that that history is connected to and bound up with, the histories of other social institutions.

Many sociologists would agree with Pierre Bourdieu's (1990: 119) analysis of this situation. He argues that the art world is like a little universe unto itself, with its own particular concerns and interests. But it is not totally sealed off from other social 'spheres' or 'institutions'. Instead, when these 'outside' spheres (or 'fields' as Bourdieu calls them) impact upon the art world (the 'field of cultural production' in his terms), they are not directly *reflected* in it but are *refracted*. In other words, influences from other fields are always indirect, and work themselves out according to the ways of operation peculiar to the field of cultural production itself. For example, a very rich businessman has a great deal of economic power, and this means he has a lot of power in the specific field called the 'economy' (i.e. business and industry). But if he fancies himself as a painter, all his money will probably not be able to buy him the approval of other painters, because what they value is what they define as 'talent', and if they think he has none, his money will make no difference to their evaluation (in fact, it might make them approve of him even less, seeing him as merely a 'rich amateur'). The point here is that factors from outside the art world do have an effect on it, but they are processed by that sphere and work themselves out according to its own 'laws' (or at least, tendencies) of operation. With this kind of analysis, we have moved very far away from a sociological approach that simply wants to find out what the effects of 'society' on 'art' are. Instead, effects on the art world from 'wider society' – that is, other social spheres, institutions and fields – are seen always to be indirect and subject to how the specific dynamics of how the art world itself operates (Anheier et al., 1995).

The 'art world'

If the modern Western phenomenon called the 'art world' is a social institution in some ways like any other, how should we try to understand how it works? Many sociologists would agree that we can see this sphere as being made up of *networks of cultural production, distribution and consumption* (Kadushin, 1976; Williams, 1981: 35). The elements of the institution we today call the 'art world' include technologies (e.g. brushes and paints), distribution and display systems (e.g. art dealers and galleries), reward systems (the means by which the benefits that accrue to the artist who has a 'successful' career are organised), systems of appreciation and criticism (e.g. critics writing reviews in newspapers), and audiences (Albrecht, 1970: 7–8). There are of course different subsystems within the overall art world, such as those oriented around particular forms of cultural production, such as painting and sculpture, novels and classical music.

We noted above that such a thing as the 'art world' is a relatively recent development, dating mostly from the middle of the nineteenth century. An excellent empirical study of how a particular 'art world' was erected at a particular time and place is provided by Paul DiMaggio, who gives an account of how an art world differentiated from other social spheres was constructed in the American city of Boston in the later nineteenth century. DiMaggio (1986: 195) notes that in the earlier nineteenth century, there was not yet a clear distinction between 'art' and 'popular culture', nor any forms of social organisation oriented around separating cultural phenomena out into these two spheres. A wide variety of cultural forms were available in a unified and not yet differentiated cultural marketplace. What were later defined as works of 'fine art' appeared alongside more 'vulgar' forms of 'popular culture' such as vaudeville shows. Yet by the end of the century, the Boston upper class had marked off for itself a distinctive cultural territory, by removing what were now labelled as the 'arts' from the commercial marketplace, and locating them inside a network of non-profit corporations. Popular 'entertainments' remained within the commercial realm and were viewed as mere commodities to be sold. Physically, the two realms were differentiated in that while popular 'entertainments' remained in the theatres they had been staged in for some time, new dedicated 'high culture' spaces such as museums, galleries and concert halls were erected to house proper 'arts'. In this way, both physical and symbolic boundaries were established between 'art' and 'popular culture'. As time went on, other cultural forms were reorganised around institutions of 'high culture', such as opera and ballet (Levine, 1988; DiMaggio, 1992). The same sorts of processes took place throughout the Western world at about the same time, both in capital cities such as Berlin, and in provincial centres like Manchester and Birmingham (Wolff and Seed, 1988).

DiMaggio's analysis stresses the role of non-profit organisations and actors, such as city councils and philanthropic donors, in the construction of the sphere of 'art'. But it is equally well the case that the creation of art worlds in different parts of the Western world involved profit-driven factors too. Perhaps the key change in the economics of artistic production from pre-modernity to modernity is the emergence of complex *art markets*. In medieval and Renaissance Europe, cultural production was carried out at the behest of powerful patrons, such as Popes or rich aristocrats. The cultural producer had to work within certain confines, in that he had to make artifacts that pleased the patron (Henning, 1960). By the nineteenth century, the patronage element in cultural production had gone into decline, and new ways of producing what was now defined as 'art' were in place (DeNora, 1991). Instead of directly producing for a patron, artists now tended to produce for art markets, which were much less personalised than the situation where the producer creates something for a specific person.

An archetypal case here is of a late nineteenth-century painter. Unlike his predecessors who would have produced works commissioned by rich patrons (Haskell, 1963), the painter now relies on other ways of making a living: selling his work to intermediaries such as art dealers, relying on displays in galleries to sell his work to prospective consumers, and making a name for himself with the critics (Taylor and Brooke, 1969; Kramer, 1970; Boime, 1976; Holt, 1981; Wolff, 1981: 139). In such cases, the relationship between 'seller' and 'buyer' has become much more impersonal and indirect than hitherto. In the context of a capitalist market in art, a whole new series of roles in the cultural division of labour appear. It is in the interests of such figures as gallery owners and auction-house managers that a certain artist's reputation be cultivated, so that they can make money out of it. 'Art' and money have always been intertwined, despite Romantic claims to the contrary (Reitlinger, 1961); but from the middle of the nineteenth century onwards, the sphere of social life called the art world becomes based in novel ways around the profit motive. Artworks, especially those in the visual arts, became forms of investment and speculation for the profit-hungry. In the present day we see many instances of this, from paintings by nineteenth-century figures such as Van Gogh selling for millions of dollars, to the activities of influential buyers like Charles Saatchi having a tremendous effect on the market value of young artists. Art today is big business and the roots of this phenomenon may be traced back to the mid- to late-nineteenth century.

A classic study that illustrates many points about how art worlds work is Harrison and Cynthia White's (1965) book *Canvesses and Careers* which charts how changes in the institutional structures of the French art world of the late nineteenth century helped encourage the development of the Impressionist school of painting. White and White note that for more than two hundred years previously, French painting had been dominated by the *Académie des Peinture et Sculpture*. Artistic Academies were set up in early modernity in many West European countries as 'official' guardians of taste and the artistic 'canon' (Pevsner, 1940). The French Academy, which was made up of mature and successful visual artists, enjoyed a monopoly not just over the training of young artists, but also over which styles of painting were allowable and decisions as to which artists were deemed to be 'great' or not. The annual competitive exhibition the Academy organised determined a pecking order of visual artists, with those winning prizes deemed to be at the top of the tree. Impressionism was most definitely *not* the kind of style the Academicians favoured. However, it came to prominence in the late nineteenth century because new ways of making and selling art had developed which bypassed the Academy and thus undercut its power and authority. There were several reasons for this development.

In the first place, far more painters than ever before were flocking to Paris, and this meant that there were more people painting than the traditional Academic system of competitive exhibition could deal with. These artists needed to earn a living and sought other means of establishing their careers. At the same time, a new middle class public with money to spend had appeared on the scene. This was a public that did not want the large canvases with 'grand' themes that the Academicians thought was the best type of painting; instead, they required paintings to hang in their homes, canvases that were relatively small, decorative, and pleasant to look at. The system that arose to meet the needs of, and to connect, these groups of cultural producers and consumers was the 'dealer-critic' system. The Impressionist painters, who could not get a foothold in the Academic system, sold their paintings to a new breed of entrepreneur, the 'art dealer'. The dealer then sold on the paintings to the middle class public, who often saw in paintings a way of earning large profits speculatively. People in this public were indirectly tutored by a new breed of art critic writing in newspapers and other periodicals not just as to what styles of painting they should like, but also to appreciate the idiosyncracies of the style of particular artists. Whereas the Academy had compelled artists to paint within the confines of certain established rules, dealers encouraged Impressionist painters to make their styles as 'personal' as possible, for that way the artworks would be more distinctive and would stand more chance of selling because the middle class purchaser would think he was buying something unique (and therefore something potentially very lucrative). So successful was the new 'dealer-critic' system that it brought the older Academic system into a situation of decline. What the Whites' study illustrates is not only how a particular art world was transformed, but also how factors such as means of exhibition and selling, and artistic 'supply' and 'demand', can have an effect on encouraging or discouraging particular styles of artistic practice.

Two of the most influential sociologists who have studied the 'art world' in recent years are Pierre Bourdieu and Howard Becker. Bourdieu's (1993a) analysis of the 'field of cultural production' is outlined by Jeremy Lane in his chapter in this book. Here we will confine ourselves to noting that Bourdieu focuses on sets of conflictual relations between different groups in that field, for example, between 'younger' and 'older' artists (in career terms, rather than personal age), between 'avant-garde' and 'established' artists (Poggioli, 1971; Bürger, 1984), between those producing 'art' and those producing 'popular works' (Grana, 1964), and so on.

Although Becker's (1984) analysis shares many common points with Bourdieu's, given that his style of sociology derives from the symbolic interactionist school with its emphasis on how people 'label' each other and what effects those labels can have, he focuses more on the 'gatekeeping' functions of institutions, persons and practices in the art world – art schools, galleries, museums, showings, art critics, magazine and newspaper reviews (Strauss, 1970; Bystryn, 1978; Shrum, 1991). Becker seeks to analyse the processes of definition within this world of who is defined as 'innovative' and 'original', and who is said to be 'derivative' within particular systems. Quite clearly, some people have more power than others to make their definition of artistic quality be accepted by others. Curators of large and powerful galleries can decide which works of art go on public display, or which are included in particular shows. Judges of art competitions have the power to define as legitimate or illegitimate not just particular works of art but also the other activities of the people who made them. In such fashions are artistic reputations made or broken. These various institutions and actors have the power to define something as 'art', even if to the general public the 'artwork' merely looks like a pile of bricks. They have the power of transfiguring an apparently ordinary object into 'art' (Danto, 1974). Whether an artist or a work retain their reputation over time is due to whether that label 'sticks'. As Becker (1984: 366) puts it, 'a work that lasts a long time is a work that has a good reputation for a long time', and reputation is malleable and subject to change as the art world itself changes.

Art worlds are made up not only of systems of production and distribution of 'artworks' but also of their consumption. The question of how the audiences of particular types of art are to be understood is a complicated one. Here we shall confine ourselves to a brief sketch of what could be said about this issue. Sociologists on the whole reject the idea that 'great art' is instantly recognisable, and that all people can spot really good art if given the chance (Hume, 1985 [1757]). They also tend to dispute claims by aestheticians such as Kant (1992 [1790]) that the proper way to engage with art is in a 'disinterested' way – that is, that one can look at for example a painting in a 'pure' way untainted by anything except wholly 'aesthetic' considerations. The sociological rejection of these sorts of views is based on the claim that different groups of people have different sets of tastes and ways of engaging with cultural products. As long as a society is made up of different groups of people with different styles of life, there will therefore never be a consensus as to what is 'good' art, nor which is the correct way of engaging with it. There is therefore no single or objective set of criteria that can identify what is 'beautiful' or not. Instead, we must ask why and how different groups of people each have different conceptions of what is aesthetically pleasing (Wolff, 1981: 97). Max Weber coined the idea of 'elective affinity' (*Wahlverwandtschaft*) to set out the problem of why certain groups of people, formed by certain life conditions, like certain types of cultural product and dislike others.

A classic analysis of these issues was provided by Herbert Gans (1978 [1966]). Instead of ranking certain types of culture and taste in a hierarchy, sociology's job is to describe neutrally what each set of tastes involves, and show how each set 'fits' the life conditions of the group that possesses it. All 'taste cultures' are to be seen as 'social facts that exist because they satisfy the needs and wishes of some people, even if they dissatisfy those of other people' (Gans, 1978 [1966]: 263). Gans argued that in modern America there are a whole rage of different taste cultures, each of which is associated with a particular social group, ranging from the 'high art' tastes of the upper middle class to the 'lowbrow tastes' of the lower working class. For Gans, one taste culture is not better than the other, they are simply different ways of engaging with the world and making sense of life.

A similar set of attitudes underpins Bourdieu's analysis of these issues. Simplifying his analysis somewhat, we can say that for Bourdieu the social position of a person, and how much power and influence they have at their disposal, is dependent on how much 'capital' they have. There are two main types of capital. The first is 'economic capital' – quite simply, this is how much money one has at one's disposal. But there is also 'cultural capital' – this is how much knowledge one has of 'high culture'. The dominant group in contemporary societies in cultural terms is the upper middle class, the *cultural bourgeoisie*. This group is made up of people in the top levels of professions like medicine and law. They are in a position of power over the other main groups in society, the lower middle class (e.g. primary school teachers, nurses) and the working class. This is not only because the upper middle class have more financial power than these other groups, but also because they have more cultural capital too. According to Bourdieu, the cultural power of the upper middle class is constantly reproduced because people in the other classes feel a sense of cultural inferiority. In a class-based society, if one does not have a 'refined' accent, then one will feel very ill at ease in the company of those with such accents (Bourdieu, 1991). Likewise, if one lacks knowledge about 'art', when in the company of those that do, one may well feel embarrassed and intimated. In this way, argues Bourdieu, the upper middle class oppress the other groups in society not just in economic terms, but in cultural terms too.

Following the line of reasoning developed by Mannheim, Bourdieu asserts that there is nothing *inherently* good or bad about so-called 'high culture'. This is simply the form of culture that the cultural bourgeoisie prefer because of their socialisation into a particular set of dispositions (Bourdieu and Passeron, 1990: 39). Each class grouping has its own 'habitus', the set of dispositions and tastes characteristic of the life conditions of that class. Because the cultural bourgeoisie do not perceive their tastes to be merely the result of such socialisation, they *misrecognize* their own tastes as both *natural* and as *intrinsically superior* to other types of tastes. People in this group exist inside a 'web of belief' whereby they take 'high culture' truly to be a realm that has a completely objective existence of its own, when actually it is only a product of the dispositions produced by their own habitus (Bourdieu, 1993a).

One of the reasons why the cultural bourgeoisie never regard the culture they favour as being arbitrary is that they periodically engage in rituals that renew their beliefs as to the apparently 'natural' superiority of their own cultural tastes. This is achieved through visiting locales that are defined as places where 'legitimate' culture can be accessed, such as museums and art galleries (Bourdieu and Darbel, 1991; Zolberg, 1992). Places like these are in essence 'temples of culture', where the 'cultured' come to worship their own refinement. Members of the cultural bourgeoisie feel comfortable in such places, as since childhood they have been made familiar with them, and they possess the capacity to 'decode' or interpret what is on offer in such places. Given such knowledge, one can talk about 'art' with great confidence, a feeling that people in other classes generally lack. Opinions can be confidently offered as to what the artworks 'mean'. Particular artists and styles can be connected to other artists and styles. In so doing, people of the cultural bourgeoisie can prove both to him/herself and others just how 'refined' she/he is. According to Bourdieu, this is generally not carried out as an ostentatious way of 'showing off', but is experienced as a completely 'natural' way of behaving. In this manner the trips to galleries and other such places are actually potent ways in which the cultural bourgeoisie maintain their cultural power over other social classes. While many criticisms can be given of Bourdieu's account, such as its possible over-emphasis on class factors and its assertion that each class has its own distinctive culture (e.g. Peterson and Kern, 1996; Warde et al., 1999), it nonetheless has become a very influential way for sociologists to think about how social relations can influence the ways in which a person's social position can effect what sorts of cultural forms they like and what they can, or cannot, get out of particular sorts of 'artwork'

Conclusion

This chapter has afforded an overview of the main themes and perspectives in the sociological study of art. Hopefully it has demonstrated the richness of this field and the many insights it has afforded into the nature of matters 'artistic', insights that other academic approaches may downplay or ignore altogether. From challenging the commonsense notions of 'art', 'artist' and 'artwork', through to macro-level discussions of the relations between 'art' and social factors and micro-level analyses of the particular dynamics of specific art worlds, sociology has developed a whole series of useful ways of thinking and analytical tools. However, as the contributions in the rest of this book show, the sociology of art in the present day cannot afford to rest on its laurels. It must constantly be in a state whereby it criticises its previous shortcomings and seeks to overcome them by developing new perspectives and analytical models. As we will see throughout the rest of the book, sociologists in the present day are seeking to do just that.

When Does Art Become Art? Assessing Pierre Bourdieu's Theory of Artistic Fields

Jeremy F. Lane

Introduction

Consider two works from the Western artistic tradition. The first, Domenico Ghirlandaio's 1488 *Adoration of the Magi*, is a panel painting of the early Florentine Renaissance. The second, *Fountain*, is one of Marcel Duchamp's infamous 'ready-mades', the urinal he first exhibited in New York in 1917. Each of these works has come to occupy a place in the Western artistic canon, the first widely recognized as an early renaissance masterpiece, the second occupying a more contested position but nonetheless seen as a founding work of the twentieth-century avant-garde, an important precursor to today's conceptual art. For a contemporary Western audience, imbued with a postromantic sensibility, the subject matter, the use of colour, the style of the *Adoration*...would surely be taken as so many expressions of Ghirlandaio's individual creative genius. Clearly, there are no such signs of skillful execution in *Fountain*. Indeed the point of Duchamp's urinal was precisely to challenge the art institution's cherished assumptions about creative genius. Yet, paradoxically, the very brilliance of Duchamp's challenge to the pretensions of artists and the art institution has itself been re-appropriated by that institution as evidence of an individual creative genius at work. In avant-garde art it is now the idea or concept, rather than the execution, that is taken as an expression of creative genius. As Peter Bürger (1984: 52–3) puts it in his study of the avant-garde, exhibiting 'ready-mades' like Duchamp's urinal 'does not eradicate the idea of individual creativity, it affirms it', so that Duchamp's protest 'against art as institution is now accepted as *art*'. Thus, despite the radical differences between the two works of art in question, a contemporary audience's response to them would tend to rely on the same assumptions about artistic expression and individual creative genius.

However, as the art historian Michael Baxandall has shown, to interpret Ghirlandaio's work in such terms is, strictly speaking, an anachronism. In the opening chapter of his *Painting and Experience in Fifteenth-Century Italy* (1972), Baxandall reproduces a selection of the contracts by means of which Florentine and Siennese merchants and priests commissioned paintings from early-Renaissance painters such as Ghirlandaio, Filippo Lippi, and Fra Angelico. As Baxandall shows, each of these contracts stipulated, frequently in great detail, the size, subject matter, and even the range of colours to be used by the painter in question. Where a contemporary audience might be tempted to interpret early-Renaissance paintings as so many expressions of individual artistic genius, the educated Florentine or Siennese merchants and priests for whom they were originally commissioned would have interpreted them in a very different way. Far from being taken as the expression of the creative genius of an autonomous artist, the selection and use of expensive colours, such as gold or ultramarine, would originally have been interpreted as explicit and ostentatious markers of the wealth and standing of the individual or institution who owned the work of art in question. Similarly, the subject matter of a painting would have been taken to perform a clearly identifiable social function, being interpreted as an exemplification of certain shared courtly values or as a tool of religious instruction. To quote Baxandall (1972: 1):

> A fifteenth-century painting is the deposit of a social relationship. On the one side there was a painter who made the picture, or at least supervised its making. On the other side there was somebody else who asked him to make it, provided funds for him to make it and, after he had made it, reckoned on using it in some way or other. Both parties worked within institutions and conventions – commercial, religious, perceptual, in the widest sense social – that were different from ours and influenced the forms of what they made.

Paintings such as Ghirlandaio's *Adoration* . . . are thus works which were originally commissioned to perform certain clear religious and social functions yet which tend to be interpreted by a contemporary audience as though they were *autonomous* works of art, things of beauty in and of themselves, to be appreciated in terms primarily of their *form* rather than their function. Duchamp's *Fountain*, on the other hand, seems to present a diametrically opposed case. For here we have a mass-produced, unmistakably functional object, a urinal, which, simply by being placed in an art gallery and declared to be *art*, demands to be appreciated in terms of its form not its function, as an autonomous work of art, an expression of an artist's individual genius.

In the series of highly influential articles and books he has published in the domain of the sociology of art since the mid-1960s, the French sociologist and anthropologist Pierre Bourdieu has returned to these two cases, Baxandall's study of early-renaissance art and Duchamp's urinal, with remarkable frequency. This is because each, in its different way, achieves a kind of de-familiarizing effect, forcing both Bourdieu himself and us, his readers, to question everything we take for granted about the way in which art is produced and received. Baxandall's study and Duchamp's urinal clearly relate to two quite different moments in the historical emergence of autonomous fields of artistic production and reception. They invite us to reflect upon the historical process whereby artists gained their creative autonomy from external forces, Church, State, or other, so that the fruits of their labours came to be seen as autonomous artworks, things of beauty in and of themselves performing no predetermined social or religious function.

The notion of 'autonomy' employed here can, perhaps, be best explained by imagining a wholly fictive traditional society whose inhabitants live from subsistence farming alone. The inhabitants of this imaginary society divide their time between ploughing the land, sowing, irrigating, and harvesting their crops and performing a series of rites and rituals in the hope of securing a good harvest. In such a society, no distinction is made between productive agricultural labour *per se* and the rites and rituals which surround it; each activity is seen as equally crucial in ensuring a good harvest. With the long process of historical development that led from traditional rural societies to urban, industrialized capitalism, the realm of productive labour proper began to differentiate itself as being the realm of fundamental importance to society's continued existence. The rites and rituals which had once been integral to productive activity thus gradually split off, as it were, to occupy the relatively autonomous spheres or fields of art and culture or religion, joining the series of other such relatively autonomous fields, justice, education, politics, characteristic of a modern, 'differentiated', capitalist society.

Thus, the art of early-renaissance Italy studied by Baxandall was produced at a moment when the artistic field possessed a low level of autonomy, when artists had yet to secure their creative autonomy from the external demands of Church or State. Duchamp's 'ready-mades', on the other hand, are clearly the products of a field of artistic production which has achieved a high degree of autonomy. In such a situation there are few explicit religious or social constraints on what artists can portray or how they can portray it, so much so that it is sufficient for an artist to exhibit a urinal in an art gallery, declaring this most banal, mass-produced object to be art, to have it recognized as such. Between them, Baxandall and Duchamp raise the question of what Bourdieu has termed 'the structure and historical genesis' of autonomous fields of artistic production and reception. They lead us to question how and when the field of production first gained its relative autonomy from external forces. They also call us to reflect upon the role played by a field of reception, composed of critics, dealers, gallery owners, and buyers, in conferring value on the products of that field of production, so that even a urinal can be 'transubstantiated', to use Bourdieu's terminology, from mass-produced functional commodity into work of art (Bourdieu, 1993a: 258–9). These, then, are some of the questions that are at the very core of Bourdieu's work in the sociology of art.

However, inquiring into the historical conditions governing the emergence of an autonomous field of artistic production forms only one part of Bourdieu's project. As Baxandall had shown, the way in which educated Florentines or Siennese responded to, or interpreted the art of their day closely reflected the conditions in which that art had been produced. There was thus, again to use Bourdieu's terminology, a close 'homology' between the historical conditions of a work of art's production and the modalities of its reception. A sociological analysis of art should therefore account not only for the historical genesis of an autonomous field of production but also for the historical genesis of contemporary modes of artistic reception, explaining how and when the art-appreciating public first became predisposed to interpret artworks as autonomous objects, things of beauty in and of themselves. A supplementary question to this would be to ask whether the ability to interpret artworks in such a way is equally distributed amongst all groups and classes in society. Many commentators, notably the Marxist philosopher Theodor Adorno, have seen artistic autonomy as fundamentally liberating. They argue that the relative autonomy gained by the field of art and culture has allowed it to become a realm in which alternative values are expressed, values not reducible to the profit motive at work in the economic field or the partial interests which dominate the political field, for example (Adorno, 1997 [1970]). Bourdieu, however, has tended to interpret artistic autonomy in rather different terms. He argues that, in a world increasingly subject to the laws of the market, to have the time and leisure to indulge in the pleasures afforded by an autonomous artistic field is something of a luxury. Familiarity with art and high culture can thus become the preserve of the leisured bourgeoisie, serving as a marker of that class's objective distance and subjective sense of distinction from the realm of brute material necessity inhabited by the dominated classes in society (Bourdieu, 1991 [1969]: 111–2).

The social conditions of artistic reception

These questions, which have been at the centre of Bourdieu's work in the sociology of art from the mid-1960s onwards, might be loosely divided into those which relate to the reception or consumption of high art and culture and those which relate to its production. Thus, *The Love of Art*, a statistical survey of attendance of European art galleries first published in 1966, saw Bourdieu analyzing the social and historical determinants behind the radically different propensity of the various social classes to visit art galleries and hence appreciate high art and culture. Bourdieu understood works of art as 'messages' requiring prior knowledge of the appropriate 'code' to be adequately 'deciphered' or interpreted. If his survey revealed those from working class or peasant backgrounds to be statistically far less likely to visit art galleries this was because, he argued, they lacked the requisite codes with which to decipher the meaning of the artworks on display there. There was little or no formal education in the principles of art appreciation. Schools were abdicating their responsibilities, failing to provide all their pupils, regardless of social back-ground, with the necessary tools to afford them equal access to 'art' and 'high culture'. Children of bourgeois or aristocratic parents were greatly favoured in this respect; born into a literate, cultured social milieu, encouraged from earliest childhood to visit theatres, art galleries, and museums, their inherited aptitudes and expectations, modes of thought and action, their *habitus*, to use Bourdieu's term, disposed them to the appreciation and understanding of art and culture. However, the social, economic, and historical determinants of the dominant classes' greater propensity to appreciate art was never openly acknowledged. Rather, this historically determined propensity was passed off as a 'natural' marker of inherent intellectual and moral superiority, hence serving to legitimize, naturalize, and reproduce existing class distinctions and divisions in society.

The Love of Art had thus sought to demonstrate that even when economic and geographical barriers to visiting art galleries were removed, through low or non-existent entry charges and policies pursued by post-war governments to improve cultural provision, the appreciation of high art and culture remained a socially exclusive practice. In the earlier collaborative study, *Photography: A Middlebrow Art* (1990 [1965]), Bourdieu had shown that a cultural practice such as photography, rendered accessible to almost all through cheap, mass-produced equipment and as yet lacking fully codified criteria of aesthetic judgement, could nonetheless also serve as a terrain of social distinction and class division. His survey analyzed the ways in which the different social classes both practised photography, selecting shots or subjects worthy of photographing, and responded to a range of existing photographs, selecting which were 'beautiful', which 'ugly', or which simply 'banal'. Bourdieu's working-class respondents were far more likely than their bourgeois counterparts to value photographs which either performed an identifiable social function, recording an important family occasion such as a wedding, christening or honeymoon, or which could be considered 'beautiful' in the most conventional way, a photo of a sunset, for example. As Bourdieu pointed out, this 'functionalist aesthetic' corresponded almost exactly to what Immanuel Kant had defined as 'barbarous taste' in his *Critique of Judgement* (1992 [1790]), the founding text of modern Western aesthetics.

In the *Critique of Judgement*, Kant defines 'the beautiful' as 'an object of delight apart from any interest'. He argues that the beautiful is that which pleases without either performing a predetermined function, appealing to particular interests, or satisfying base sensual desires. Appreciation of the beautiful calls for an aesthetic gaze purified of such narrow subjective instincts and interests, a 'pure', 'disinterested gaze' which appreciates the beautiful artistic object on the level of form rather than function, as an object of beauty in and of itself, with no regard to its possible function. In purifying the aesthetic gaze of subjective desires and narrow, partial interests in this way, Kant sought to establish the 'universal communicability' of the aesthetic experience, distinguishing, therefore, the universality of aesthetic taste from the wholly subjective, sensual taste for wine over beer, say, or cream cakes over sardines (Kant, 1992 [1790]: 41–89).

However, as Bourdieu has sought to demonstrate in a critique of Kant first elaborated in *Photography* and *The Love of Art* and which culminated in 1979 in his massive study of taste, class and lifestyle, *Distinction*, the aesthetic experience as described by Kant is anything but universal. On the contrary, according to Bourdieu, to adopt the pure aesthetic gaze, to contemplate a work of art on the level of form alone, 'bracketing off' any question of its possible function, presupposes an ability to 'suspend' any immediate material needs or interests, to take up a leisurely, contemplative distance on the social world, an ability that was the preserve of the dominant classes in society. Writing at the very moment feudal regimes were giving way to Western bourgeois democracies, Kant had placed a specifically bourgeois attitude to the social world at the core of his supposedly universal criteria of aesthetic judgement. In so doing, Bourdieu argued, Kantian aesthetics elevated a socially and historically determined predisposition to appreciate works of high art and culture to the level of a universal measure of moral and intellectual worth (Bourdieu, 1992 [1979]: 485–500). The bourgeoisie could thus 'legitimize' and 'naturalize' its political and economic domination by invoking its refined cultural tastes as evidence of its inherent superiority; 'culture', 'taste', and 'refinement' performing the same legitimizing function as had birth and bloodline for the nobility under feudalism (Bourdieu, 1991 [1969]: 110–11).

Distinction was thus the culmination of Bourdieu's enquiries into the social, historical, and economic determinants of the way in which art is received and consumed. Because of its role in legitimizing the social status quo, Bourdieu named high art and culture 'legitimate culture', and the prestige accruing to those equipped to appreciate its 'cultural capital', a form of capital which could elicit real material benefits for those who possessed it without, for all that, being directly reducible to economic capital proper. *Distinction* did not limit itself to the domain of legitimate culture but analyzed the social determinants of taste across a wide range of cultural practices, from the most elevated to the most apparently banal. According to Bourdieu, just as in their preference for Bach's 'Well-tempered Harpsichord' over Strauss's 'Blue Danube', so in their taste for *pâté de foie gras* over steak and chips, for understated interior décor over garish ostentation, as in their characteristic bearing and patterns of speech, the bourgeoisie demonstrated a collective ethos and attitude to the world dependent upon their material well-being. Each of these tastes and lifestyle 'choices' exemplified a typically bourgeois, leisurely, contemplative attitude, which was determined by and expressive of the bourgeoisie's distance from material necessity, yet which was taken to be a natural sign of their innate refinement, culture, and hence moral superiority. It was this distance from material need which formed the defining characteristic of the bourgeois habitus.

The habitus, for Bourdieu, forms 'a durable and transposable structure of dispositions', a set of internalized 'practical taxonomies', modes of viewing the world and acting in it that have been 'picked up', 'incorporated', through the experience of growing up in and inhabiting a particular socially marked cultural milieu. It was the assumptions, attitudes, and schemes of perception incorporated through being brought up in a cultured bourgeois environment, then, which formed the basis of the bourgeois habitus, a structure of dispositions which could be 'transposed' into any number of social contexts, finding expression as much in a taste for fine cuisine as for high art. The familiarity with high art and culture, the facility with language and the manipulation of theoretical concepts, which formed an integral part of the bourgeois habitus were moreover, Bourdieu argued in studies such as *The Inheritors* (1979 [1964]) and *Reproduction* (1977 [1970]), precisely those attributes recognized and rewarded by the institutions of French higher education. Playing on the etymology of the word 'scholastic', from the Greek *skholè* meaning leisure, he thus maintained that the bourgeois habitus manifested itself in a 'scholastic point of view', a leisurely, contemplative distance on the world, the pre-condition for adopting the pure, disinterested aesthetic gaze described by Kant and a strong contributory factor to the higher rates of academic success amongst the offspring of the bourgeoisie.

The social conditions of artistic production

In studies such as *Photography, The Love of Art*, and *Distinction*, then, Bourdieu has sought to trace the social and historical genesis of the scholastic point of view and the pure aesthetic gaze, the propensity to appreciate legitimate culture, it engendered. However, tracing the historical genesis of current modes of receiving or consuming legitimate culture forms only one half of Bourdieu's project in the sociology of art. For he has argued that it is only with the emergence of a relatively autonomous field of cultural production that works of art are produced which demand to be apprehended by a pure, disinterested gaze, appreciated in terms of form rather than function. Any sociological account of art would therefore have to account not only for the historical genesis of the pure aesthetic gaze, but also for the historical genesis of an autonomous field of production producing works which demand to be apprehended by such a gaze. As Bourdieu (1993a: 256) puts it:

> From the angle of phylogenesis, the pure gaze, capable of apprehending the work of art as it demands to be apprehended (i.e., in itself and for itself, as form not as function), is inseparable from the appearance of producers of art motivated by a pure artistic intention, which is itself inseparable from the emergence of an autonomous artistic field capable of formulating and imposing its own ends against external demands. From the side of ontogenesis, the pure gaze is associated with very specific conditions of acquisition, such as the early frequenting of museums and the prolonged exposure to schooling, and to the *skholè* that this implies. All of this means that the analysis of essence which overlooks these conditions (thus universalising the specific case) implicitly establishes as universal to all aesthetic practices the rather particular properties of an experience which is the product of privilege, that is, of exceptional conditions of acquisition.

In a series of articles from the mid-1960s onwards, a selection of which have been anthologized in English translation as *The Field of Cultural Production* (1993), and all of which fed into the 1992 study *The Rules of Art* (Published in English in 1996), Bourdieu has therefore sought to trace what he terms 'the structure and historical genesis' of an autonomous field of artistic production.

Bourdieu's approach to the sociology of art thus focuses as much on histori-
cizing changing modes of artistic production as it does on analyzing the
sociohistorical determinants of particular modes of artistic reception. For
Bourdieu, a sociological analysis of any work of art would have to pay attention
to history of the field of production which produced it, as much as to the
historical genesis and structure of the field of reception into which it emerged.
Any such sociological account would also have to reflect upon and historicize
the point of view of the sociologist undertaking the analysis, questioning to
what extent their response to the artwork in question might be determined,
and hence rendered anachronistic, by the unquestioned assumptions about art
and artists internalized in their habitus, itself acquired in specific social and
historical conditions (Bourdieu, 1996 [1992]: 306–12).

Thus Bourdieu rejects what he terms 'internal' readings of artworks which
take their meaning and value to be transcendent of the historical conditions in
which they were originally produced and received. Yet he also rejects traditional
modes of sociological analysis, which he dubs 'external' readings, charging
that these all tend to reduce the genesis of an artwork to the social origin of its
creator, thus 'short-circuiting', as he puts it, the vital mediating force of the
field of production. A work of art, for Bourdieu, is therefore neither the
solitary expression of an artistic genius nor the simple reflection of that
artist's social origins. Rather works of art are produced by the meeting of a
habitus, which reflects the social origins and personal trajectory of a given
artist, and a field, a structured space of possibles, of competing genres and
styles, possibles themselves determined by the historical evolution of that field.
No artist or writer simply invents genres or styles *ex nihilo*. Rather, they take
up a position in terms of an already-existing range of genres and styles,
choosing to repeat existing successful genres, in the case of cheap romantic
fiction for example, or to take an existing genre and push it to its limits, in the
case of an experimental modernist novel such as James Joyce's *Finnegan's
Wake*. Edouard Manet's formal innovations in painting, for example, only
make sense, were only possible, given the sterile academicism against which
they rebelled. Thus, every artistic statement implies a kind of 'position-taking'
in relation to existing works and positions in the field and the range of
positions any artist can take will depend upon the prior history of the field.

For Bourdieu, the field of artistic production is a realm of 'permanent
revolution' (Bourdieu, 1996 [1992]: 239). Adopting the terminology of Max
Weber's sociology of religion, he distinguishes between the 'priests', 'consecrated' artists with an established reputation who seek to defend their position
in the field, and the 'prophets', avant-garde artists whose stylistic and generic
innovations define themselves in opposition to existing artistic conventions.
However ferocious, these struggles between priests and prophets within the
field conceal an objective consensus over the value of what is at stake in the
field and thus contribute to the continued reproduction of that field. Priests
and prophets alike share an unquestioned 'interest in the game', a pre-reflexive
'investment' in the stakes of the artistic field, which Bourdieu terms the *illusio*
(ibid.: 227). To adopt an avant-garde position within the field requires not
merely an investment in its stakes but a firm grasp, a 'mastery', to use

Bourdieu's term, of that field's history. An artist cannot rebel against stale convention, stage a return to the 'purity' of an artistic practice compromised through routinization or commercialization, without a deep understanding both of the history of the field and its products and of the range of positions occupied by predecessors and peers. Hence Bourdieu's insistence that a sociology of art should not seek to explain the genesis of an artwork simply by reference to the social origins of its creator. Stylistic choices and aesthetic innovations can only be explained by taking into account the historically determined range of possible positions on offer to any artist and not by reference to 'external' factors such as social origin alone. Social origins may have a role to play but only inasmuch as, incorporated into the structured dispositions of the habitus, they are mediated or 'refracted' through, 'retranslated into the logic' of the artistic field at a particular historical moment. These rather general statements can be elucidated by returning to the example of Duchamp's urinal.

As Bourdieu points out, Duchamp was born into a family of artists; grandfathers, brothers and sisters were all practicing artists. He grew up, therefore, surrounded not only by artists, but also by critics, dealers and art buyers. From this particular social milieu, Duchamp inherited a peculiarly developed artistic habitus, a detailed, almost intuitive understanding of the artistic field, of its history and competing positions, as well as that investment in the stakes of the field Bourdieu terms the *illusio* (ibid.: 246–47). Duchamp's 'ready-mades' were born at the intersection between his highly developed artistic habitus and a field of artistic production which had already undergone a long history of gradual autonomization; from Manet's rejection of the generic conventions of the Academy, to the formal innovations of the Impressionists, Paul Cézanne, and the Cubists, artists had gradually imposed the notion that their art should be subject to no external constraints, simply expressing their own aesthetic vision. In exhibiting a urinal as though it were a work of art, Duchamp demonstrated his understanding of this history of autonomization. He also demonstrated his understanding of the effect that history had had on the field of reception, predisposing critics, commentators, and dealers to confer artistic value on this apparently worthless, purely functional, mass-produced object. The entire history of the artistic field was thus immanent in Duchamp's urinal, itself the unmistakable product of a field which had reached a high degree not only of autonomy but also of self-reflexivity, since the provocation of Duchamp's 'ready-mades' lay precisely in their ability to force us to reflect upon the structure and genesis of the field, the status it attributed artists, and the value it conferred on their work. As Bourdieu (ibid.: 169) puts it:

The artist who, in attaching his name to a *ready-made*, confers on it a market price which is not measured on the same scale as its cost of fabrication, owes his magic efficacy to a whole logic of the field that recognizes and authorizes him; his act would be nothing but a crazy or insignificant gesture without the universe of celebrants and believers who are ready to produce it as endowed with meaning and value by reference to the entire tradition which produced their categories of perception and appreciation.

The phrase 'magical efficacy' has more than purely rhetorical force here. Indeed, elsewhere Bourdieu has argued that to question the way in which value is conferred on art is to ask a series of 'questions quite similar to those raised by Mauss when, in his *Theory of Magic*, he pondered the principle of magic's effectiveness', moving back 'from the instruments used by the sorcerer himself [...] to the belief held by his followers', finally 'to confront the entire social universe in whose midst magic evolves and is practised' (1993a: 258). These allusions to the work of Marcel Mauss, like the Weberian terminology of 'priests' and 'prophets', or the references to 'transubstantiation' and 'consecration', emphasize the extent to which Bourdieu sees himself drawing on the classical sociological tradition, extending and refining its findings in the sociology of religion to apply them to the sociology of art. Just as in the sociology of magic or religion the efficacy of beliefs was located not in the specific nature of rite or dogma but in the society which gave birth to and fostered them, so Bourdieu argues that the source of artistic value is not to be found in artworks themselves but in the social institutions, the *fields* in which they are produced and received. If Duchamp's urinal exemplifies an artistic field which has reached a very high degree of autonomy, much of Bourdieu's effort, most notably in *The Rules of Art*, has been devoted to examining how and when that autonomous field first emerged.

The historical genesis of an autonomous field of production

Bourdieu's analysis focuses on three central figures of French nineteenth-century art and literature, namely the painter Edouard Manet, the poet Charles Baudelaire, and the novelist Gustave Flaubert. What these three figures share is that they all came into direct conflict with those state institutions which attempted to control what could be artistically represented and how it should be represented. Manet had to confront the state-run *Académie des beaux-arts*, a jury of whose members selected which works would be exhibited at the (after 1863) annual *Salon*, the primary means for aspirant artists to gain wider critical and public recognition for their work. In challenging the stylistic and generic conventions upheld by the *Salon*'s jury, Manet faced, alternately, the jury's outright refusal to exhibit his works or public ridicule of those of his works which were exhibited. Baudelaire and Flaubert, on the other hand, both faced obscenity trials, risking censorship for the depiction of adultery in *Madame Bovary* (1856), in Flaubert's case, and of prostitution and lesbianism in *Les Fleurs du mal* (1857), in Baudelaire's case. According to Bourdieu, the efforts of Manet, Flaubert, and Baudelaire to secure their creative autonomy in the face of *Salon* refusals and obscenity trials represent key moments in the emergence of an autonomous field of artistic production. Much of *The Rules of Art* is thus dedicated to an analysis of those efforts drawing on the concepts of 'habitus' and 'field'.

Bourdieu argues that the family backgrounds of Baudelaire, Manet, and Flaubert show certain common characteristics which, internalized into their habitus, predisposed them to take up certain positions within the artistic field of their day. Flaubert, for example, was the son of a doctor, Baudelaire the son of a bureau chief in the high legislative Assembly. Both, then, came from cultured bourgeois backgrounds which afforded them not only material security but also a respect for intellectual and high cultural endeavour. These artists, 'almost equally endowed with economic and cultural capital', were thus disposed to treat commercially successful art forms, the 'bourgeois art' directly subservient to its audience's expectations which had flourished under the Second Empire, with a kind of aristocratic disdain. Yet if their cultured habitus disposed them to reject 'bourgeois art', one of the positions available to them in the field of artistic production, it also encouraged them to reject the opposing position, the politically engaged artistic and literary forms of 'social art'. Such engaged art, Bourdieu argues, could only strike those of a cultured disposition as 'demagogic', identified 'with the journalistic plebs of bohemia' (Bourdieu, 1996 [1992]: 85–6). Disenchantment following the failure of the Revolution of 1848, the Bonapartist coup of 1851, and the establishment of the conservative Second Empire further discouraged these artists from using their art to transmit explicit political messages.

The habitus and trajectory of Manet, Flaubert, and Baudelaire thus disposed them to reject the two dominant positions on offer in the artistic field, those of 'bourgeois art' and 'social art', respectively, encouraging them to create a new position for themselves, that of autonomous artists, free of the 'external' forces of money or politics, pursuing their own creative ideas. Through this 'double rupture' with, on the one hand, the 'temporal' rewards of wealth and fame offered by 'bourgeois art' and, on the other, the political engagement of 'social art', Manet, Flaubert, and Baudelaire thus made a decisive contribution to the emergence of the modern figure of the autonomous artist. The sons of wealthy bourgeois, they were able to live off their inherited economic wealth, sacrificing immediate economic reward or wider public recognition in the name of a set of higher artistic ideals. Where practitioners of 'bourgeois art' worked within what Bourdieu terms a 'field of large-scale production', aiming to attract the biggest possible audience for their work, autonomous artists worked within a newly formed 'field of restricted production', where immediate commercial success would be taken as an index of the superficial or degraded nature of that work. Within the field of restricted production, artists produced work which was destined not for a wide or popular audience but rather for an audience composed of their peers, other artists, a select band of critics, and the growing body of journalists and commentators working on the edge of the cultural and artistic field proper. The field of restricted production was 'an economic world turned upside down', it functioned according to 'an inverted economy', whereby those works which achieved most commercial success would be treated with suspicion but those works which struggled to find an audience would receive the greatest prestige, their very lack of success being taken as a sign of their artistic purity. Participants in the restricted field of production were thus characterized, Bourdieu argues, by their relative lack of economic capital, a lack 'compensated' by their high levels of cultural capital. Within the field of large-scale production, the positions were reversed; participants in this field enjoyed relatively high economic capital but low levels of specifically cultural capital, having 'sacrificed' this to the demands of the market.

This division between fields of restricted and large-scale production, what Bourdieu terms 'the emergence of a dualist structure' of artistic production, was not solely attributable to the efforts of Manet, Baudelaire, and Flaubert to secure their creative autonomy, however. On the contrary, a series of broader historical changes need also to be taken into account, a set of 'morphological' changes to the size and sociological composition of the potential audiences for the products of those two fields. In particular, Bourdieu points to increasing literacy and the extension of formal education under the Second Empire as being 'one index amongst others of an unprecedented expansion of the market for cultural goods'. Qualified school-leavers were being produced faster than either business or the public sector could absorb them and they flooded into Paris in increasing numbers, hoping to make a living as artists or writers, frequently eking out an existence in journalism, living a typically 'bohemian' lifestyle. It was this 'intellectual reserve army', as Bourdieu puts it, who formed the basis of the field of restricted reception, affording autonomous artists such as Baudelaire, Flaubert, and Manet such minimal support, economic and spiritual, as was necessary to their survival (ibid.: 54–7).

Conclusion

Bourdieu's account of the historical emergence of an autonomous field of artistic production in nineteenth-century France thus involves taking into account a wide range of different historical and social determinants and analyzing how such determinants are mediated or 'refracted' through the field of artistic production at a given historical moment. As has been stated, this account of the emergence of a field of autonomous production compliments his studies of the reception or consumption of the different forms of legitimate culture, studies such as *The Love of Art* or *Distinction*. In these earlier studies artistic autonomy, the propensity of art and artists to stand at a distance from the realm of material necessity, was viewed as an essentially negative attribute, allowing high art and culture to play their role in signifying, legitimizing, and naturalizing social distinctions. By the publication of *The Rules of Art*, Bourdieu's thinking had undergone a significant shift. Whilst continuing to acknowledge the socially distinctive nature of the products of an autonomous or restricted field of production, Bourdieu now argued that such products nonetheless possessed a 'universal' value inasmuch as they stood opposed to the narrow, partial, or particular interests of politics and the market, of the 'field of power'. He maintained that the autonomy of the artistic field was increasingly threatened by the 'heteronomous' forces of the media and the market, forces to which a current generation of artists and intellectuals were all too willing to sell out in search of the immediate 'temporal' rewards of wealth and fame (Bourdieu, 1996 [1992]: 339–48). To trace the historical emergence of an autonomous field of artistic production, as he had done in *The Rules of Art*, was thus also to return 'to the "heroic times" of the struggle

for independence, when the virtues of revolt and resistance had to assert themselves clearly in the face of a repression exercised in all its brutality (especially
during the trials)', in the hope of 'rediscovering the forgotten – or repudiated –
principles of intellectual freedom' (ibid.: 48).

Surprisingly, then, for someone whose sociology of art seemed to pose such
a radical challenge to existing hierarchies of aesthetic value, Bourdieu seems
ultimately to have left those hierarchies firmly in place. The canonical figures
of Manet, Flaubert, and Baudelaire are the heroes in Bourdieu's account,
representatives of a 'universal' aesthetic value now threatened by the media,
the market, and the politics of neo-liberalism. Nowhere does Bourdieu question
the process whereby those figures became canonized nor examine what social
or political factors may have conspired to prevent female artists or minority
and popular art forms from attaining such canonical status. Moreover, the
works Manet, Flaubert, and Baudelaire produced in the autonomous field of
production, works of apparently 'universal' value, demand, according to
Bourdieu's own account, to be appreciated by a 'pure', 'disinterested' aesthetic
gaze which itself is the preserve of the leisured bourgeoisie. Paradoxically,
Bourdieu's account of universal aesthetic value would seem to reproduce the
very exclusions he had uncovered to such devastating effect in his critique of
Kantian aesthetics. Thus, if Bourdieu's 'field theory' undoubtedly has much to
offer the sociology of art, it nonetheless leaves certain philosophical questions,
namely that of the precise nature of aesthetic value, unresolved.

The Female Body in Women's Artistic Practice: Developing a Feminist Sociological Approach

3

Alexandra Howson

Introduction

My task in this chapter is to suggest some ways in which an avowedly *feminist* sociology of art might be augmented and extended. This undertaking raises two immediate questions for me. First, is there not already a feminist sociology of art (the work of Janet Wolff springs to mind)? Second, how does the feminist sociologist embark on a feminist sociology of anything? Moreover, my qualifications for the task are not immediately apparent. I have no training or education in aesthetics, I am not a sociologist of culture, and there are days when my affiliation to either feminism or sociology is equally tested.

However, I do have two main interests in visual art. First, I have used visual images in my teaching on the body, gender and health as supportive and/or illustrative material, particularly images produced by women or those that I interpreted as referring to what I will call here the *vicissitudes of female embodiment*. Visual art practice has been an important point of cultural intervention for twentieth-century feminists in order both to challenge the masculine privilege of the artistic canon, and to create images that refer to and draw on the concerns of women's lives. Many of these images draw on and offer comment on issues central to the development of the women's movement.

Second, my research on body concepts in sociology and feminism has led me to engage with contemporary feminist analyses of women's art. Visual culture is privileged in modern Western societies as evidence of social reality, and the sociological approach to art has in the past largely reflected this view. In Western culture there is a tendency to base what we know on what can be seen, rather than on the relations, processes and contexts of viewing. However, recent feminist analyses of contemporary women's art disrupt that association by insisting on the power of the unconscious. The female body bears a particular form of value within visual systems of representation and this value is reflexively mobilised by contemporary feminist theories of the body. Whereas academic feminism (or feminists in the academy) use women's art as supportive and/or illustrative material, contemporary women's art implicitly and explicitly builds insights from feminist theory into its representations.

Hence, the substantive focus of this chapter is both on representations of the female body in 'women's art', clearly a contentious notion, and on how academic feminist audiences have responded to this body of work. As feminist art historians observe, the term 'women's art' can be applied to those traditions of art associated with a domestic context of production, such as tapestry or quilting. Although the bodies of women labour in the production of such art, representation or acknowledgement of the female body is not necessarily central to the final product. Yet women's art also denotes an art which, as Wolff (1990) notes, assumes and affirms the ontological difference of women's knowledge and experience. I use the term here as a shorthand way of referring to visual images of the female body, which are produced by women. I am particularly interested here in the significance of feminist theory for artists' work on, through or with the female body and will argue that in reading/interpreting contemporary artistic practice it is difficult not to draw on readings of feminism past and present. Feminism both implicitly and explicitly informs the work and in my view it is very difficult to separate theory and practice in the context of women's art. This insight could be used to inform the development of a feminist sociology, not *of* art, distinct and distant from its perceived object, but a feminist sociology sensitive to and working *with* (women's) art.

The chapter is organised as follows. First, I outline the changing structural context in which women produce visual art. Second, I describe changing representations of the female body and highlight some of the debates accompanying these representations. Third, I identify how the fragmentation of feminist theory has transformed feminist analyses of women's art. Finally, I reflect on the implications of this fragmentation for pursuing a feminist sociology of art.

Making women's art

Prior to the middle of the twentieth century, few women were admitted to art schools or acquired formal art training. However, the gradual expansion of citizenship for women in relation to civil, political and social entitlements (Walby, 1995) affirmed the entry of women into formal institutions at the turn of the century, and grounded the 'struggle over the representation of women's bodies' (Betterton, 1996: 3). The general expansion of higher education in the 1960s and 1970s further improved women's access to education and to art institutions, which were increasingly influenced by the language and frameworks of critical disciplines such as sociology (Cottingham, 1989). Moreover, by the 1980s, feminist theory had gained a place on the curriculum of disciplines that contribute to art education (McRobbie, 1990). This opened up visual practice and theory to feminist critique and established the conditions for feminist interventions, such as those represented by the work of Pollock (1988).

As McRobbie (1990) notes, artistic practice and critical analysis generally inform each other, and this cross-fertilisation is especially potent in relation to women's artistic practice and feminist theory. This process occurs in formal and informal ways. Whether women view themselves as feminists or not, feminism provides an important reference point for women acquiring a formal education in artistic practice. For instance, women artists born between 1940–55 are likely to have been exposed to feminism's claims and/or influenced by the women's and other social movements (see Seidman, 1994) in ways which make it difficult for women artists both to avoid 'admitting gender' to their work (Cottingham, 1989) and which had an impact on ways of working within the academy. In the 1980s, in particular, the establishment of women's art groups and publications provided a specific network for the development and exchange of ideas (McRobbie, 1990: 7). Moreover, whilst later cohorts of women artists are less likely to have been exposed to the activism of the women's movement, they are nonetheless still likely to encounter feminist theory in the academy. As Stanley (1999) has noted, academic feminist theory is the primary mode of exposure to feminism for a generation of women in higher education. The work of many contemporary women artists draws directly on this developing body of theory, particularly feminist theories of the body, in which there has been a rapid growth since the late 1980s. Hence, although artists themselves may disavow the extent to which such theory informs their work, nonetheless, modern(ist) academic feminism provides an irrefutable framework through which to represent and critique the politics of the female body (Cottingham, 1989).

Feminist critique of and intervention in the visual arts has taken a variety of forms, which follow a trajectory similar to feminist disquisition in other academic disciplines. First, feminist art historians have cultivated accounts of the historical absence of women from the production of visual imagery. Revisionist accounts identify 'missing women' (e.g. Harris and Nead, 1978) and 'herstories', as well as those strategies which excluded women from art institutions and the production of visual art and knowledge. Second, just as feminist critiques have challenged the assumptions of other disciplines (see Finch, 1993, for the case of sociology), so too has feminist critique challenged the artistic canon 'by reclaiming a hidden tradition of female art' (McRobbie, 1990: 5) and by posing a redefinition of what counts as art. Third, influenced by post-structuralism in particular, feminists have increasingly directed their attention to the content and meaning of visual imagery, particularly in relation to the female body and sexuality, in pursuit of a distinctly (though contentious) feminine visual language. It is important to consider the *form* of feminism to which women artists have been primarily exposed, and which has been translated into a feminist visual vocabulary or aesthetic. This has a bearing on the nature of artistic practice and accordingly visual representations of the female body and their interpretations. The following section now traces the forms of feminism (whether movement-based or academic) which have influenced the production of and responses to women's art.

The politics of the female body in women's art

Why did some women artists begin to focus explicitly on the female body in the 1970s? In order to answer this question, we need to look at the status of the female body in the history of art, the influence of the women's movement and the impact of new knowledge about aspects of women's lives. First, the female body occupies a specific position in the history of art. Its representation has largely been the province of male artists, whose practice has tended to objectify women for a male audience (Mulvey, 1975), render the female nude in idealised terms (Williams and Bendelow, 1998), and represent woman as the alien Other and as 'uncharted and peripheral wildness' (McRobbie, 1990: 12). Second, the 'personal is political' provided a nodal point of reference within the second wave of the women's movement in the Anglophone world (Seidman, 1994). Although the precise origins and meaning of this term are contentious (see Holmes, 2000), it is usually taken to refer to the various ways in which those relationships and experiences we consider to be private and personal are constituted through social and political relations and conditions. For instance, this view of the personal and private as political and open to public scrutiny informed the activism associated with the women's health movement. In particular, this movement, especially in the USA, emphasised the need for women to develop an awareness of the specificities of their own bodies as a way of resisting the colonising tendencies of the medical profession (Ruzek, 1978). Concomitantly, body consciousness emerged as an implicit theme within women's art of the 1970s.

Third, women's writing in the 1970s focused explicitly on relationships between the personal and political in order to make visible and to politicise those aspects of female embodiment which were culturally deemed private and effaced from the public sphere (Rose, 2000). This writing provided a new and accessible source of knowledge for many women, and highlighted the various ways in which the social, economic and political world was divided along the fault lines of gender. In the 1970s, a predominant theme of women's writing was the ways in which patriarchal culture worked to suppress female ways of being, women's knowledge and understanding. It is unlikely that this literature did not influence the visual work of many women artists during that period. The production of images of the female body, by women, needs to be understood as part of a more generalised response to the social and cultural world which viewed and treated women as objects, and which concealed and denied the rhythms, emissions and vicissitudes of female embodiment. What appeared to be new and significant about such work was the explicit evocation and, in some cases celebration, of female corporeality, in contrast to its treatment within other traditions of artistic practice.

There are precedents in the history of art for the evocation of female corporeality and of the female body as a colonised, occupied body in visual art of the 1970s (Tickner, 1978), particularly in the work of Frida Kahlo. However, women's art of the 1970s shared the assumption that *experience* provided epistemological privilege; that women commonly shared material experiences; and that the *different* rhythms and pains associated with female embodiment were concealed and distorted by patriarchal culture. First, for instance, some women artists used 'vaginal iconography' in their work in ways that made visible the 'cordon sanitaire' installed around female genitalia in Western culture. The Anglo-American women's movement argued strongly that the only available images of their own genitalia were produced in clinical and scientific contexts. Consequently, images of what would now, in the twenty-first century, be identified as female interiority, had resonance in the 1970s as a reclamation of those aspects of the female body typically concealed and shrouded in shame by Western culture. This kind of reclamation continues in, for instance, dramatic work such as *The Vaginal Monologues* staged in New York involving many high-profile women in politics as well as in the arts.

A second approach in women's art in the 1970s was associated with female 'transformations and processes' and used images and performances to make private experience available for public consumption. For instance, Eleanor Antin's *Carving: A Traditional Sculpture* for the Whitney Museum, consisted of 144 photographs of the artist's naked body in different profiles, which documented weight loss over a period of 36 days (Tickner, 1978: 244). As Tickner observes, the artist herself noted that her work built on the sculptural methods of antiquity based on carving layers away to 'reveal' the aesthetic ideal, and, as such, observe how the feminine aesthetic ideal is achieved by removing layers from the female body. One major effect of such images and performances was the production of responses of disgust from audiences, who viewed them as forms of obscenity and vulgarity, thereby reproducing the disgust associated with the female body. As feminists have observed, while women are not expected to be disgusting, the female body nonetheless has long been designated a source of shame in Western culture.

A third approach that began to emerge in the 1970s and developed more fully in the 1980s was the use of art (and representations of the female body within that work) as therapy and critique. Much of this work was very personal and explicitly politicised through interpretation and social commentary. Jo Spence's photography is paradigmatic of this approach. Spence deployed a realist documentary format to address the politics of women's health and the female body, in ways which expand the parameters of photography in terms of what it can show and be used to show. Like Kahlo before her, Spence addressed issues of personal pain and suffering, the values of biomedicine and dominant images of disease and decay. Her work is interpreted as directly challenging medicalisation through the advocacy of self-help (thereby re-emphasising the importance of the women's health movement). It relies on the practice of confession as therapy through the representation of the 'grotesque' female body, or by 'making a spectacle of oneself' which, as Wolff and others note, provides a means of saying the unsayable.

Despite the optimism accompanying women's art of the 1970s and the pursuit of female authenticity through realist and revisioning strategies, celebratory approaches to the female body and attempts to develop a specifically 'feminine' visual language also attracted criticism from feminists. First, such work was viewed as reinforcing the biological basis of femininity and sexual difference, in which women's social, emotional and psychical characteristics were understood as fixed, static and inferior to those of men. The work of Judy Chicago is most often cited as typical of an approach that is reductive. For instance in *The Dinner Party*, she organised vaginal motifs into a work representing the lives of women she herself identified as socially and politically significant. However, many feminists responded angrily to Chicago's work as the reduction of the hard-won life of the minds of women to compartmentalised genitalia (Williams and Bendelow, 1998). Chicago herself did not necessarily share the view that she was contributing to the development of an explicitly feminist visual language, and insisted her work be viewed as art and not as a political statement. Second, some feminist commentators noted the difficulties of giving visual expression to female experience, given the patriarchal context in which female desire and experience is constructed. If ontological difference is constructed through patriarchal relations, how then can women artists represent a female ontology that does not simply reproduce those relations? Hence, whilst women's art implied a distinct ontology, some writers began to raise epistemological questions concerning access to that ontology.

Third, issues of power embedded within the process of making art have been obscured by preoccupations with the correspondence in women's art between representations of the female body and women's experience. For instance, Judy Chicago's *The Dinner Party*, reportedly drew on the labour of 'thousands of unpaid volunteers' (Woodley, 1985: 97) in an effort to create a 'collective approach' to making art. Yet, the women involved in contributing to *The Dinner Party* remain nameless although Chicago arguably has reaped the rewards of fame that accompanied the project. Moreover, while Chicago is seen by some as the epitome of 'woman's art', she has been criticised for the absences of particular women in some of her work. *The Dinner Party* makes very little reference to black women and where black women are represented, they are so with no reference to internal differentiation. Finally, by the early 1980s, women who had been influenced by academic feminism had begun to question the stability and ontological basis of experience and this had a direct impact on the nature of the visual art they produced.

Psychoanalysis, postmodernism and visual culture

In the 1980s, women's art moved away from an explicit focus on the politics of the female body towards an emphasis on the deconstruction of meanings and the interrogation of signs. This development was underpinned first by the influences of psychoanalytic theory, which was used to emphasise the politics of looking and of the 'gaze'. As Nead (1992) notes, the gaze 'regulates' the female body by presenting it as intact, flawless, idealised and contained, concealing the fleshy, messy leaky experiential female body. Feminists have observed how women are encouraged to treat their bodies as raw material for manipulation and display (see de Beauvoir, 1972 [1949]), and to subject themselves to constant scrutiny (Berger, 1972; Synott, 1993). This masquerade of femininity was subject to visual critique through the work of Cindy Sherman.

Through her photographic transformations 'female objectification becomes both the subject and the object' (Cottingham, 1989: 94) through the exposure of the 'narcissism implicit in femininity' or the exaggeration of body parts. Moreover, her use of parody demonstrates the series of interplays between text and image, and between the removal of flaws and blemishes in order to smooth out the feminine body in which women engage on the one hand, and feminist critiques of the oppressive effects of those processes of cosmetic transformation on the other. This reflexive manipulation is also evident in the work of women artists in the 1990s who 'emphasized the transforming process' and used their own bodies 'to make of that material "art"' (Betterton, 1996: 244) and emphasise 'woman as object in life *and* art'. For instance, the French artist Orlan has become famous for her participation in cosmetic surgery according to prevailing notions of Western beauty in ways that also offer critique of those standards of beauty (see Davis, 1995 for an extended discussion of Orlan's approach). In a similar fashion, Jenny Saville's paintings comment on how a feminine aesthetic is achieved by peeling layers of skin from the female body and reshaping or remoulding skin into new idealised features. Such art highlights the ways in which the female body is treated as a project (Shilling, 1993) by both women themselves and by the artist. Here the body is shown both as being transformed to create the appearance of femininity and as embodying its 'own' critique of such processes.

Beyond psychoanalytic theory, a second influence on women's art in the 1980s was postmodernism, which provided a platform for a 'new ontology'. This ontology highlighted difference, using the tools of appropriation, subversion and self-conscious irony (Cottingham, 1989) and though many feminist art critics initially disregarded postmodernism's possibilities for women, some women artists began tentatively to view it as a way of constructing new meanings about femininity (McRobbie, 1990; more generally see also Flax, 1986). A key challenge was the representation of female embodiment without 'using' the female body as an object or reducing femininity to the body, and without reliance on the visualising techniques of those institutions and practices which fragment and objectify the female body (such as the medical gaze) (Betterton, 1996). The 'new ontology' used patriarchally defined femaleness in ironic ways: the representation of difference was not the representation of an essential, biologically defined difference, but a difference grounded in patriarchal thought and structure. Such art eschewed painting which was deemed a privileged masculinist reserve (Cottingham, 1989) and associated with a modernist objectification of the female body and instead, used a range of media such as photography and installation. The postmodern approach to the production of visual images engaged with the female body, without reducing femininity *to* the body, and relied on tactics such as reframing, juxtaposition and reflexive manipulation to highlight the various ways in which ideas about the female body and femininity are constructed.

Hence, although postmodernism offered ambiguous interpretations, multiple readings and explicitly incorporated theory into practice, some of the work produced in these new media was seen to be less confrontational, 'less politically directed' and more 'aestheticized' than previous 'women's art'

(Cottingham, 1989). In part, this had to do with the way that postmodern art in general deconstructs things in ways that are specific to and accessible for an 'art literate' audience. Moreover, by the end of the 1980s, although feminist theory occupied a place in art education, the visible and collective presence of women in the arts was undermined by under-funding and masked by a postfeminist individualism which suggested that women had made a greater impact in the visual arts than ever before (McRobbie, 1990). Many feminist commentators remained unconvinced by the political effects of postmodern women's art and saw it as a force that stifled the radical potential of women's art rather than providing it with a new direction.

For instance, McRobbie (1990) argues that the *feminism* in such art is somewhat less than palpable and hence a feminist reading of it is not the only possible reading. This is so because, in the first place, the ironic and gender-neutral readings favoured by postmodernism contribute to a lack of interpretative clarity, which has implications for critical responses to the art. Second, the privileging of ambiguity makes it difficult to identify the presence and form of feminism in art and for women artists engaging with feminism to be interpreted as feminist. Third, the (constructed) difference between men and women, lived in the body, is effaced as a source of inequality and/or as a resource for critique (McRobbie, 1990). Difference becomes incidental rather than pivotal in the art and postmodernist theory does not provide a means of analysing women's art, because 'women's art' is defined (by the artists themselves as well as by audiences and critics) 'in relation to, and against, 1970s feminism' (1990: 11). That is to say, it is difficult to see how women's art could be created and interpreted *as* women's art, without some reference to feminism in one form or another. While a postmodernist framework does not rule out this emphasis, it does not make a feminist interpretation explicit and therefore, compromises the radical potential of women's art. So while on the one hand, there appears to have been a partial inclusion of women as producers of art within a postmodern turn, the inclusion itself effaces the political potential of such art and jeopardises the extent to which such art can be interpreted *as* women's art.

Poststructuralism, philosophy and psychoanalysis (again)

Women's art and feminist analysis shifted in the 1990s from normative questions about whether or how the female body should be represented to phenomeno-logical questions concerning meaning and experience. Betterton describes this shift in feminist analysis as one from 'the problem of *looking* (distance) to the problem of *embodiment* (touch)' (1996: 7) and in visual art production, a return to an explicit focus on the female body. Moreover, the production of women's art and feminist analysis of it follows a more general shift towards what Gatens (1996) terms an 'embodied perspective', itself a reaction to the rationalisation and regulation of the social body in modernity, which has been '*disembodied* in modernist art practices' (Betterton, 1996). The re-embodying move identified here is 'part of an attempt to visualise the repressed, corporeal and unregulated aspects of ourselves' (1996: 19). Although this aim has similarities with the aim of women's art in the 1970s, what makes it different is that it is accompanied by feminist theories of the body, which provide it with academic legitimacy.

Feminist theories of the body have developed rapidly in the last decade, and the move to an 'embodied perspective' is now shared by feminists in many disciplines, as part of a reaction against the disembodied practices and knowledges they identify as constitutive of their respective disciplines (for instance see Rose (1993) for an explicit account of the disembodied knowledges of geography). Though feminist perspectives on the body differ, and there is considerable debate about what materiality means and what it refers to, there is also substantial convergence around the notion of the body as discursively and symbolically produced. This convergence insists on the constitution of matter through social practices and discourses (Foucault); on viewing language as constitutive of reality rather than as a medium of expressing reality (Derrida); and refuses a phenomenological distinction between subject and object. In particular, feminist theories of the body refute a stable, reductive bodily basis for gender (or rather, sexual difference). This is because, in the first instance, feminist historians (such as Duden, 1991; Oudshoorn, 1994) have demonstrated how interpretations and understandings of the female body have changed. Second, female biology has changed. For instance, women now begin to menstruate at a younger age than at the turn of the twentieth century (Brumberg, 1997) as a consequence of changes in diet and health. Thus, the body has a history (Illich, 1986) and any feminist consideration of 'women's knowledge' must account for the social and historical constitution of both such knowledge (Wolff, 1990) and the experiences from which it develops. Third, feminists have by and large accepted that the experience of *being* embodied (or how we inhabit the body) is socially and politically inscribed (Bordo, 1989). Moreover, predominant understandings of the self in Western thought are premised on a model of heterosexual masculinity, and feminists have used phenomenology and psychoanalytic frameworks to demonstrate how this model of the self shapes female embodiment according to a male symbolic order (e.g. Irigaray, 1985; Young, 1990).

This kind of claim is most tenaciously associated with the poststructuralist readings of psychoanalysis that became available to Anglo-American feminist audiences in the 1980s. New French feminism is largely associated with the work of Hélène Cixous, Julia Kristeva and Luce Irigaray, although there are many other French feminists associated with poststructuralist thought (Vice, 1998). Psychoanalytic theory is dense and extensive but of most relevance to the development of feminist theories of the body are claims concerning how the '*matter* of women's bodies underpins the social order' and how the specificities of female embodiment are repressed within this order (Game, 1991: 64). French feminists have argued that the female body can be deployed strategically in visual art as a means of challenging the binary arrangement of the symbolic order (Betterton, 1996: 16).

For instance, Irigaray's work has been interpreted as reversing traditional psychoanalytic views of the feminine (Davidson and Smith, 1999) by challenging

Lacan's theories of the female as the 'passive recipient of the male gaze' (Carson, 2000: 43) in which she uses the metaphor of two lips speaking together as a textual strategy through which to positively represent feminine sexuality. Both she and Cixous advocate textual strategies that emphasise the specificities of female embodiment (which for Irigaray is summarised in terms of the multiplicity, fluidity and decentred nature of experience). Other feminists (e.g. Grosz, 1994) argue that these characteristics contribute towards the deconstruction of binary opposites and in particular, dualisms between mind and body. Kristeva (1982) places emphasis on the semiotic, pre-linguistic, pre-Oedipal phase in which 'bodily encounters' in the maternal-child relationship shape the Imaginary but are repressed on entry into language. For Kristeva, culture or cultural objects provide the space in which the Imaginary finds expression (Wolff, 1990) and in which, therefore, there lies the possibility of revisioning the feminine. Accordingly, in painting, photography, sculpture and installation in particular, metaphors of touch have been deployed, the 'maternal' retrieved and the concealed, marginalised corporeal aspects of Western culture re-emphasised as a means of 'imagining' a feminine subject. As recent feminist reviews and analyses of contemporary women's art observe, the incorporation of feminist theory into visual work has revitalised and matured the representation of the female body. It seems generally accepted by academic feminism that women artists across media now represent the female body with the *intention* of raising questions about the masculinist values that shape female lived experience and of highlighting the ways in which the feminine is repressed in the symbolic order.

Feminism and art today

I have thus far outlined the development of women's art over three decades and reviewed the ways in which feminist theory has provoked and influenced women's artistic practice in relation to both what is represented and to the process of representation. I have traced how feminist theory has been applied to visual images as a means of addressing the politics of representation. These theories highlight the gendered, sexualized and feminized nature of representation and the difficulties of establishing alternative modes of representation beyond dominant cultural codes. However, there have been significant shifts in both the nature of women's art and in feminist analysis. Where much of the art of the 1970s sprang directly from the women's movement and as such, from material and political engagement with the objectification and coercion of the female body, in contrast, women's art of the 1990s and beyond takes feminist writing about sexual difference as its starting point and in particular, the writing of contemporary French feminists. Interpretation of women's art begins from text and reads visual art through the themes and concepts derived from the writings of feminist theory. As with other areas of feminist inquiry, analysis of visual art is predominantly characterised by a deconstructionist framework that privileges psychoanalytic interpretations of visual imagery. Indeed, it is striking that feminist analyses across a range of media produce a convergence concerning the '*effects* of representation in terms of ideology and power' (Evans, 2000: 105). Moreover, the prevailing mode of feminist analysis tends to address 'representation' in terms of the effects of a particular image, rather than pose questions about the 'the specificities of a medium, its conditions of production, distribution, consumption and practical use' (ibid.: 107). There are both advantages and disadvantages associated with the current position.

What are the advantages? First, contemporary visual art, produced by women and interpreted by feminist scholars, contributes to the wider project of reappropriating corporeality for women (Bordo, 1989), by exploring the possibility of feminine ontology and asking what a distinctly 'feminine' culture might look like. This is a highly significant and pressing question for contemporary feminism, and its pursuit contributes an ongoing challenge to formal, expert masculine forms of knowledge. Second, contemporary feminist visual analysis is supported by a predominantly deconstructionist approach that privileges a post-Lacanian psychoanalytic framework. The emphasis placed on the imaginary body by such an approach both offers a theory of the (non)visual and a theory of the acquisition of gendered subjectivity and in doing so, provides a universal framework for visualising and interpreting what Elaine Showalter (1985) has called the 'wild zone'. This wild zone is characterised by that which is concealed, abjected and obscured from public (and implicitly masculine) consideration. Such a tactic pulls the female body back into the visual frame via theory and allows feminists to address the question of how the body enters into the constitution of female subjectivity. Moreover, it insists on revealing the ways in which female corporeality underwrites the symbolic order and is repressed in the process of constituting that order. The application of feminist theory as an interpretative grid invites us to consider women's visual art in terms of a particular set of feminist issues and to see such art as a critical space in which difference is more positively (and legitimately) imaged and imagined.

However, there are in my view, distinct disadvantages accompanying current feminist commitment to deconstructionist approaches and the emphasis on imaginary corporeality that a psychoanalytic framework supports. First, as Janet Wolff and other writers have noted, any feminist visual strategy that attempts to reassert female corporeality is politically problematic. Modern Western culture is characterised by contradictory tendencies which, on the one hand, culturally deny the significance of women's corporeality as a basis for knowledge and understanding, yet, on the other, impose corporeality on women as the basis of female subjectivity. Although Irigaray's corporeal tactic places analytic and interpretative emphasis on the distinctiveness of the (imaginary) morphology of the female body, corporeal specificity already contains an essentialist potential because of the way that the female body has been historically and socially constituted in Western culture (Wolff, 1990). Hence, although an emphasis on (imaginary) corporeality may have the effect of politicising that which has been hitherto obscured, that political force can too easily be compromised. Whatever the intentions of artists themselves, the context in which images are consumed effects their interpretation, and (imagined) female corporeality is always open to reading against the grain.

Second, although feminists have criticised the privileged status of the visual in psychoanalytic theory, non-visual feminist readings of psychoanalysis are bound to an epistemology that *presumes* the corporeal nature of the maternal/ infant relationship as the basis for the acquisition of gendered subjectivity. This presumption allows feminist theory to develop the speculative nature of post-Lacanian psychoanalytic models into an interpretative grid that is applied to a variety of media. The application of this grid has a tendency to establish a closure against consideration of the particular and treat the visual under analysis as a general claim. For feminist sociologists this is problematic because of (1) the normalising tendencies inherent in psychoanalytic frameworks; (2) because of the way in which the (heterosexual) Oedipal triangle is priv-ileged in the constitution of the unconscious (Barrett, 1992); and (3) because a knowledge of text is a necessary precondition of access to such interpretations. Moreover, although the poststructuralist impulse within feminism springs from a critique of the universalising tendencies of the grand narratives of modernity, paradoxically, contemporary feminist analysis of women's art is in danger of reproducing grand theory, by investment in the language of theory. Despite a commitment to the specificities of female corporeality by feminist appropriations of post-Lacanian psychoanalytic theory, the repetitious enunciation generated by this theory reduces the imaged body to the general-ised object of theory.

Third, while psychoanalytic models may provide a means of analysing the 'wild zone', they do so at the expense of experiences lived and differentiated on many levels (Wolff, 1990). While the poststructuralist impulse that under-pins much contemporary feminist analysis of visual culture provides a formal critique of a discursively produced imaginary body, this body has become detached from contexts, times, places and relations. The corporeality of the women who produce, view and consume such imagery is bracketed out. In contrast to women's art and feminist interpretation of such art in the 1970s, contemporary images are rarely treated as situated knowledges. Nor does feminist analysis acknowledge the power relations that constitute art and its critiques, and in particular, how the feminist gaze is located within and consti-tutive of a particular, dominant, interpretation of women's art. Concomitantly, not only is the lived body excluded from discussion but also, and more problematically for the feminist sociologist, the social.

Now, many sociologists as well as many feminists have acknowledged a shift in understanding the nature of the social. As Game (1996) observes, the 'sociological social' invites methodologies that allow the sociologist to represent the real, maintaining clear boundaries between the sociologist and the knowledge she creates about the real, which in turn exists independently of both the sociologist and the knowledge created. Many currents and impulses, including feminism, have challenged this clarity of relation between the real and the represented. Hence, the *feminist* sociologist may be more committed than other sorts of sociologist to methodologies that allow her to examine how a relation between real and represented is constituted, how knowledge is produced about that relation and how her relation to the afore-mentioned relation is constituted. Indeed, a feminist sociology of women's art and feminist responses to it might examine how feminist theory itself operates as a textual apparatus that produces certain effects (Rose, 2000), a gaze that visualises female corporeality in particular ways, but possibly at the expense of aspects of corporeality that evade visualisation.

Hence what I am arguing here is that feminist theory has itself become a disciplinary apparatus, which is put to a certain kind of work. Feminist theory, particularly that influenced by post-Lacanian psychoanalysis, actively constructs a particular way of seeing women's art. While on the one hand this may be productive for academic feminism (visualising the hitherto unseen, verbalising the hitherto unsaid), it may also operate closures for feminists inside and outside the academy and for women who do not consider themselves affiliated to feminism in any form. This need not matter if feminist theory considers itself only to be participating in an internal dialogue with feminist theory. But it does matter, if feminist theory is to remain both part of a wider feminism as a social and political movement and if it wishes to contribute to interdisciplinary conversations. A significant effect of feminist theory as a textual, disciplinary apparatus in its current poststructuralist, philosophically and psychoanalytically influenced form is that conversation and exchange between feminists in different disciplines is stifled. As other feminists have noted, the language of theory generated by these intellectual currents makes the subject matter intelligible only to those fully conversant with that language. This seems counter-productive for a feminism that seeks to re-emphasise the specificities of lived embodiment. In contrast to the investment in the discursive as linguistically produced (as illustrated by feminist interpretations of contemporary women's art) that start from the standpoint of theory, a sociologically informed feminist methodology might more productively begin with lived experience, or what is 'real' and 'lived' for women involved in the production and consumption of visual art. Given the persistent conceptual difficulties with the category of experience, this approach need not bracket out the socially constituted nature of experience, but rather address the social relations, circumstances and contexts in which experiences are formed (Smith, 1987, 1990). This would allow feminist sociologists not only to address corporeality in women's art but also avoid reducing corporeality to an already objectified body, because analysis would also focus on the diverse ways in which corporeality is constituted and understood.

Conclusion

While feminist interpretations of women's art in general are currently persuaded by the linguistic turn and the investment in psychoanalytic frameworks for the analysis of the politics of representation, *sociologically* informed feminist approaches to the analysis of women's art need to begin from and proceed towards an understanding of the *social*. This need not preclude acknowledgement of the significance of text because a sociologically informed feminist analysis of art would acknowledge the ways in which the textual becomes part of and shapes the social. But text alone does not constitute the social. As a contributor to a recent volume on feminist visual culture remarks, it is 'difficult to imagine art without politics, ideology or social context' (Evans, 2000: 26). This is more strongly the case for women's art than other categories of art because of the way in which feminism as a social and political movement has materially and symbolically shaped the production and consumption of art by women. Hence, in relation to women's art, to view the social only in terms of text is to view gender (or sexual difference) as textual, as inscribed, as written, as imaged, and while gender may be all these things, a sociologically derived understanding of gender breaches the text and insists on the existence of phenomena that are not purely textual in form. This space beyond the text – occupied by relations, practices, thoughts, feelings, actions – is excluded from current feminist approaches to the analysis and interpretation of women's art, which is typically driven by the internal logic of poststructuralist deconstructionism and intertextuality. A sociologically informed feminist approach begins from this space beyond the text, and proceeds by acknowledging its own contribution both to the production of women's art itself and to the identification of the latter *as* an object of feminist inquiry.

A 'New' Paradigm for a Sociology of Aesthetics

Robert W. Witkin

Introduction

Artistic revolutions like scientific revolutions involve 'paradigm shifts' that are closely correlated with major social and economic changes. One such shift certainly occurred with the development of a so-called 'naturalistic' style of representation in the visual arts in the late fourteenth and early fifteenth centuries. Another occurred in modern times during the late nineteenth and early twentieth centuries. In the earlier period, Renaissance painters adopted, as an ideal, a model of picture-making in which a painting aimed at simulating the optical values that would be obtained in natural perception. There were certain technical developments necessary to achieving high degrees of perceptual realism. The invention of oil paints allowed a more lustrous and realistic depiction of the surfaces of all kinds of materials, including the depiction of flesh-tones. The discovery of 'linear' perspective – the convergence of parallel lines, as they recede from the viewer to a point on the horizon – facilitated the realistic depiction of size–distance ratios and opened up the deep space of the picture allowing the depiction of three dimensions on a flat surface. Finally, the development of 'chiaroscuro' in which objects are modelled in tonal gradations of light or shade in accordance with their orientation in relation to a unified light source, gave a solidity and depth to depicted objects that rendered them with more realism than had been possible hitherto.

But how are we to see the significance of such developments in technique? A simplistic account would have it that the technical discoveries referred to above were the cause of the paradigm shift that took place in art; that artists painted in this way because it became technically possible for them to do so as though the revolution in art could be ascribed simply to technological progress, ignoring changes at the level of social formation in which such technological developments are grounded. The history of art should lead us to doubt this view of causation. For one thing the ideal of making visual representations approximate to natural perception was not new. While it is true that in the Renaissance, European art developed the techniques involved to a higher level of sophistication than had earlier societies, those of classical Greece and Rome had also produced something approximating to a perceptual-realist art. Why did later European societies give up that classical heritage? The art of the early Christians, for example, followed the same broadly perceptual-realist path as that of Rome but as early as the second century AD, Christian art was undergoing a stylistic change that was making depicted images less realistic, less volumetric. Space was flattened and depiction became formalised and schematic and for centuries this situation prevailed. We then have to explain why so many societies, originally subject to Roman influence, chose to abandon its 'technical advances' and actively pursue non-realistic modes of representation.

Even at the time there were those who, like the neo-Platonist thinker Plotinus, eschewed reference to technical factors and justified the retreat from realism and the flattening of depicted surfaces as a spiritualisation of art. Clearly what holds a style in place or triggers the development of a new style cannot be attributed to the mere presence or absence of certain techniques. The more recent paradigm shift, which occurred in the late nineteenth century, is also evidence of this same type of reversal. The volumetric realistic styles of European art that evolved over a period of five hundred years were abandoned in the paintings of Manet, Cezanne and others in favour of a type of art-making in which 'flatness' became an aesthetic imperative and in which the depiction of objects and of spatial arrangements was a complete negation of Alberti's ideal of a painting being like a scene depicted through a window.

Cezanne did not paint apples so that we would be able to find our way around a fruit bowl, nor just to show us how pleasing to the eye an arrangement of apples can look. Aesthetic means are employed in painting to do 'ideational' work. If we ask precisely what semiotic possibilities are afforded by a given perceptual system, we will have moved away from the notion that suggests that pictures are made purely to realise ideals of beauty and of sensory preference where the latter are seen as divorced from the realm of ideas. If we are to account for stylistic change on the scale of an artistic revolution, it will not do to see such changes as merely the pursuit of a kind of sensory preference. Painters of the fifteenth-century did not typically paint pictures in order to show us what something looked like. In painting the face of the Virgin they certainly sought to express an ideal of beauty but in pursuit of the expression of an important idea. We need to take seriously the question of precisely what type of ideation a given stylistic change makes possible. What type of ideation, for example, did the production of the perceptual-realist art of the Renaissance make possible that an earlier art could not? We should not be looking primarily, here, at the content of paintings. The Renaissance painter was a visualiser of the holy stories as had been the painters of earlier centuries. Content, alone, will not serve to differentiate painters before and after an epochal change in style. We need to consider the *process of ideation*, the mode of constructing reality, and the way in which important values are thought under given social conditions. I shall argue that paradigm shifts in aesthetic styles corresponded to new modes of understanding and experiencing values that reflected changed social conditions.

Abstraction

'Styles' of art are held in place by the 'demands' made by societies to think their key values at a level of abstraction appropriate to their principles of social formation. Consider the case of a perceptual-realist painting, one that successfully simulates a three-dimensional reality on a two-dimensional surface, allowing the receiver to see the frame as a kind of window through which a scene may be viewed, much as one might view a scene in real life. No matter how fascinated artists were, at the time of the Renaissance, with the technical wizardry that surrounded the production of such pictures, the raison d'être for such developments is best sought in the semiotic possibilities that they afford for raising the level of abstraction at which values could be ordered in thought. A perceptual-realist art clearly alters the structural possibilities for representing figures and objects and the relations among them in important ways. For example, to the extent that the space depicted simulates a real optical space, and figures and objects are represented *as they appear from a particular point of view*, the attributes of depicted figures and objects will be determined by the system of optical transformations into which they enter. No figure in such art comes complete and self-contained in its visual values, as it does in archaic art. Rather, the optical values that describe a figure are functionally relative and are determined by the figure's position and relations within a larger system of transformations and relative to the assumed point of view of an observer (e.g. the figure varies in size and distinctness depending on its position; all such perceived dimensions are a function of the total system of relations in which the figure participates).

This represents, in my argument, a raising of the level of abstraction at which values may be represented and, therefore, thought. My claim, here, runs counter to the usual sense in which we speak of art as abstract. Thus many use the term 'abstract' to describe both primitive art and modern art because they mean by it a departure from realism, the assumption being that the more art looks like real things the less abstract it must be. In contrast, I am arguing that so-called 'perceptual-realist' art is of a high order of abstraction because it deals not in objects *as such*, something I would claim is true of primitive art, but in objects *as seen*, that is the appearances of objects from a distance. This construction of reality at a distance and relative to a point of view means that 'knowledge' of things is abstracted not from the things themselves (that they are hard or soft to the 'touch', for example) but from the system of optical relations, constituted by the eye of the observer, into which objects are inserted. This more abstract and more comprehensive system of relations is also, therefore, a more subject-centred system. The raising of the level of abstraction in art is synonymous with a heightening of the subject-centredness of art.

Semiotic systems

In the modern theory of signs as it has developed in Europe, particularly in the writings of French post-structuralist thinkers such as Baudrillard, a distinction is drawn between the elements of the semiotic process, the signifier, the signified and the referent (Gane, 1991). Moreover, the tendency has been to see the modern period as one that has witnessed a substantial shift of 'value' towards the signifier and away from referent and the signified. By the *signifier* is meant the marks on paper, the sound or 'voicing', the 'pure symbol' as it were, considered independently of anything symbolised. By the *signified* is meant the idea or value that is symbolised by such signifiers, what the symbol is intended to communicate. Finally, by the *referent* is meant the object or thing referred to in the signification. Consider a famous painting such as Louis David's *The Death of Marat*. The painting depicts the murdered Marat in his bath. The pigmented forms that fill the canvas constitute the 'signifier', the aesthetic symbol itself. Clearly Marat, the man himself, together with the bath and other objects and details *referred to* in the pictorial text, constitute the 'referents' of the sign. However, the values and ideas that David sought to communicate in this painting – the idea of nobility, of heroic composure, of sacrifice and martyrdom (with all its implicit parallels with another story) – constitute the 'signified'.

The relations among the elements of the semiotic process are inherently problematical. It is possible to analyse the development of these relations in terms of a historical theory of signs by linking it to an analysis of the development of relations among the elements of the perceptual process on the one hand, and relations among the elements of the social process on the other. Baudrillard, for example, sees capitalism as reflecting, at the level of economic relations, the abstract symbolic code that emerged at the time of the Renaissance and characterised by the 'emancipation' of signs from their referents. This abstract code is even likened by Baudrillard to money, as an abstract medium of equivalences. In late twentieth-century society, Baudrillard sees the separation of signs from referents as virtually complete and modern consumer society as dominated by an endless circulation of signifiers (Gane, 1991). The development of semiotic systems from the predominance of the referent, through predominance of the signified to the predominance of the signifier can be seen, as will be argued below, to mirror the development of the perceptual system. In both, development is from lower to higher levels of abstraction and from more object-centred levels of organisation (semiotically, more referent-centred levels) towards more subject-centred levels of organisation (semiotically, more signified/signifier-centred levels).

Social systems

The line of development that I am tracing – from lower to higher levels of abstraction in the thinking of values – is closely bound up with changes in the social order itself, changes in the relations of social production. Marx claimed that human societies are distinguished from non-human societies by the fact that they must produce the means of their subsistence. However, in the process of doing so, different types of society clearly stand in different types of relationship to nature. That is to say, social organisation and social formation reflect a variety of possibilities with respect to the distancing – and, therefore, the abstraction – of the 'agency' of social actors from nature. We can thus differentiate societies, albeit crudely, on the basis of the degree to which agency, in a given social formation, is *embedded* in nature. In a hunter-gatherer society, for example, the 'distancing' of social agency from nature is relatively low. Such societies do not produce nature or even occasion it; they organise themselves to make efficient use of what nature produces. In a society based upon settled agriculture, however, there is a greater degree of distancing of agency from nature. Although such societies do not produce nature they do 'occasion' it through the practice of building settlements, seasonal planting of crops, the construction of drainage, fortifications for defence and so forth. Such societies can also develop significant urban centres, as was the case in all the great agrarian empires.

Where city-based production is decisively distanced from nature, where it involves a significant degree of manufacture, the society becomes a producer proper. Such production takes place at a remove from nature. It involves individuals not only in 'freely' initiating and developing production and commercial enterprise but also in their entering into cooperative relations with others to produce the environment – political, social and economic – in which the projects of 'free' citizens can be fulfilled. That is, in truly bourgeois societies, the very construction of society itself is the construction of a 'second nature' which is the ground of all the projects of individual producers and merchants. Society becomes the producer of this second nature.

Ideal-typically, this second nature must be made through negotiation and cooperation among free individuals. It is inherent in the construction of bourgeois societies that individual freedom and social cooperation and constraint must somehow be harmonised, that the social order constructed through cooperation among bourgeois producers must be the means of realising and fulfilling the individual projects of those producers. The reconciling of individual and society, personal freedom and collective constraint, subject and object, part and whole, is not merely ideological; it is an urgent practical problem in the construction of bourgeois life. To some extent, bourgeois societies have, as a matter of practical daily life, to achieve an accommodation between these poles, a degree of equilibration, however tense or imperfect. Failure to cooperate adequately in the efficient construction of a social order in and through which the projects of individuals can be realised, means the failure of those projects. Thus bourgeois societies tend to 'democratic' forms of political structure and the development of 'universalistic' systems of law. According to Arnold Hauser (1991) it is this aspect of city cultures that accounts for the tendency to 'naturalistic' styles of art.

Any such approximation to equilibrium between individual freedom and social constraint was only ever partial and only transient. Moreover, it constituted the ideal (and ideology) of higher social classes. As bourgeois societies developed, the problems of constructing 'second nature' grew more complex and the organisational process threatened to submerge individuals and to achieve an end to the antinomy of individual and society, not through an equilibration between the two, as sought in the earlier phase of bourgeois development, but through penetrating the boundaries of the individual and entirely subsuming its constitutive elements in the collective order – in other words, through becoming totalitarian. It is possible to see the artistic revolution and accompanying paradigm shift at the turn of the twentieth century as a response to this situation.

In the classical model of a bourgeois society, individuals must interact with others to construct the system of social constraints and conditions through which their free choices are exercised. Social interaction, therefore, has an inherently teleological character. The material order of bourgeois life demands of its texts a historicity, a textual suspense, with which to furnish itself with ideas, with consciousness and with reflections on experience. One implication of this textual suspense is that we cannot identify an element or part (a character in a story, for example) with its immediate appearance, presuming that what we actually see at one instant is all there is; what appears of the subject, at any given instant, only has meaning in virtue of its historical unfolding (retrospective and prospective) and that historical development (suspense), which stands back of what appears of a subject's actions, shapes and determines those actions, imparting meaning to them. This suspense divides the world into foreground and background, into what we can immediately see and what we perceive to lie 'behind' what we see; suspense invests appearances or 'surfaces' that are in the foreground, with depth. To the extent that a subject in a story has depth, she/he has an interiority, a personality that can be 'perceived' in outer appearance and expression. Thus, the 'depth' of the subject in a story can be thought of synchronically – as the personality of the subject and diachronically, as the biography of the subject. Corresponding to the individual's personality and biography is a society's culture and its history.

In his monumental study of the representation of reality in Western literature, Auerbach (1968) begins with an analysis of Homer's Odyssey. He argues that the world of Odysseus is one which is entirely foregrounded, a world lacking background and depth; Homer's characters exist in an eternal present without biographical suspense arising from their past and determining their actions. They appear, in Auerbach's memorable phrase 'as though on the first morning of their lives'. Odysseus has a character – we know that he is cunning and brave – but he is without an interior life extending into the background. By contrast, the classical bourgeois novel is steeped in background, in suspense, both at the level of the personalities and biographies of its main characters and at the level of the larger culture and history which shapes their existence.

The representation of reality in terms of an articulation of foreground and background, of outer appearance and inner meaning, makes of the immediate visible surface of a representation the sign of an underlying dynamic stretching back into the past and forward into the future. The 'whole' or the 'totality' – society, culture, history, personality – is identified with what lies 'behind', 'beneath' or 'within' appearances, that is, with the 'idea' disclosed in appearances or – to express it semiotically – the 'signified'. European societies from the time of the Renaissance developed, in all the arts – in painting, architecture, literature, theatre and music – a systematic dialectics of foreground/background relations, of inner/outer. It was an art that aimed at disclosing the depth, the inner meaning of experience – its psycho-logic, its socio-logic – in and through the systematic articulation of 'external' or 'surface' appearances. This disclosure depended crucially for its success upon systematics, upon the rational articulation of all the differentiated elements in a work such that the entire work appears to arise organically from the movements and relations among its parts. It is this identity relation between whole and part which puts suspense or historicity into the work, making the development of the parts, in their mutual relations, unfold towards the completion of the whole. The refinements through which this system was developed were centuries in the making but the principle technical means appeared as far back as the fifteenth century.

Perceptual systems

The assignment of art works by art historians to epochal categories such as Archaic, Classical, Mediaeval, Renaissance, Modern and so forth is more than a system of temporal classification. It also describes marked and 'characteristic' changes in the mode of 'picturing', in the 'styling' of art works adopted by artists. Each of these epochal changes might be termed an 'artistic revolution'. And each of these revolutions poses what Gombrich referred to as 'the riddle of style', the puzzle of how ways of depicting the world in pictures squares with ways of seeing the world in everyday life.

In his book *Art and Illusion* (1959), Gombrich reproduces Alain's witty cartoon of what purports to be an ancient Egyptian art class in which ancient Egyptian art students are painting ancient Egyptian models in the ancient Egyptian manner; each figure, whether an art student or the figure s/he is drawing or the model being drawn, appears as a composite of frontal and profile views that could never occupy the same picture plane in any realistic portrayal. There are three components to the riddle. What did the ancient Egyptians actually see with their eyes when they looked at a person? Assuming that what they saw was, optically, more or less what you or I would see, why did they depict people in the way they did, with eyes and torso facing front and head and legs in profile? Finally, what role does the society in which this art is produced play in conditioning both the perceptual process that is to be used in picturing and the semiotic process that organises such picturing as a symbolic or signifying of ideas and values.

In every age, including archaic times, artists have paid close attention to the perceptual world and to perceptual truths. They have not been indifferent to such relations nor seen themselves as free from the demands of perceptual truth. We have only to think of the intensity with which Cézanne actually *observes* the nature he paints – an intensity that is all the more marked as he transforms the way of seeing that predominated in European art for five centuries – or, to consider the equally studied observation of landscape that results in the flattened articulation of forms produced by Braque. Perceptual values are always of importance in realising new ways of picturing. Nor is there any necessary contradiction between having a concern for perceptual truth, for real material 'sense' values, and the need of the artist to construct works that will realise important cultural values, not only in the content of the work but also in and through its formal construction.

Because a work of art is an organisation of *perceptua* and is only able to organise the *body* of the subject in and through sensuous means, perceptual relations and perceptual truths determine what kind of organisation of the body (here, equivalent to an 'understanding') is possible and, therefore, what kind of organisation of social and cultural values can be realised in a work of art. Returning to the riddle of style posed by the Alain cartoon, we can resolve the matter by recognising that neither the ancient Egyptians nor the modern Cubists were moved by a concern to reproduce the perceptual relations governing optical experience. Such optical perception places the world at a distance from the subject and renders it subject to fluctuations in appearance in accordance with the disposition of the observer. Objects and figures, in themselves, lose their absolute unchanging and self-sufficient solidity. Societies for which this absolute and unchanging solidity is perceptually an important value can have little use for a perceptual-realist art that relativises the 'sacred' at a perceptual level and renders it dependent upon a point of view.

On the other hand, these archaic artists were concerned to abstract from their everyday perceptual relations those perceptual modes that answered to the semiotic demands that they sought to meet; perceptual modes that would enable them to inscribe the unchanging and absolute solidity of 'real' things. In our everyday perceptual relations, different sensory modalities are involved together and are mutually confirming. We see with our eyes what we grasp with our hands, for example. The *contact* values yielded through grasping and touching objects are visually reinforced by the *distal* values yielded in seeing those same objects at a distance. These, in turn, should be distinguished from the *proximal* values that make up the purely visual qualities – colour, texture, shape and so forth – values that are 'closest' to the eye as a sensory system. Thus a visual scene may be resolved into recognisable objects and figures which can be 'handled' (yielding contact values), seen at a distance (yielding distal values) and sensuously apprehended as a patterning of shapes and colours, of visual qualities (yielding proximal values). Each of these perceptual modes can be abstracted from the total system of perceptual relations. Each mode affords unique possibilities for aesthetic ideation and its appropriation by artists in a given type of society is secured by its affordance of these possibilities. The fact that the process of picturing is visual does not mean that it centres itself on an optical mode of perception. The ancient Egyptian artists adopted a mode of picturing that appropriated the possibilities of a *haptic* mode of perception based upon contact values. Renaissance artists, by contrast, appropriated the possibilities of an *optic* perceptual mode based upon distal values. Modern artists have grounded aesthetic process in a *somatic* mode of perception based upon proximal values. The semiotic requirements for thinking values in a given society are decisive for determining the appropriation of perceptual systems in the production of art.

While the semiotic function is key, it will not do simply to argue that perceptual values are (arbitrarily) distorted in order to accommodate the requirements of the art work to symbolise important values. There is good reason to believe that this is not the case. The depicting of figures as a composite of frontal and profile views was not simply semiotically convenient to ancient Egyptians seeking to signify important values; it may also have been sensuously and perceptually meaningful to them. Their concern was to aim at a genuine depiction of 'real' figures where reality was identified, not with the distanced view of an object – its appearance from a single point of view – but with the object itself in some absolute sense. If the ancient mode of picturing had been governed purely by the demands of sight then the picturing of such a composite figure might be described as a distortion of perceptual values. On the other hand, if the figures depicted existed for the perceiver as 'contact' values, that is as objects of 'touch', of what is disclosed to the tracing finger and enclosing hand or grasp, then the visual representation of such 'haptic' figures as composites of frontal and profile views makes sense. Such a claim effectively distinguishes between the visual process of *picturing* and the perceptual system that it models; in this case, I argue, a *haptic* system.

Haptic systems

To the extent that art appropriates a haptic mode of perception – that is, deals with the world at the level of contact values – it is 'thinking' values at a relatively low level of abstraction. Those values must be carried in the depiction of the outer form. The saintliness of Saints or the majesty of Kings must be made fully visible in the exterior of the form itself. The king may be depicted as being very much larger than his enemies as though his majesty and superiority were a matter of absolute value and therefore visible in the attributes of his depicted person – in this case, his size.

If we consider only the kind of knowledge that comes through touching and 'manipulating' objects, it is very much knowledge dominated by the material character of things themselves, as disclosed to touch. It is the objects themselves that are hard or soft or more or less massive, and so forth. The object in the hand is complete and self-contained. We can feel its bounding and enclosing surface. Different objects as disclosed by touch are *beside* one another. In their completeness and self-containedness, they do not interact. Rather they *coexist* and are ordered *coactionally*. Such a perceptual system is of a low order of abstraction. It does not permit the subject to construct a system of perceptual relations that is distanced from objects themselves. There is no possibility, therefore, of realising within a haptic perceptual mode a more comprehensive level of (semiotic) ordering of the kind that is possible when perception operates at a remove from the objects in question and can have a *point of view*. At the haptic level perceptual process is embedded in material things. Because a *haptic* system is low in abstraction, its selection as a principle of aesthetic construction is secured under those conditions where a society must necessarily think its important values at a low level of abstraction. The level of abstraction of the perceptual system can be said to correspond, therefore both to the level of abstraction in the ideas to be realised in a work of art and to the level of abstraction from nature at which social relations (social action) are realised.

Ivins (1964), in his study of Art and geometry, analyses the effects of 'tactile' (I prefer 'haptic') perception. Ivins (1964: 3) notes the extent to which truly optical experience is marked by continuous change, fluctuation and transition. Optical experience is thus dynamic and relativistic:

> Objects get smaller and less brilliant as they get further away. Very distant objects are mere shapeless nubbins. Near objects continuously change their shapes as we move about them. A pine wood close up is a mixture of deep greens and browns, but at a distance it becomes diaphanous light blue. In the course of the day the whole landscape drastically changes its colour. As the light decreases, the different objects disappear from view at different times. Parallel lines as they recede from us tend to come together.

Against all this fading in and out, this 'shifting, varying, continuity of quite different visual effects', Ivins (1964: 3) sets the discrete and absolute quality of tactile perception:

> Tactile awareness, for practical purposes, is not accomplished by a gradual fading in and out of consciousness, but by catastrophic contacts and breaking of contacts. My hand either touches something or it does not. My hand tells me that something is light or heavy, hot or cold, smooth or rough. I can measure an object that is simple in form against a phalange of my thumb or a stick, and by counting my motions I can tell how many phalanges or sticks high or wide it is. Short of accidents, my muscles tell me that these measurements always require the same number of movements, i.e. that the object does not change in size or shape. If the object is a molding, I can run my fingers or stick along it and determine that within the reach of my hand, its lines are always the same distance apart and do not come together, i.e. that the lines are parallel. Furthermore, the fact that I can touch an object, hold it, push it, pull it, gives me the sense that there is really something there, that I am not the sport of a trick or an illusion and that this something remains the same no matter what its heaviness or lightness, its hotness or coldness, its smoothness or roughness should be. Moreover, the shape of objects as known by the hand do not change with shifts of position as do shapes known by the eye.

It is little wonder that Arnold Hauser (1991) was to argue, in his *Social History of Art*, that the geometrised art of archaic societies was an art that emphasised the eternal and enduring aspects of an order, that it was produced by societies that were aristocratic and hieratic rather than democratic and individualistic. The haptic principle is actually found more purely in the archaic art of the ancient Egyptians, while Ivins himself was actually discussing classical Greek art. The art of classical Greece made many concessions to the optical and, although it did not perfect a perceptual-realist art of the kind that developed in Europe from the time of the Renaissance, the Greeks did travel a long way in that direction. However, none of these qualifications precludes acknowledging the value of Ivins' description of the contrast between the tactile and the optical. Such a description helps make sense of a great deal of theorising in respect of the social history of art.

The emphasis of haptic perception is on the bounded and continuous surface of the object – objects tend to be experienced as isolated, self-contained and self-sufficient. To the extent that this element is stressed such objects appear predetermined, marked by the possession of a 'fate' or 'destiny' but devoid of historical development, background and suspended biography. From a haptic standpoint, there is no true *interaction* between figures or objects. Relations are *coactional*. The objects and figures are part of an ideal arrangement. They approximate to the form of *ritual*. Objects are experienced, not in their becoming what they are but as fully complete in the here-and-now. Haptic presentation justifies Max Weber's famous description of traditional societies in terms of 'the authority of an eternal yesterday'. Scenes, in depiction, are uniformly lit and there is an absence of cast shadows or chiaroscuro – both, in different ways, would, if present, serve to undermine the predominance of the 'object' depiction, to make it a less than substantial presence. God is described in the biblical book of James as 'The Father of Lights in whom there is *neither variableness nor shadow of turning*'. Any use of chiaroscuro – light and shade variation reflecting the object's disposition with respect to a unified light source – would lose the (substantive) reality of the object and subject it to the rationality of appearances. Colours in haptic art tend to be monochromatic, flat and crystalline. When an object is given strong local colour it is often 'symbolic' in character. Blue is the colour of the Virgin Mary's robes, for example. Again this has to be seen as part of the same 'haptic' perceptual mode. The values to be depicted cannot be suggested by the work but must *be directly shown* in it. Realistic appearances must be sacrificed in order to *invoke* the presence of the 'real'. This constitutes, as I have suggested above, a low level of abstraction.

Optic systems

The advent of a perceptual-realist art in the city cultures of Renaissance Europe was a decisive stage in the development of an art dominated by an optical perceptual mode. In an optical relationship, an object undergoes continuous transformations as it moves through space or changes in position relative to an observer. Throughout these transformations the object remains recognisably the same object. Objects and figures thus acquire their solidity, their 'reality', from their fluidity, their very changeability; from the fact that they are inserted into multiple frames of reference and yet remain identifiably the same object (with changed appearances) throughout. An optical space is, therefore, a dynamic interactional space as distinct from a static coactional space.

A truly optical space provides a constitutive ground for the interpretation of every fragmentary appearance of a thing. Thus, when a figure is seen from one position in one of its aspects, all the other positions and aspects that constitute the full reality of the figure – its plenitude as a visual thing – are present and active in determining what is perceived. We 'see' a whole cup even when most of it is hidden from view. The third dimension is clearly important as a device or means for signifying this plenitude in the object or figure. Roundly modeled objects exist in a three-dimensional space. While only one aspect may be seen, the promise of all the other aspects making up the plenitude of the object is indicated in the projection of this continuous three-dimensional space. Objects and figures are perceived as being *in* space; their continuity is presupposed.

The system of optical transformations of objects, that constitutes a 'rational' continuous perceptual space, can be appropriated in the semiotic process in order to signify values and ideas at a level of abstraction in which the signified is no longer embedded in the referent but has gained its freedom. In a haptic perceptual mode, significant values have to be shown as integral to depicted figures. For example, in van Eyck's painting of *The Virgin in the Church*, the Virgin is a truly gigantic figure, out of all proportion to her surroundings. In a fully optical perceptual mode, however, important values can be depicted as a function of interactional relations among the figures and objects within a visual space. Figures assume a more 'natural' size and attention shifts from the perception of value in the formal attributes of the figure as such, to the perception of value in the organised system of relations and interactions into which objects and figures enter. Interaction brings suspense and background into representations, a sense of an unfolding historical development, of inner lives expressed in outer actions; it constructs historical and biographical trajectories.

The characters in a novel or in a drama have both depth and background; they have inner lives and biographies that operate as a kind of 'suspended reality' which is, nevertheless, present and effective in determining their actions and they participate in an external situation which is also experienced in terms of its cumulative suspense. In a painting we can observe the same suspense, both in the depiction of the inner lives of individuals as reflected in their outer forms, movements and expressions – personality as suspense – and also in the depiction of a background in which events and relations build cumulative suspense.

The emergence of the autonomy of the 'signified' with the advent of a perceptual-realist art did not go unnoticed among the theoreticians of the Renaissance. Alberti (1966), in his famous treatise *On Painting*, introduces the concept of the *istoria*. The *istoria* is identified with the 'themes' the painter is seeking to realise in the work. For Alberti these would be suggested by the stories of antiquity as well as the stories of the Bible. Alberti does not mean to imply that the work of the artist is simply that of illustrating stories. The *istoria* is brought to life in a painting and becomes a 'virtual' reality, permitting the emotions of depicted bodies and events to be projected onto the observer.

The construction of the *istoria* is here identified with the rationalisation of a three-dimensional pictorial space:

> The greatest work of the painter is not a *colossus* but an *istoria* ... bodies are parts of the istoria, members are parts of the bodies, planes parts of members. The primary parts of painting, therefore, are the planes. Bodies ought to harmonise together in the istoria in both size and function. It would be absurd for one who paints the Centaurs after the banquet to leave a vase of wine still standing in such a tumult. [We would call] it a weakness if in the same distance one person should appear larger than another, or if dogs should be equal to horse or better, as I frequently see, if a man is placed in a building as in a closed casket where there is scarcely room to sit down. *For these reasons bodies should harmonise in size and in function to what is happening in the* istoria. (Alberti, 1966: 72; my emphasis)

The conquest of representing three-dimensional space objects through linear perspective, foreshortening, chiaroscuro harmony and colour interaction did not of itself mean that the art produced would be immediately a realist art. Bourgeois society was centuries in the making and the styles of art that developed may be marked, from one point of view, by the radical break involving a paradigm shift in the fifteenth century. Development also had its continuous and gradual aspect and reflected the gradual evolution of a bourgeois order. The social system that emerged in the city cultures of the late Middle Ages was superimposed upon an older system of feudal relations. To that extent, the styles of art through which its values were expressed and thought, bore the same marks of superimposition and transition.

Somatic systems

In the taken-for-granted visual world, objects are clearly differentiated from each other and from the surrounding and continuous space. What is true of objects themselves is also true of the parts of objects. The face consists of nose, mouth, chin, eyes and so forth. When Picasso asserts pictorially that a face is eyes, nose, mouth, and so forth, and that it does not matter in what order one places them, he calls into question our ordinary understanding of the visual world. When he annihilates the illusion of depth created by linear perspective in painting and the stable relation of masses achieved through chiaroscuro; when he uses light and shade freely to generate complex tonal rhythms rather than to model objects; when he tears open volumes and renders them in a complex articulation of facet-planes, flaps and flanges linked by passages or hung on 'scaffolding'; when he ties the foreground to the background, tipping everything up onto the surface of the picture plane; when he uses colour as a free creative element in itself, without reference to the properties of the object being depicted; when he incorporates 'real' things as well as painted representations of things in his compositions and when he fractures the unity of appearance by combining different viewpoints, and even material from different contexts (collage), in a single depiction, then ordinary everyday optical understanding finds itself in the presence of a visual and aesthetic earthquake.

The sustained and systematic undermining of the optical coherence of visual representations, carried out by artists like Picasso, at the turn of the twentieth century, was no perverse attempt to experiment for the sake of it, nor to worship novelty or contradiction. If objects and figures in such paintings became subject to massive deformation and fragmentation, it was perhaps less a statement about the object *as such* (the object of Archaic art) or even the object *as seen* (the object of Renaissance art) as it was an exploration of the *seeing* of the object; that is, an exploration of the constitutive process through which sensuous perceptual relations are made. This paradigm shift involved a quantum leap in the level of abstraction. With Cubism, the elements of aesthetic experience, colour, tone, line and plane were divided from one another and given new functions. They ceased to serve the demands of the distal object and moved over to meet those of the somatic subject. Colour, light, shade and line came to describe the *experiencing* of things rather than things as experienced. Colour became a language of expression in itself. Tonality became a free rhythmic element in the construction of pictorial space. Line was freed from its role in describing the ordinary distanced objects of perception and became both a means of expression and a means of constituting a new spatiality, a new type of 'object'. Depth was renounced and the picture plane, together with the purely pictorial business of painting, was made central.

With the emancipation of the aesthetic elements of line, shape and colour from the business of describing objects, the centre of aesthetic organisation moved to the *intra-actional* and intra-personal level of experience. There was a further heightening of subjectivity. Each element in the work of art had to arise from a continuous *somatic* ground, which it shared with other elements. That somatic ground was the constitutive perceptual process in which all the differentiations and distinctions of time and space and context – differentiations that keep the objects of everyday experience bounded off from one another – were overcome. When objects and forms have dissolved into the elementary shapes, lines and colours from which all forms can be constituted, it becomes possible to abstract the constitutive machinery for doing seeing, itself, and to depict the 'emerging within it' of the forms of experience.

It is no longer the *distal* stimulus of the object-as-seen that is the focus of the perceptual process, but the *proximal* stimulus yielding the visual qualities and sensations through which the perceptual process itself is realised. To focus upon the proximal stimulus is, therefore, to make the perceptual process itself – that is, the seeing of things – an object of special perceptual attention. If contact values provide knowledge of *objects-as-such* and distal values knowledge of *object-as-seen*, proximal values provide knowledge of the *seeing-of-things-seen*. Perceptual understandings of this type can be said to be *somatic* in the sense that they are centred on the *arising of a world of 'objects' in the (perceiving) 'body' of the subject*. This represents the highest level of perceptual abstraction.

At the somatic level of perception, the perceptual system attains a degree of autonomy as a locus of ordering and is no longer *embedded* in the world of objects. This growing autonomy of the perceptual process is identified, semiotically, with the growing autonomy of the signifier (as distinct from the signified) and, sociologically, with the emergence of a subject-centred locus of ordering in social relations. Relations among elements in a haptic space are *coactional* and, in an optic space, *interactional*, relations among elements in a somatic space are *intra-actional*. The movement to a somatic level of perception is movement to the most subject-centred mode of organisation. This has nothing to do with becoming egoistic or unsocial. Rather, it is a claim concerning the level of abstraction at which social experience is ordered, a level at which meanings are fully relativistic and in which all foundational forms are subject to a reflexive vision. Art itself cannot complete this process, cannot become truly deconstructive unless it overcomes itself, living only to provoke the activity that it demonstrates, to provide 'glimpses' of the process by which everyone can become his or her own artist in the praxis of everyday life.

The modernist artist demanded a heightened engagement on the part of the subject receiving the work. The latter was not offered a picture of some portion of reality for her appreciation. Rather, a modernist picture made visible, tangible almost, the 'sensuous machinery' through which the subject realises a 'mode of being'. The artist was no longer representing a world but making one; the art-making process did not point beyond itself. The significance of this is to be found in the fact that art – which made the constitutive sensuous process the focus of the work – could be so constructed as to *provoke* or awaken this same constitutive process in others. The implication of such a strategy is, therefore, that the ultimate purpose does not lie in the work itself nor in its contemplation; it lies, rather, in the mode of being in relation to the world that the work provokes; the vision and possibility of the aesthetic as an ordering of everyday experience. We might say that anti-art is at the heart of all the most important movements of art in the twentieth century – a case of 'Art is dead, long live art'.

The subject, in reception, has to be something of an 'artist' in respect of everyday experience to make use of what is offered. More than this, however, the line between the aesthetic in everyday life and the work of art disappears. The work of art, in this sense, provides a means for provoking, through aesthetic means, a sensibility that answers to the varieties of experience that arise in disparate social contexts. This changed role of the subject in *reception* is also a profoundly changed role in respect of the influence of the work of art. The influence of modernist art lies less, perhaps, in the appreciation of art objects, as it does in its power to provoke an aesthetic sensibility which affects creation, construction and design in every aspect of modern life. The diffusion of the sensuous intelligence offered by modern art is a complex one and passes through every kind of reproductive and mass-produced process of image making; what is an abrupt transition at the level of art is, to some extent, a gradual preparation for such an abrupt transition in other spheres of life. Even the advent of new forms of writing and of relativistic and deconstructive critiques in modern sociology, can perhaps be seen as a late development in the diffusion of the same revolution that appeared in art under the label 'Modernism'.

Conclusion

This chapter has offered an outline framework for conceptualising the relations that pertain in different historical epochs between social relations, modes of perception and cognition, and stylistic innovations in the visual arts. The chapter argues that paradigmatic shifts in aesthetic styles are driven by the demand to think values at a level of abstraction that is required by a given type of social organisation. Thus, changes in aesthetic styles are seen, themselves, to be reflective of changes in the nature of social relations and as integral to social formation. In this way the chapter has sought to provide a framework for a sociology of the aesthetic in which the arts, in the broadest sense, are viewed as central rather than peripheral to social formation.

Acknowledgments

Thanks are extended by the author to the Leverhulme Trust for the support given to the writing of this chapter by the award of a Major Research Fellowship (2001–2003).

This chapter is a re-working of arguments originally presented in Chapters 2 and 3 of R.W. Witkin (1995) *Art and Social Structure*, Cambridge: Polity Press, and R.W. Witkin (1993) 'From the Touch of the Ancients to the Sight of the Moderns: Social Structure and the Semiotics of Aesthetic Form', *Real Text*, pp. 89–113, Verlag Ritter, Klagenfurt.

Invisible Aesthetics and the Social Work of Commodity Culture

5

Paul Willis

Introduction

This chapter calls for the reformulation and transcendence of established categories of understanding 'aesthetics', as these are currently established in both everyday and academic discourses. It argues that although there are evident differences in how art history and philosophy on the one hand, and sociology on the other, conceptualise aesthetic matters, all of these disciplines nonetheless share certain assumptions about what 'aesthetics' involves and how the social realm, in which aesthetics is located, is to be studied.

The received view of aesthetics suggests that the aesthetic effect is internal to the text and a universal property of its form. This places the creative impulse squarely on the material and symbolic productions of the 'creative' artist with the reception or consumption of art wholly determined by the aesthetic forms, so drawing to them only privileged 'art world' minorities composed of those with the fine dispositions and the cultural resources necessary to appreciate (de-code) the timeless beauty of art. 'Reception' palely reflects what is timelessly coded within the text. Although it is no longer useful to speak of them as at the centre of culture in the age of the instant cultural media, the essentially nineteenth-century fixation on unitary forms, contents and performances still leads institutions, despite passing concessions to post-modern levelling and 'democratisation' of the arts, into their false pursuit of monuments, organisational and material.

The sociology of art is fully alive to the effects of the institutionalisation of art, to the selective traditions they promote and the self-confirming fields they support. Sociology points an accusing finger at art, and the associated institutions which crust, crystallise and glassify its motile surfaces, indicting them for making and maintaining the social distinctions which allow social hierarchies actually based on unequal power and exclusion to self-effacingly constitute themselves as the innocent and normal consequence of naturally occurring differences in the disposition of groups and individuals. Sociologists have cracked the enigma of the social coding of the aesthetic – but have mistakenly assumed that it is a unitary not a polyvalent code. The pressing danger here is of throwing the creative baby out with the aesthetic and artistic bath water. Sociology has exposed how 'art' functions as a social marker at the upper reaches of social space within the current web of historical, institutional and determinant conditions, thus exposing it, apparently, to the universalistic charge that it is *only* a social marker: merely the carapace of that creativity to which it pretends. Critique has reduced the aesthetic to its carapace! But the forensic depictment of the latter's dead presence on the embroidered social cloak kills what once lived inside and could live, does live beyond the shell – human creativity.

Sociology, as much as its academic 'rivals' in understanding 'artistic matters', fails to acknowledge that far from being explicable only as a bounded and delimited entity synonymous with 'art worlds', 'aesthetics' is actually contiguous and continuous with the overall flow of everyday life practices, carried out not only by specialists called 'artists' but by everyday actors in mundane contexts of activity. In other words, the sociology of 'art' is far too narrow an enterprise to grasp the flip-side of 'aesthetic' matters, namely the fact that aesthetic elements are thoroughly embedded in, and constitutive of, everyday lifeworlds and practices. The sociology of 'art' in fact helps reproduce the fallacy that 'aesthetics' is synonymous with 'art', so-called 'high culture'. The critique is a partial one, for, in denying a living content to aesthetics, sociology fails thoroughly to locate 'aesthetics' (without the shell) as a characteristic of *ordinary* and *everyday* social contexts. As such, it unintentionally reproduces elitist discourses as to the somehow 'special' nature of 'high art', discourses that it thinks it has transcended.

I argue that the boundaries between arts and non-arts need to be redrawn or declared entirely defunct. It is necessary not only to critique the view that participation in 'art' produces 'culture' (for the few) but to proclaim, as a comparative or historical view readily grants, that actually, if we are forced to use the terms, 'culture' (as ways of life) produces 'art', not vice-versa – or at the very least that there is a dialectic tension between them productive of our very communicativeness as human beings. Cultures are intertwined with and produce everyday forms of aesthetic experience, only a small part of which is precipitated textually, only a small part of which survive as or are composed into texts, only a small part of which is preserved, only a small part of which is consecrated as 'art'. Why do we concern ourselves so much with critiquing the very last link of this chain, in breaking it, breaking the unit chain link connecting all? Where is the profane testing and vesting of the aesthetic in rumbustious daily life? If the term 'arts' is given an altogether wider definition as sharing daily terms with its equal partner, culture, then it will be seen that everyday life is full of expressions, signs and symbols through which individuals and groups creatively establish their very presence, as well as important elements of their identity, purpose and meaning. Young people, in particular, are all the time expressing, or struggling to express, something of their own – or hoped for – cultural significance. This involves a wide range of creative activities and forms of expression and communication which people find relevant to their lives – fashion and pop music, room and personal decoration, the rituals of romance, subcultural styles, magazines, radio, television. We need a view which accepts a continuum of expressive forms, practices and resources and materials through which people symbolically portray their meanings, which they press into play as symbolic languages for the expression and formation of their identities. Themselves, at least initially, the result of such fragile conjurings, even the 'sacred' texts of the hallowed traditions and the canonical performances of the 'central cultural repertoire' are most note-worthy, not for what they bring to or displace from, but for what they bring out of the human soul. I would argue that received musical and literary forms should be recognised not for the disputed and cloudy trophies of their sealed-in aesthetics, still less for their dismal social functions, but for their living capacity to incite different formations within the sediments of the terra incognita of the self; stirring 'new' meanings and understandings within the viewer/ listener/receiver which were there but not in the same way before, now discovered as things never meant to be there, concealed or configured by other powers, but which can go forward in new ways. All kinds of symbolic materials, profane as well as sacred, can have these effects.

Perhaps we should see the 'raw materials' of cultural life, of communications and expressions, as always intermediate. They are the products of one process as well as the raw materials for another – whose results are raw materials for successive groups. The law of copyright recognises that every time an artefact changes form or content, a new product is created on which copyright can be established. Where is our cultural realisation of this principle? Why should not bedroom decoration and personal styles, grounded appropriations of new technology, master mixes produced by teenagers for circulation to friends – all combinations of the productions of others – as well as creative writing or song or music composition, be recognised as fields of aesthetic realisation?

In this chapter, then, I call for a radical re-visioning of the study of aesthetics, a reworking of dominant paradigms of sociological (and other) forms of analysis, such that what comes to light are the 'invisible aesthetics' of everyday life. Setting aside limitations of their imaginings of what 'art' and 'aesthetics' are or could be, sociology and other disciplines must learn to see the 'art in life' that hitherto has primarily remained hidden from their purview. This chapter sets out epistemological and methodological re-imaginings of the necessary elements of how a revivified study of aesthetics might proceed.

Everyday meanings

I posit that we must now be alive to the presence of 'lived aesthetics' in everyday life. But where do the 'aesthetic' forms of daily life come from, how do its creativities arise? It is inadequate to explain creativity away as an aspect of human essence. Creativity arises, in part at least, from a dialectical and immediately sensuous relation to the materiality and determinacy of surrounding 'non-human' forms and materials which have their own nature and history. It is commonplace to say that we produce and reproduce ourselves indirectly whilst we directly produce and reproduce our conditions of life in paid and unpaid work. However, such a dichotomous view tends to ignore the 'art in life' which involves the *direct* – even if 'decentred' – production of aspects of the *expressive* self. Such production occurs through 'necessary work' on the provided materials, symbolic and other, most of which today arise from the alienated labour processes of capitalism – the cultural production from 'necessary work' thus occurs behind the back of 'formal' capitalist production. The irony of 'necessary work' is that it thrives on the production of the cultural goods, objects and services of capitalism, while putting these items to creative, indeed often subversive cultural use (Willis et al., 1990: 9–14). 'Necessary work' assumes the most democratic understanding of 'aesthetics'. In common cultural life – built on 'necessary work' – the 'artistic' and the 'social' are all of a piece. Aesthetic feelings are not conflated with 'art', still less with 'textual art', still less with 'high art'. In a sense, then, 'necessary work' shatters, at the epistemological level, cultural exclusion and aesthetic privilege. The arts of daily life flicker in and out, unseen: everyday aesthetics are invisible aesthetics, ignored deliberately or unintentionally both by social elites and most academic analysis.

Perhaps the main characteristic of the aesthetic practices of the everyday is their 'sense-full-ness' in relation to social-structural location. They provide alternative groundings and practices for an ability to make a 'lived' assessment of *particular positions as humanly occupied*, the symbolic possibilities of their sensuous materiality existing beyond ideologically loaded or idealised sociological accounts of 'structural relations'. The aesthetic forms of everyday cultures concern sensuous and concrete practices and processes which allow the contextual *human* apprehension of wider structures and structural relations, their possibilities and potentials, *as locally experienced and explored*.

But they are not, themselves, usually, verbalised abstract constructs. Rather, they are more expressive of certain 'attitudes', the *lived experiences* of social practice *from below*. 'Alternative knowledges', or, better perhaps, states of 'knowingness', exist separately from dominant forms of meaning, both textual and institutional. These 'alternative knowledges' are based on the *sensuousness* of the practicality and lived-out-ness of relations to real conditions. Meaning comes about not as an abstract expression nor as an asserted human universal, but as an experienced and creative form of exploring the possibilities of the concrete with the resources and potentialities of a given culture. Sensuous powers indicate possibilities within the self for creative autonomy and independence. Outside ('sociological') and ideological definitions of the self are exposed by sensuousness as one-sided and partial, tending to limit or close wider potentials. Meanwhile these potentials, from their own sidedness, explore the objective structural limits and possibilities of the conditions under which they operate relatively unrestricted by ideology. Their own sustenance and reproduction, in turn, rest upon how well they illuminate these conditions.

As collective and working-class institutions decline or become more individualistically orientated, as radical political economic discourses become ever more marginalised, so are lost from 'the popular' legible means and resources for explaining the location of individuals and groups in respect to larger structures.

Correspondingly, the burden of collective 'thinking' and representation will fall ever more onto informal life and onto lived cultures and cultural forms. We must now be alive to the necessary social work of lived aesthetics. The arts of daily life may flicker in and out, unseen but their continuous re-kindlings depend not only on their own guttering combustion but also on what they cast light upon.[1]

Commodity culture and informal meaning-making

In the present day, we are condemned to live the fraudulence and endless double takes of capitalist culture. We make our meanings lost on the surface of things and under conditions *and with materials* not of our own making. What is inescapable now and has to be grappled with, not bemoaned, is that cultural life and communications are mediated more than ever through objects and forms not of local making, in no way supplied out of responsible interest in development or improvement. The rise of commodity culture moves objects and human-objects relations to the centre of our lived culture just as present-day communication, mediated by electronic signs, floods over local relations not least investing with fraudulent, intimate and mystical powers the commodities and gadgets that surround us even though they are actually produced by strangers for profit, often with palpably cynical motives.

To gain our bearings in such a world, we need to acknowledge that the electronification of culture must be viewed in the context of the overall domination of capitalist relations in communication, cultural production and distribution. The academic field of 'political economy' is important in this regard, both for examining *specific* mechanisms and for explaining the conditioning of general possibilities arising from the symbiosis of economy, society, politics and culture (commercial, electronic and mass mediated). Criticisms of my previous work as indulging a 'cultural populism' (McGuigan, 1992) – celebrating a creative capacity apparently to make absolutely anything of any cultural commodity unrestrained by wider structures and power relations – have hit the target and partly inspire the current (revised) commentary.

However, in many ways political economists seem to be *assuming* a similar Olympian role to that of real capitalists and their agents – enjoying their own 'No *Financial Times*, no comment' mentality – deploying their elite knowledge to understand what the plebs never can. However, unlike *Financial Times* and *Wall Street Journal* readers, academic cultural analysts are only too painfully far off from the levers of real cultural power. If we really were close to these levers then we could test 'live' for differences arising from alternative owner-ship. As it is, we are actually living through a world historic defeat for the aims of common ownership. Now our tasks are, at best, truly subaltern. The issue now is, surely, accepting the field of domination as it is, to try to under-stand, much more inwardly, the nature and alienated potential democracy of our actually existing and emergent commodity and electronic culture, the 'common culture' as it actually is, or is becoming. The point is to understand the new and emergent conditions of culture generally, the new formative and pre-disposing tendencies within the whole system including the creative, *upon conditions*, activities of those who are economically subordinate in the system.

From this viewpoint, a 'political economy' route to understanding cultural processes is at best limited and partial and at worst deeply flawed. This is because the whole process of commoditisation involves a situation where materials are not only packaged 'for the masses' but also in important ways transformed in the process of becoming a commodity. Further, one must take account of the stage of contextualised, *on terms*, creative and transformative consumption by *users*, not consumers. *Really* to understand audiences we need to know how modern cultural materials, commoditised in form, are taken up *creatively* into everyday life, as this is itself articulated with some of the main structures and contradictions of modern society and to understand how from here (not from direct 'media effects') overall power structures and relations of dominance are lived and reproduced. We must direct attention to the unseen but foot-worn pathways, the practical moments of an unlikely and invisible aesthetic realisation in sensuous activity in cultural life, in life as it actually exists, however debased it might seem to middle-class onlookers, both academic and not. The 'dirty' practices of informal cultural production in everyday life continue apace, making their own priorities and choices, shifting their own fields, choosing their own sites for contestation. They find new uses and social possibilities – multiple and centrifugal, not limited to sociological constructs such as 'work', 'neighbourhood' and 'class'.

My point is simply that the 'fast' political economy route misses out on three important areas in the dynamics of cultural consumption and creativity: (1) the openness of the commodity stage (2) the creativities and differences, upon conditions, of 'mass' experience (3) how this experience relates finally and with great complexity, penetratingly and reproductively, to structural conditions and restraints. Rather than whistling up 'old community' in a forlorn attempt to run backwards the 'capital logic' monochrome film, these real 'future side' processes and activities should be the focus of critique and for beginning to understand what may be new kinds of base for what kinds of communality.

From British political economists to French post-modernists, the cultural pessimists miss the point that commodity communication, however much in bad faith or fraudulence, still concerns expanded communication: the passing between humans of information and meanings, materials which, no matter what their source, are then always available for creative and contextual meaning-making. Against the apparent odds, communication remains. The pessimists also overstate and exaggerate the 'homeliness' of traditional communication and related cultural materials. Part of the critical sensibility arising in and from the commodity age is a massively increased awareness of the mediatedness, rebarbative, selecting/rejecting nature of *all* communication and symbolic materials in whatever cultural form at whatever stage of social development. Though carrying within them a sided interest in communication, even the 'pure' communications we imagine to have been involved in the mutuality, co-operation and solidarity of older 'sacred' working-class 'organic' communities cannot now be seen as expressing or reflecting a genuine 'essence' or undistorted picture of social conditions/relations. They did not, for instance, express hidden gender and race experience. They worked through symbols, images and icons which helped to produce rather than simply reflect the 'raw material' of directly experienced social conditions. The autonomies of communication and symbolic form have always operated and had their effects, even if hidden; you could say that we are now released from the blinkers of parochialism and 'folk idiocy' in the way we understand these processes; equally you could say that, always actually freer than we thought, cultural forms are now freer than ever to find new attachments to 'real' conditions, producing their own new putative senses of authenticity and essence.

Cultural commodities

Although sympathetic to the culturalist tradition in Cultural Studies, which is inspired by humanism, I remain critical of that tradition's implied notions of authenticity and essence in relation to community and cultural life. These notions – feelings really – are always fabrications of historical hindsight. If we come to accept the commoditised and fetishized nature of culture over a considerable period of time – the twentieth century at least – we strip away the hindrance of romance. Analysis of everyday aesthetics should neither condemn nor celebrate the commoditised and fetishized nature of culture but should seek to understand it, especially for what commodity fetishism brings to communications materials. Fetishism of the commodity has to be understood in relation to that other main characteristic of commodities: they have to sell. The uncertainty of whether commodities will sell, has to be negotiated time after time as a condition of the circuit which produces them, and they will only sell if they can offer meaningful use in some kind of shared symbolic world. The prior semiotic, material and human factory of the production of cultural commodities cannot be cut off from – in the manner of the factory – the material commodity. It is these connections that actually allow the commodity to be sold in the ever-repeated cycle of capital accumulation. The commodity is ever repeatedly revalorized not only with respect to value (embodied human labour time) but also with meaning, new, extra or differently more relevant meaning, meaning at any rate whose pre-requisite is that sharedness which the fetishised commodity form denies. Moreover, it is the capitalist obsession of the ever driven circuit of accumulation (this being a commodity circuit too) that ensures the never ending and restless search for precisely that social connection which the capitalist commodity form denies.

The fundamental contradiction of the cultural commodity form is that such a 'hieroglyph' must, simultaneously, be not a hieroglyph. Fetishism must defetishize itself. Here we encounter the hypnotic polysemy of cultural commodities. The commodity bears an internal and constant tension between meaning and meaningless. The dialectic of this tension works towards its own resolution – the impossibility of decipherment offers up decipherment. However, the semiotic social promiscuity of commodities offers amnesia for the sacred and passage for the profane. Fetishisation strips 'meaning objects' of their previous histories and accretions of socially determined norms of consumption. Fetishistic acid burns away history, so revealing open possibilities making it easier for new users to adapt them to their own, new or emergent norms of consumption. Commodity meanings which survive beyond the fetishism are maximally open to finding new articulations, new homes. Commodified social semiotics get through to receivers/viewers/users without being framed through traditional forms of social dependency. They carry over fractured, through lens-darkly, pictures of their original social meanings and social relations impossibly seeking wholeness in future social relations of consumption. General commodity fetishism produces an estrangement, lack of home, loss of parentage and loyalty, an in-turnedness which is strangely fertile territory for a communicative anti-fetishism to solicit any use, any possible attachment in a guiltless, never ending semiotic promiscuity. Fetishism cuts the past; anti-fetishism opens the future.

Cultural commodities must deal in social meaning and connection but they do not enforce particular meaning. They exist without organised semiotic policing. Though carrying over some of the semiotic and symbolic resources from the circumstances of their formation, the forces of their original location do not fix their messages and meanings; texts do not bring along old 'con-texts'. The alienated offer of meaning in the commodity object is quite different from the despotic command of the auratic 'art' object. The former can be taken into many homes, regardless of the decoding capacities of the people living therein. The nature of cultural commodities is that new users can adapt them to their own, possibly new or emergent, norms of consumption. If objects and artefacts seem to belong to someone else, then they cannot be yours. But if they are orphaned, they can be adopted.

It is therefore the case that commoditised materials and practices, for all the worst reasons, are available for informal meaning-making because they are broken off from past dependencies and limiting norms of consumption. Cultural commodities are the semiotic harlots of communication systems. Tawdry it might be, but here are grounds for understanding a 'late modern' route into everyday practices of creativity and meaning-making. The half formings and semi-decodings of cultural commodities and the re-codings they incite, can play an important part in making meaning from below, supplying multifarious sensuous raw materials for the creation of new social identities and possibilities – forms of *lived difference*, even superiority, in the face of subordination. They provide a field, a contingent ground, a field of at least partly possess-able symbols and practices for 'seeing through' the illusions and apprehending and sensing the flatness of ideological-discursive placings and formings. Of course this is not to say that commodity production and mediated communication do not carry ideological messages, not least in their very commodity form, but it is to assert that meanings which are exported 'down' are not re-exported back up or anywhere else in social space in the same form. The commodisation of cultural materials changes them in ways facilitating a further transformative stage of concrete use in local context and purpose. Here resides a real resource for creating and knowing with a critical social edge, all in the unlikely soil of exploitative commodity relations.

The processes involved in this more cultural production are essentially collective and social in nature, though they may occur on the site of the individual or small group. The 'social' need not move around in mass semiotic army units empirically matching the size of originally locating social groups. It is possible to see the contradictory social relations of consumption playing out inside one body and head as the impacted histories, contradictions and social relations of cultural commodities limit and channel, ignite and incite, certain kinds of meaning. The varieties of artistry in lived cultural forms practically exploit the intrinsic contradiction that even though, perhaps because, commoditised meanings are fetishised, they are actually highly suited to forms of meaning-making within informal everyday life.

Making the invisible visible

This is not to argue, however, that all is for the symbolic best in the best of all possible cultural worlds. We are still no nearer to true depth in useable information for all, no nearer to the genuine understanding of other cultures in context, no nearer to the democratic control of the agendas and material production of cultural resources. There are practices and materials towards a 3-D view of daily life and its dilemmas but not towards a 3-D view and control of the real political economy of the conditions which make the everyday arena.

I emphasise the importance of concrete use by way of creative informal practices not out of populist zeal but for a recognition of their nature, social location, and social meaning for their bearers and participants: for the 'social work' they do but through an 'invisibility' which changes the very function of their operation. To be crude, though I emphasise the social and potentially critical content of practices of informal cultural production, the misrecognition or invisibility of these practices all too easily renders *social* or *socially derived* meanings into individual meaning which in turn becomes a magical property of the cultural commodity rather than an ordinary feature of located, informal practice. In fact the changing states and statuses of 'things' in *actual practice and practical experience* becomes a steady state for *conscious experience* of the 'always already', 'singular' nature of a singular category of the mystically endowed cultural commodity. The purpose of analysis, in part, is that by clarifying the links in the chain of the 'changing states of things' – under the invisibility – we might find clues for turning the associated practices inside out to render them visible. The process of cultural consumption is not simply one involving the reappropriation of commodities by users and that is the end of the story. The process must be rendered in this way:

Cultural object > commodity > possession > commodity

Capitalist conditions of production and distribution turn an object into a commodity and the creative informal practices of consumption turn a commodity into a possession. Ever more devious and cunning marketing practices try to insert commodities ever more accurately into the interstices of informal production (retail theatre, interactive media, product placing, fluid logos, 'experiential products'), also learning from and expropriating the nature of 'possessions' in order to moderate and calibrate their seamless and invisible insertion as commodities into informal production. These can all be understood as attempts to recommodify 'possessions'.

Nonetheless, the analysis of everyday aesthetics asserts the existence of the 'possession' element in the commodity production–consumption chain, because that is precisely where the 'creative' aspects of cultural practice are today to be found. The 'aesthetic' aspects of life are today located at the interface of capitalist commodity culture and the appropriations thereof in everyday contexts by everyday actors. These are the 'artists' of the present, rather than the self-proclaimed elite cultural creators who claim that appellation and who are thus honoured by elitist discourses, various forms of academic discourse included.

Despite the multiple forms of creative practice in everyday contexts, academic analysts of all varieties still lack a language to name the specificities of such forms of 'informal' cultural production. The possibilities of recognising and naming informal practices are further obliterated by the dominance of the languages for talking about the symbolic forms which are highly valued, languages which are mobilised for controlling or attempting to control the understandings of 'art', understandings which pertain both in the academy and in everyday parlance. The 'aura' of the art object is both granted and reproduced by the all too visible aesthetics of self-proclaimed value, which are held in place by monumental art histories, institutional practices first developed in – and remaining relatively unchanged since – the nineteenth century, and Arnoldian liberal arts educational regimes with their emphases on the 'greatness' of 'great works'. These understandings and related practices are not neutral in any sense, for they control the fields of subsidy, access and influence in the 'aesthetic' realm, narrowly defined. Consequently, the invisible aesthetics of 'the masses' are rarely seen, recognised, analysed or taught.

Representing the invisible

Everyday practices are centred around particular, located forms of meaning-making. Our task in the comprehension of 'everyday aesthetics' must be to *make meaning of meaning-making*. Meaning-making is a profane activity, not yet, and no doubt never fully, adequately named, existing within the liminal spaces characteristic of everyday practice. The problem here is that we still possess only a clumsy 'social scientific' vocabulary (no equivalents yet of 'the social poem') in order to describe and situate the creativity and complexity of everyday aesthetics. We can talk of 'lived experience', 'actual experience', 'everyday meanings', 'lived meanings', 'authentic roots', 'symbolic creativity', but everyday meanings are inherently difficult to express in analytic language. Nor are they embossed on the surface of things, awaiting only a methodological brass rubbing to reveal what is signified. Verbal language certainly plays a privileged part in everyday meaning, but not always as the main, certainly never the only, carrier of meaning, so agents' self-reports are necessary to, but not adequate as, a full account. The full account must recreate the tension created when language, aesthetics and the everyday are understood as compressed together in the same life space. It may be as well to think of especially subordinated cultural meaning as not being of a logo-centric (reasoned speech) type at all, but as the frequently asymmetric and eccentric logic of connection (what makes sense of the connection) between the different elements of a cultural form or practice judged sensuously for *lived* satisfaction and psychic pay-off rather than for abstract coherence.

We do, however, need the already existing, clumsy social scientific terms and vocabularies to try to unpack, take apart, name and conceptualise the manner of how these parts relate, impact on each other and produce simultaneities of meaning traceable to no individual part alone. Yet at the same time we also need terms derived from traditional 'artistic' discourses to indicate unity and elegance, and to show a commensurate respect in at least some of the vocabulary used to represent the experience of others. In the academic imagination of the twenty-first century, *the 'artistic' imagination and the sociological imagination will have to be fused together*.

This fusion would lead to forms of ethnographic study of everyday aesthetics which are sensitised to the nuances of the mundane practices under study. Yet even with such a sensitive ethnographic approach attuned to the particularities and peculiarities of the everyday, we must always be on our guard. Acknowledging the aesthetic meanings of everyday life carries with it the contradiction and irony of making a text out of – textualising – what was often implicit before, perhaps doing a kind of violence to situated meanings, and certainly carrying them in a different way to a wider and/or different audience. Questions thus arise of purpose, effect and responsibility.

Nor should it be overlooked that often a vigorous and deliberate methodological act of practical (fieldwork) intervention, and frequently of intellectual inversion, is required in order to access and textualise the 'data' which is in solution in daily life. The quality of meaning-making is especially difficult to locate, represent and interpret in subordinated or dominated cultural forms because their presence on the underprivileged side of the mental/manual division of the social, and the fear of punitive or controlling surveillance, drive meanings further down, or impact them deeper, into other and different forms. Not that the arts of the subordinate, at least in their own time and place, are ever likely to be recognised by their super-ordinates, or seen as anything other than 'in – subordination', or even as pathological and 'mindless'. Hence the need for a sensitive and carefully attuned ethnographic method, rather than a reliance upon secondary reports almost always mediated through the meanings, problems and definitions of the powerful.

Private and public 'art worlds'

My comments here on invisible aesthetics contain certain implications not just for how academics should understand 'aesthetics', but what academics as *public intellectuals* might strive for vis-à-vis future forms of social organisation of 'artistic' life, defined both more narrowly and more widely. Dominant institutional practices in the present day try to freeze the 'art' object in aspic, while commercial practices try to launch the art object as a commodity in the cultural marketplace. Against both these grains, everyday practices hitherto under-explored by academics may launch objects and artefacts of all kinds carrying symbolic meaning of all kinds into invisible chains of 'possession'. But these are processes barely touched upon by sociology and other disciplines that think they understand 'aesthetics'.

An interesting question arises as to how informal practices facilitate or might facilitate an intervention in the chains or stasis of 'high culture'. Everyday actors may appropriate objects defined by dominant discourses as 'art' in different, often complex ways. From here we might see how creative practices might be strengthened, and observe what crossovers or parallels there might be with transformative programmes for aesthetic development, in both the public and private, formal and informal, aesthetic spheres.

After all, we are all the invisible and unacknowledged curators of our own material culture: from clothing and presentation of our bodies to decoration in and out of the home, to the outside and inside of our cars; from the paintings to the posters we hang; from Beethoven to the Beatles to Basement Jaxx. More focused thought might expose some of the curatorial criteria of our everyday life, and show how the range of what is to be selected from can be widened, and kept wide. It might show how sophisticated selection principles grow unseen from responses to the ordinary things of material culture, and suggest ways in which the self-conscious knowledges of art history and other formal discourses might make more vibrant and critical the webs of meaning which bind everyday choices and preferences into cultural wholes and ways of life.

An agenda of many possibilities may open up between formal and informal curatorships. This might include, for instance, mixing items from collected and private worlds, technical 'morphing' of the images of collection and everyday items to explore their similarities and differences with respect to the organising principles of selection, mixing 'art' collection items with private creative work, and encouraging gallery displays drawn from the objects and practices of private material culture. It is to be hoped that the informal world of everyday aesthetics will inspire the formal world of 'art', and that a genuine sensuousness can be injected into a more self-conscious professional curatorship, informing the decision-making on how 'art' exhibitions are selected and displayed.

The best chances of encouraging an artistic democracy are not through 'democratisation' of the existing arts but through an identification, recognition and support of existing creative experiences and activities not at present regarded as 'artistic' but which are now part of our common culture. There is surely a sound policy basis for aiming to recognise, support and develop forms of cultural creativity, which are already rooted in the social milieux and interests of those at whom policy is directed. The central thrust would be to strengthen, facilitate and provide more conducive conditions towards helping people to do better what they do already, understanding and exploring their conditions of existence and possibility. If we can accept that this already proceeds largely through the creative consumption of cultural commodities and the cultural media, then one important starting point for encouraging further creativity is simply – through new kinds of embedding 'intermediate' institutions (not traditional or 'top down') – to widen, deepen and make more self-aware the access to and use of these things. Through such means the hegemony of 'official' art institutions, and the reflections of these in academic analyses, could be transformed into something more vital and expressive of the everyday conditions whereby social actors engage in forms of aesthetic practice hitherto excluded, both analytically and practically, from the mandarin world of 'high culture'.

Conclusion

In this chapter I have argued that the sociology of art differs little from other academic forms of comprehension such as art history in its privileging of official 'art' spaces and practices. In so doing, 'aesthetics' is understood as a bounded entity unconnected to the broad mass of people in a contemporary society and the cultural commodities that they take up and appropriate. It is in fact in those acts, individual and collective, of appropriation that the 'invisible aesthetics' of the everyday rest. Sociology must turn away from its – no doubt unintentional – privileging of the visible 'aesthetic' realm of established art institutions and move towards ways – both ethnographic and 'artistic' – of comprehending the role of aesthetics in mundane lifeworlds. Sociology and other disciplines should recognise, and thus bring out into the light, the myriad, but unseen and 'invisible', creative aesthetic practices of informal life. In doing so, it would make the communities and cultures in which such practices are embedded more knowable and more visible, a potent contribution in the service of the democratisation of cultural life, a project to which sociology has hitherto only paid lip service.

Acknowledgement

Thanks to John Hughson for tenaciously commissioning this piece and for such a sympathetic editing that amounts almost to co-authorship.

NOTE

1. A metaphor drawn from gas heating technology helps me to think this through. When you light a gas fire, a safety mechanism called a 'thermo-coupler' transfers heat along a tube back to the gas supply to keep the supply valve open, so maintaining the burning of the gas. The flame is its 'own thing', its own combustion, a unique and singular reaction of oxygen and carbon, but the heat it produces, through none of its own intended purpose, maintains the conditions of its own

functioning. If for any reason the flame goes out, the thermo-coupler goes cold, contracts and switches the gas valve off, so cutting the supply and preventing the free escape of un-burnt gas – so with the informal creativities of common culture. The flame of creativity is its 'own thing' but survives only so long as it really burns producing heat and light which are useful for other purposes in context. As soon as an apparent systemic usefulness is lost, the flame dies. The flame is not lit by social usefulness, but it will not burn in isolation; its autonomous functioning is conditional. Ultimately, the potential of the flame is to spark a connection in the contemporary collective imagination, fusing the literary and sociological imaginations and providing a guiding light for the appreciation of life as art.

Cultural Studies and the Sociology of Culture

Janet Wolff

Introduction

Ten years ago, I moved from Britain to the United States. Before that date, I had taught for thirteen years in a department of sociology in Britain. My geographical move also entailed an apparent change of disciplines (and, given the nature of the academy in Britain and the United States, also a change of academic divisions, from the social sciences to the humanities). But the change *was* only apparent, except in the material sense of my institutional location. My work did not change radically (though I hope it has developed in the past decade). I did not retrain, or take another Ph.D. This biographical fact is interesting, I think, not for its own sake, but because of what it says about the organization of disciplines in Britain and America, and about the study of culture in the late twentieth century.

There are a number of issues here. First, given my background and training in a certain kind of European sociology and my involvement already in inter-disciplinary work, I am not sure that many departments of sociology in the USA would have been prepared to give me a home. The discipline here has, as far as I can see, remained resolutely *intra*disciplinary as a collective project; moreover, it has manifested a strong attachment (in some cases, a growing one) to positivist scholarship, including quantitative and mathematical methods. For the most part, this has also been true of that subspecialization called the sociology of culture, many of whose practitioners continue to operate with untheorized and unexamined categories of social analysis.

Second, new emphases have emerged in the humanities, which have rendered certain sociologists welcome – new historicism, the new art history, postcolonial and feminist approaches to literature and culture, and so on. And third, the success and proliferation of cultural studies in the United States, in academic programs and in publishing, has provided new opportunities for such cross-departmental moves. Given my alienation from much American sociology, my lifelong interest in the study of culture, and the hospitality of the humanities, my current situation makes plenty of sense. Nor in my own change of discipline-home unique. Simon Frith (1998: 3), delivering his inaugural lecture as Professor of English at the University of Strathclyde, opened his talk this way:

> I ought to begin by saying that I am honoured to be giving this lecture, and indeed I am, but I have to confess that my dominant emotion is surprise. I haven't studied English formally since I did O levels, and I still find it a peculiar turn of events that I should now be a professor of English. My academic training was in sociology, and I'm tempted to treat this lecture as a sociological case study: what does it tell us about the present state of English studies that a sociologist can chair an English department?[1]

Nevertheless, since taking over in 1991 as director of an interdisciplinary humanities program[2] I have somehow felt that my "mission" was to encourage a "sociological imagination" among graduate students in a program, after all, initially founded by the collaboration of colleagues in art history, film studies, and comparative literature, and only more recently including the participation of colleagues from anthropology and history. (There is no longer a department of sociology at the university.) I have wanted to direct students to the texts and methods of sociology and social history, and to urge them to supplement their interpretive and critical readings of visual texts with attention to the institutional and social processes of cultural production and consumption.

In my opinion, cultural studies at its best is sociological. Yet, in the continuing cross-disciplinary dialogue that has characterized cultural studies in the decade or so of its progress in the United States, the discipline of sociology has been notably absent. At the same time, within sociology, the study of culture has expanded enormously in the last twenty years among sociologists of culture, and among those who have more recently been calling themselves "cultural sociologists" – which is not the same thing. (I will come back to these terms later.) Some of these sociologists have themselves adopted the term *cultural studies* to describe their work, thereby claiming (mistakenly, as I shall suggest) to have pre-empted the newer field, and ignoring the possibility of a productive encounter with cultural studies in general and with related developments in the study of culture in the humanities. Within the past couple of years, this has begun to change, and some of the newer work in this area has begun to bridge the hitherto radical divide between sociology and cultural studies.

My main intention here is to stress the advantages that will ensue if sociologists enter into the interdisciplinary dialogue that constitutes the ever-changing field of cultural studies. A good deal of what I have to say consists of a critical review of recent developments in sociology, a discipline which for the most part has still not come to terms with the fact that, as Avery Gordon has put it, "the real itself and its ethnographic or sociological representations are... fictions, albeit powerful ones that we do not experience as fictions but as true" (1997: 11). I review this work not so that I can simply dismiss it, but because, first, it retains a very high profile in the study of culture within the discipline of sociology; and second, because, as I shall show, it makes claims either to supersede or to displace cultural studies. (I should point out here, though, that other branches of sociology, less visible and less influential, offer more promising approaches to the field, especially work influenced by the Frankfurt School.[3]) My critique of trends in sociology is motivated entirely by my hope for a productive encounter between cultural studies and sociology. The benefit to both fields will be the mutual recognition that – again to quote Avery Gordon – "the increasingly sophisticated understandings of representation and of how the social world is textually or discursively constructed still require an engagement with the social structuring practices that have long been the province of sociological inquiry" (1997: 11).

Between 'social life' and 'texts'

What sociologists can contribute to the project of cultural analysis is a focus on institutions and social relations, as well as on the broader perspective of structured axes of social differentiation and their historical transformations – axes of class, status, gender, nationality, and ethnicity. You do not, of course, have to be a sociologist to pay attention to these analytic dimensions, and there are certainly cultural studies scholars who do just this kind of work. (Stuart Hall, Tony Bennett, and Angela McRobbie come to mind.) For example, the focus on the ideology and practices of the museum has been prominent in some important works in recent years in what is usually called "museology" or "museum studies", most of it done by people who are not trained in sociology. My suggestion, rather, is that the fact that such questions constitute the *raison d'être* of sociology is enough reason to want sociologists to contribute to the debate about the study of culture.

The sociological perspective is invaluable in directing attention to certain critical aspects in the production of culture. But my concern to see sociology figure more centrally in visual studies, and in cultural studies more generally, is expressed in a context in which institutional and social issues are too often ignored, and in which as Steven Seidman has put it, the social is often "textualized" (1997: 41). A lot has been written about the "Americanization of cultural studies", much of this writing critical of the trend (Budd et al., 1990; Pfister, 1996). Some writers object to what they perceive as a depoliticization of the project in its move from Britain (and originally, of course, the Centre for Contemporary Cultural Studies at the University of Birmingham) to the United States – its detachment from social movements and its increasingly professionalized and rarefied life in the academy. Others have noted that the proliferation of cultural studies scholarship and teaching through the 1980s and 1990s has occurred largely (though not solely) in humanities departments, especially departments of English and Comparative Literature; and they see an abandonment of the more sociological approach, which understands culture in terms of axes of stratification and inequality (primarily class relations in the early years of the Birmingham Centre, but later also relations of gender and race). Cary Nelson, in one of the more impassioned critiques of this trend, describes American cultural studies as a kind of textualism – a set of ingenious, and perhaps politically informed, new readings of texts, but readings that are ultimately ungrounded, arbitrary, and shallow (Nelson, 1991).[4] Sociologist Michael Schudson makes a similar point through a careful and serious analysis of what he takes as a paradigmatic text in American cultural studies: Donna Haraway's "Teddy Bear Patriarchy", a study of the American Museum of Natural History in New York, specifically its African Hall (Haraway, 1989; Schudson, 1997). In particular, Schudson takes issue with Haraway's use of synecdochal conversion to link display, ideology, and politics, on the grounds that such links are not based on social–historical study or attention to actual viewing practices of museum visitors.

Schudson's general point is that contemporary cultural studies is "sociologically impoverished", to its detriment. Although he is not particularly devoted to the Birmingham tradition in his own work (in media studies), Schudson concludes by predicting that "the works of cultural studies that will last will be the sort that follow Williams and Hoggart and Thompson, in close attention to lived experience" (1997: 395). This invocation of the "founding fathers" of British cultural studies reminds us that despite the particular disciplinary affiliations of these writers (literature and history), Birmingham cultural studies was firmly grounded in sociology – Weber, Marx, Mannheim, the symbolic interactionists, and other sociological and ethnographic traditions (see Hall, 1980). Throughout its theoretical transformations – its continuing revisions of neo-Marxist thought through the work of Althusser, Gramsci, and the Frankfurt School, its radical rethinking of its critical and conceptual framework in response to feminism and ethnic studies, and its rapprochement with post-structuralism – "Birmingham" work retained its primary focus on the structures of social life.

Let me be clear, though, that I am emphatically *not* recommending a return to origins, or an uncritical resumption of a pre-critical sociology. The critique of the early Birmingham model from the point of view of poststructuralist theory, first made, famously, by Rosalind Coward in an article in *Screen* (Coward, 1977), has been definitive. In short, a sociological model that takes categories of "class" and "gender" as unproblematically *given*, and that reads cultural activities and products as *expressions* of class (and other) positions, is revealed as fundamentally determinist and theoretically naïve. As Coward shows, cultural studies must address questions of representation, signification, and the nature of the subject if it is to deal adequately with its chosen field.[5] But this poststructuralist turn in cultural studies, which renders at least problematic any talk of "real" social relations, can be taken as opening the way to exactly the kind of cultural studies that Nelson, Schudson, and others have rejected: the interpretation of cultural practices undertaken without a grounding in identifiable social categories. Once we acknowledge that those social categories (class, race, gender, and so on) are themselves discursive constructs, historically changing articulations, and, ultimately, no more than heuristic devices in analysis (and, of course, in political mobilization), then where is that solidity of the social world on which a cultural studies that is *not* "purely textual" can depend?

Sociology and 'culture'

In my view, this necessary rethinking of the sociological project does not translate into license for "wild interpretation". Indeed, in the past few years encouraging signs have appeared within the discipline of a determination to engage with critical theory in the humanities and in cultural studies. Two sociology journals have devoted special issues to the subject of postmodernism (*Sociological Theory*, 1991; *Theory and Society*, 1992). A series of conferences initiated at the University of California, Santa Barbara, in February 1997 by two sociologists (*The Cultural Turn Conference*) was designed explicitly to address the impact of cultural studies and theory in the humanities on "cultural sociology".[6] In Fall 1997, Blackwell published *From Sociology to Cultural Studies*, edited by sociologist Elizabeth Long, and sponsored by the Sociology of Culture Section of the American Sociological Association (Long, 1997). Contributors include cultural studies scholars – Richard Johnson, Andrew Goodwin, Tricia Rose, George Lipsitz – as well as sociologists and anthropologists whose work is based in cultural studies – Herman Gray, George Marcus, Jon Cruz. Long's introduction reviews developments in British and American cultural studies and in critical theory in the humanities, as well as in the sociology of culture, and asserts her intention, with this volume, to facilitate the dialogue across these fields. Sociologist Steven Seidman proposes the "relativization" of sociology by its encounter with cultural studies (for him, primarily the Birmingham tradition, and including its own "semiotic turn" and its turn to psychoanalysis) (1997). Such a relativized sociology, in his opinion, would have a theory of the subject and of subjectivity, a critical-moral role that rejects the traditional sociological standpoint of value-neutrality, and, as a result, "more productive ways of handling problems or concerns which are considered important by some American sociologists, for example, relating social structure and culture, meaning and power, agency and constraint, or articulating a stronger notion of culture" (Seidman, 1997: 55). Other contributors take Elizabeth Long's invitation to contribute to the book as the opportunity to stress the other side of the relationship – cultural studies' need for a firmer sociological grounding. But of the 17 contributors, almost all of them, as Long points out in her introduction, have "minimized territorial bickering" (1997: 1), and have engaged seriously in the work at the intersection of sociology, the humanities, and cultural studies.[7]

These developments, though, are occurring on the margins of the discipline of sociology, and I am not especially optimistic about either a more extensive re-evaluation of the field or a more widespread enthusiasm among sociologists to engage in cross-disciplinary dialogue. I want to consider in particular two branches of sociology, both relevant to the study of culture, and each indifferent or hostile to cultural studies. Since between them these two fields account for most of the sociological work on culture, it is important to look closely at their practices and assumptions. The first is *the sociology of culture*, or the sociology of the arts. This subspecialization has gone from strength to strength in the past two decades, now constituting one of the largest sections in the American Sociological Association. At annual meetings, the Culture section regularly merits about five sessions and 15 roundtables, on the basis of membership numbers. It has a quarterly newsletter, which publishes short but often important articles, and it has embarked on a series of volumes, published by Blackwell, of which the book edited by Elizabeth Long is the second. This work is represented most strongly by the study of arts organizations and institutions, known since the mid-1970s as "the production-of-culture approach". Two special issues of journals appeared with that title in 1976 and 1978 (*American Behavioral Scientist* and *Social Research*). Although this is not the only model for the sociology of culture, I have chosen to discuss it, since it continues to be prominent in the field.[8]

Moreover, its limitation are shared by most other works within the subdiscipline. A typical study, for example, investigates publishers' decision-making criteria in two commercial publishing houses. Another looks at the role of the radio and record industries in relation to changes in the world of country music.[9] Other work has taken its departure from Howard Becker's classic essay, "Art as Collective Action" (1974), and is devoted, like that essay, to the investigation of the social relations of cultural production, though not necessarily within one institution – the roles of composer, performer, instrument-maker, bureaucrat, fund-raiser, and so on.[10] As I said earlier, most sociologists of culture and the arts base their work on pre-critical, sometimes positivistic, premises. The typical methodology is to select for analysis a specific arts organization (an opera company, an art school, a gallery) and identify its social hierarchies, its decision-making processes, and, often, the aesthetic outcomes of these extra-aesthetic factors (though it is rare that questions *of* aesthetics are permitted in this discourse, or indeed any discussion of works themselves).[11] But usually the institution is detached from both its social and its historical context, since the sociologist is dealing with the microsocial sphere. Ironically, the result is that this work is often both ahistorical and unsociological. The tenacious social-scientific commitment to "objectivity", even in qualitative (rather than quantitative) work, blocks such scholarship from addressing certain questions of interpretation, representation, and subjectivity.

It is instructive to compare contemporary work in museology, much of it founded on these very questions, with a recent special issue of a social science journal on the theme of "Museum Research".[12] Here are a couple of titles from the volume: "Art Museum Membership and Cultural Distinction: Relating Members' Perceptions of Prestige to Benefit Usage"; "The Effect of School-Based Arts Instruction on Attendance at Museums and the Performing Arts"; and "The Impact of Experiential Variables on Patterns of Museum Attendance". (It is striking, by the way, that even Bourdieu, whose influence may be detected in a couple of these titles, can be turned into a tool for empiricism – as if he were represented simply by the tables and correlations in *Distinction* (Bourdieu, 1992 [1979]). The complex analysis of cultural taste (in terms of class, habitus, and cultural capital) and the social critique of the Kantian aesthetic that underlie his empirical work take second place to the enthusiasm for surveys, number-crunching, and what C. Wright Mills once denounced as "abstracted empiricism.") One of the more quantitative studies in the volume considers museum-goers' responses to 94 questions about their social, cultural, and political values and attitudes, using multiple classification analysis to explore the implications (DiMaggio, 1996). Here it is not so much that the statistical model seems inappropriate to the subject matter – after all, interesting correlations can be found that way – but rather that the categories of analysis are themselves untheorized.

The second area of sociology that foregrounds culture is sociological theory itself – that is, the theory, or theories, of society. Here in the past couple of years the term *cultural sociology* has become prominent. But this term, and its associated reference to "the cultural turn", has nothing at all to do with language, semiotics, or poststructuralism. It describes a sociological theory whose central focus is culture – here with the broader meaning of values, beliefs, ideas, and so on, and not (as in the sociology of culture) the arts in particular. Cultural sociology, then, might be the approach employed in other sub-specialities – the sociology of law, the sociology of education, industrial sociology – which have nothing to do with culture in the narrower sense.[13]

The objective of these sociological theories is to emphasize the centrality of cultural aspects of everyday life, which proponents believe have been rendered secondary to economic, material, structural factors within the discipline. Several of these authors are fully aware of the tradition of cultural studies, but they either consider it intellectually inadequate or maintain that anything worthwhile to be found in cultural studies was done earlier (and usually better) by sociologists.[14] It is worth considering how *language* sometimes operates to stake a claim to such authority (at the same time making the implicit assumption that doing something first also means doing it *better*). Note the not-so-subtle adverbs and other indicators of priority in these examples. A short article in the ASA Culture Newsletter by Michele Lamont (1992: 8), past Chair of the ASA section on Culture, states:

> Of course, the relationship we have with cultural theory, and with theory more generally, is very different from that of academics working in Comparative Literature, English, or History departments. While sociological theory has *always* been at the centre of our common enterprise, the interest of those scholars in "theory" – to say nothing of their interest in power, class, etc. – has developed from the *relatively recent* encounter with European texts. (Foucault, Ricoeur, Derrida, and others; emphasis added)

and

> We need to painstakingly explain the place of theory in our field, and how issues that are *being appropriated* by New Historicism, New Cultural History, Cultural Studies, and "Race Theory" have been conceptualized and studied empirically by sociologists. (Lamont, 1992: 9; emphasis added)

Sociological theorist Jeffrey Alexander employs the term *cultural* to claim, using the same rhetorical device, that this is nothing new to sociology, but dates from the classical sociological tradition, particularly the work of Emile Durkheim and his followers: "Both as theory and empirical investigation, poststructuralism and semiotic investigations more generally can be seen as *elaborating* one of the pathways that Durkheim's later sociology opens up" (Alexander, 1988: 6; emphasis added).[15] And another example is to be found in a collection of essays on Symbolic Interactionism. The book, incidentally, is titled *Symbolic Interactionism and Cultural Studies* (McCall and Becker, 1990), though nothing in it really has anything to do with either the Birmingham tradition or cultural studies work within the humanities in the United States. In their introduction, the editors say this:

> We use the term *cultural studies* to refer to the classically humanistic disciplines which have *lately* come to use their philosophical, literary, and historical approaches to study the social construction of meaning, and other topics *traditionally* of interest to symbolic interactionists. (McCall and Becker, 1990: 4; emphasis added)

The sociological focus on the social construction of identity and of meaning does sound something like the project of a poststructuralist cultural studies. But the interest in social constructionism, as in work in the symbolic interactionist tradition, does not amount to the embrace of the radical rethinking mandated by poststructuralist and psychoanalytic theory, which exposes the constitutive role of culture and representation in the social world, as well as the discursive nature of social categories themselves. In addition, the "identity" understood in the Meadian tradition of symbolic interactionism is a socially variable, but psychically fixed entity, whose coordinates are the traditional sociological ones of social position and social role.

Although Jeffrey Alexander appropriates the term *cultural studies* for sociology, his views on Birmingham cultural studies are clear – and totally dismissive – in a review he cowrote in 1993 of the *Cultural Studies* reader that came out of a major conference on cultural studies; actually, they are *immediately* clear in the title of the review, which is "The British are Coming... Again! The Hidden Agenda of 'Cultural Studies'" (Sherwood, Smith, and Alexander, 1993). Like the symbolic interactionists, Alexander uses *cultural studies* to identify the type of sociological theory and sociological analysis he proposes.[16] In 1988, he edited *Durkheimian Sociology: Cultural Studies*. The book is premised on an argument spelled out in his introduction: that the later work of Durkheim – especially his work on religion – provides an excellent model for contemporary sociology, given its primary focus on symbolic process. Alexander claims that Durkheim turned to the study of religion "because he wanted to give cultural processes more theoretical autonomy" (1988: 2). He suggests that there are "parallels" with the work of Saussure, Levi-Strauss, Barthes, and Foucault, and that in some cases this is more than coincidence, but rather the unacknowledged influence of Durkheim. He goes on to review the work of certain sociologists, and some anthropologists, who have pursued Durkheim's later theory (Edward Shils, Robert Bellah, Victor Turner, Mary Douglas), and he outlines a project for a late-Durkheimian sociology, which he calls "cultural studies". But despite the names of structuralists and poststructuralist writers, this project is innocent of some central theoretical insights of those writers. This is Alexander's (1988: 11) formulation of such a sociology:

> [T]he major point of departure is *The Elementary Forms of the Religious Life*, which functions as a model for explaining central processes in secular social life. The other shared emphases follow naturally from this. They concentrate, first, on what might be called motivated expressive behavior as compared conscious strategic action. This emotionally charged action, moreover, is not seen psychologistically, but instead as the basis for ritualization. It is conceived as action organized by reference to symbolic patterns that actors – even if they have a hand in changing them – did not intentionally create.

The vocabulary here – "motivated expressive behavior", "the basis for ritualization", "action organized by reference to symbolic patterns" – reveals a fundamental conception of culture and society that is at the same time humanist, potentially mechanistic, and grounded in the sort of "layered" model of the social world which the crudest notions of base and superstructure once gave rise to. In fact, some of the essays in the book are extremely interesting and quite sophisticated.[17] But Alexander's theoretical formulae, and his conception of sociology as cultural studies, continue to operate with an understanding of discrete layers – the social/institutional and the cultural/ symbolic.

Conclusion: Towards rapprochement

I have spent some time discussing what has been called "the cultural turn" in sociology to try to identify the grounds for a possible rapprochement with cultural studies which, as I argued earlier, needs to work within a sociological perspective. I have pointed out that the sociology *of* culture (the study of the arts) has, for the most part, little interest in the critical revision of its categories of analysis. Cultural sociology, or sociological theory which foregrounds culture, on the other hand, claims both to pre-empt cultural studies and to improve on it. This applies to both symbolic interactionism and late-Durkheimianism. But in doing so, it retains the fatal weaknesses produced by ignoring a central aspect of cultural studies – namely, a theory of representation. As Steven Seidman has put it, "American sociology, even today, has not made a semiotic turn" (1997: 43). And, in the words of Roger Silverstone, a British media studies scholar, "the sociology of culture still finds comfort in the modernist securities of classification both of approach and subject matter" (1994: 993). This means, among other things, that sociologists, while understanding the social construction of meaning and even of the social self, retain a concept of the subject as coherent, unified, and stable. It also means (and this is a point made by Seidman) that they renounce the moral-critical role of cultural studies, maintaining the traditional social-scientific conception of the scholar as objective and value-neutral. And, of course, it means that sociologists cannot (yet) grasp the discursive nature of social relations and institutions. Obviously sociology, even after the "cultural turn", will not do as a model for cultural studies.

In the context of this disciplinary intransigence, I base my hope for a growing dialogue between sociology and cultural studies on two things: first, what seems to me to be an increasing acknowledgement within cultural studies of the importance of ethnography, of the study of social processes and institutions, and of the understanding of those structural features of cultural life which the sociological imagination has the ability to illuminate; and second, the work of some sociologists, few and marginalized though they might be, who have extended their view and their conceptual frameworks in new engagements with critical theory. I am not asking literary critics or art historians to become sociologists, or, for that matter, sociologists to become cultural studies scholars. We will continue to have discipline-based interests and discipline-based training. But cultural studies, after all, has always been the cross-disciplinary collaboration of interested scholars, and the body of work produced within that field is the product of those intellectual exchanges and influences. By now it is a cliché to say that cultural studies is not one thing – even that it cannot be defined. Stuart Hall, director of the Birmingham Centre throughout the decade of the 1970s, and still a major figure in the field, has said this (1990: 11; 1992: 278),[18] as have the editors of various volumes of essays on cultural studies (Grossberg et al., 1992: 3).[19] It is in the nature of cultural studies to proceed in symbiotic relationship with other disciplines. (I leave aside the question of whether or not cultural studies can itself be called a discipline.) And that relationship is, and has always been, an *ad hoc* affair.

This serendipitous nature of cultural studies, which I see as nothing but a great advantage, means the discipline continues to be an open venture. My hope, then, is that sociologists will increasingly participate in its conversations. Historians and anthropologists are already part of the collective project, but to date sociologists have, for the most part, refrained from taking part.[20] At the risk of sounding as though I *were*, after all, recommending a return to origins, I would point out the productive collaborations in Birmingham, which both in the early years and later have included sociologists. Such conversations would both guarantee the re-sociologizing of cultural studies and ensure the long-overdue theoretical development of sociology.

NOTES

1. In England, O-level exams were taken at age 16.
2. The Program in Visual and Cultural Studies at the University of Rochester.

3. Paul Jones made this point to me, as an important corrective to what might seem to be a too generalized account of American sociology.
4. Nelson describes this work as a "recycled" semiotics, which he equates with textualism; however, as Keith Moxey (1991) has pointed out, semiotics at its best is not merely a "textual" enterprise.
5. See also Burgin, 1996. Burgin reviews the development of cultural studies in Britain, and addresses particularly the turn to semiotics and psychoanalysis by those in the field.
6. This initial conference is being followed up by further such conferences at UCSB, including organized exchanges on a conference Web site.
7. See also two recent articles by Gregor McLennan (1998a,b).
8. See, for example, Peterson, 1994.
9. Essays by Walter W. Powell and Richard A. Peterson in *Social Research* (1978).
10. Becker, 1974. The article was later expanded in his book *Art Worlds* (1984).
11. I have written at greater length about these characteristics of US sociology of culture. See, for example, Wolff, 1993 [1981], Chapter 2.
12. *Poetics: Journal of Empirical Research on Literature, the Media and the Arts* (1996).
13. Indeed, one session at the 1997 ASA meetings was devoted to reviews of the 'return to culture' in a number of subspecializations, under the general panel heading 'The Return to Culture in American Sociology'.
14. Herman Gray also makes this point, in passing: 'Professional mainstream theorists strongly identified with specialties like social theory and the sociology of culture hold fast to the claim that sociology long ago dealt with the issues and questions that now appear under the sign of cultural studies' (1996: 210).
15. See also Alexander and Smith, 1993.
16. He uses the term interchangeably, and therefore confusingly, with the term *cultural sociology*. See Alexander, 1996: 1, 3–5.
17. For example, Eric Rothenbuhler's study (1988) of mass strikes as ritual and interpretation, whose discussion of the symbolic meaning of such conflict has quite a bit in common with Birmingham work on subculture.
18. "Cultural studies has multiple discourses; it has a number of different histories . . . It included many different kinds of work" (Hall, 1992: 278). Also, "Cultural studies is not one thing, it has never been one thing" (Hall, 1990: 11).
19. For example: "[I]t is probably impossible to agree on any essential definition or unique narrative of cultural studies" (Grossberg et al., 1992: 3).
20. The University of California, Santa Barbara, is one exception to this generalization.

The Sociology of Art: Between Cynicism and Reflexivity

David Inglis

We are now living in the day of the sociological interpretation of cultural achievements.

– Arnold Hauser, *The Philosophy of Art History*

> *Hollow and dull are the great.*
> *And artists envious, and the mob profane,*
> We know all this, we know!
> Cam'st thou from heaven, O child
> Of Light! but this to declare?
> Alas! to help us forget
> Such barren knowledge awhile,
> God gave the poet his song.

– Matthew Arnold, *Heine's Grave*

Introduction

One can understand a great deal about a particular form of analysis if consideration is given to the temperament that animates it. The animating drive behind most forms of the sociology of art is one of *exposure*. Just as the *philosophes* of the Enlightenment wished to expose the ways in which kings, priests and other functionaries cloaked their temporal power in otherworldly mystique, so too does the sociology of art seek to reveal the various means by which beliefs in 'art' as a superior and quasi-holy entity operate in the interests of particular powerful social groups. The mystique of 'art' is understood to be based upon the suppression of its connections with the vulgarities and mundane aspects of social life. As Pierre Bourdieu (1992 [1979]: 11) puts it, the world of art is 'the area par excellence of the denial of the social'. But by bringing the 'social' into contact with 'art', the spell that the latter casts will be broken, and the true nature of things will be revealed. The revelation thus brought to light is that 'art' is a label put on certain objects with those with the power so to consecrate them, rather than a neutral ontological category reflective of the intrinsic properties of those objects themselves. Moreover, art worlds are analysed not only in terms of the reproduction of 'bourgeois power', as in the analyses of Bourdieu (1993a, 1996), but also by focusing upon the prosaic means of cultural production and distribution, as in the work of Becker (1984), where artistic work is seen to be organised in ways analogous to the making of any other type of goods. Bringing art 'down to earth' is the keynote of most, if not all, forms of the sociology of art.

The sociology of art is therefore concerned to demonstrate the roots in forms of social power of the beliefs, attitudes and practices not only of persons in the 'art world' such as gallery owners and critics, but also of those academic groups who take 'art' as their object of analysis, such as aestheticians and art historians. While the sociology of art has expended much effort on analysing the social bases of the ideas of these groups, it has given much less attention to the project of examining *its own* assumptions. The ways of thinking, inherited from wider forms of sociological discourse, clearly inform the way sociologists conceive of artistic matters. Yet the 'sociological gaze' is as much a product of social and historical contingency as any other form of knowledge, including art history and aesthetics. But these sociological ways of thinking are themselves rarely subjected to reflexive scrutiny by sociologists of art. What I seek to do here is to begin to outline the contours of a critique of sociological critiques of art. My critique will itself be sociological in nature, and thus the paper is concerned to show what a sociological analysis of sociological analyses of art might entail. My intention is to show that only by subjecting their own views of art to reflexive self-critique can sociologists avoid lapsing into cynicism towards, and derision of, matters artistic and aesthetic.

I will first set out the tacit and often unexamined epistemological assumptions upon which sociological ideas as to art are based. Then I will examine the plausibility of charges that sociology is guilty of 'disciplinary imperialism' when it comes to artistic matters. I will then proceed to turn the sociology of Bourdieu against itself, showing how his sociology's dispositions towards art could themselves be seen as the products of particular social life conditions. By way of conclusion, I will suggest ways out of the various forms of impasse I have identified in the current sociological comprehension of artistic phenomena.

Tacit assumptions

Despite the variations between different positions within the sociology of art, there is nonetheless an identifiable 'meta-discourse' that unites all these strands (Inglis and Hughson, 2003: 35). I would argue that the idea that there is really no such thing as 'art' per se, but that the very word 'art' is a label put on certain things by certain interested parties (intentionally or unintentionally), has come to be a default position in sociology. Such a view has become the 'commonsense' of the discipline, its automatic response to the issue 'what is art?' The answer to that question has become ever more unquestioned – there is no such thing as 'art', if this means objects that are somehow more 'refined', 'sophisticated', and 'meaningful' than other cultural forms, because 'art' is just a tendentious label put on certain objects and not on others by those who have at their disposal the power of definition.

We can trace the historical genesis of this 'commonsense' that informs the sociology of art to the trajectory that much Western philosophy has taken since the beginnings of modernity, and especially since the later eighteenth century. The most singularly dominant figure in modern Western philosophy is undoubtedly that of Kant. The Kantian philosophy sees each object as having two separate manifestations – on the one hand, there is its *noumenal* side, which is its essence and which exists beyond human perception, and its *phenomenal* side, which is the object as it appears in human perception (Bennett, 1966). Kant (1999 [1787]) sees the human mind as playing an active role in organising the world that the human being sees presented before it. The mind shapes the phenomenal aspect of things, and thus constitutes the world as we perceive it. However, Kant holds that all human minds are alike, and hence the world as perceived by me is found to be the same world as perceived by you – or by anyone else – because our minds process the world in the same ways (Korner, 1955). The history of post-Kantian developments in thought, especially as the social sciences are concerned, breaks down this position, denying the existence of *noumena* at all, and seeing the world only as a series of *phenomena*. Different groups of people are seen as possessing 'their own' culture, and it is through this cultural gauze that the world not only is perceived, but is constituted. The mainstream currents of both French and German sociology have each, in their own particular ways, emphasised the phenomenal rather than noumenal qualities of the world. Thus Durkheim (2001 [1912]) in his late work *The Elementary Forms of the Religious Life*, revises the Kantian philosophy such that he regards the perception of phenomena rooted not in the individual mind but in the cultural structures of particular groups or 'societies'. According to this account, it is the set of classifications that make up the group's 'culture' which specify what is perceivable and not perceivable within the purview of all of the members of the group (Durkheim and Mauss, 1969 [1903]). Out of this way of thinking comes one of the main tenets of contemporary sociology, the notion that all forms of 'reality' are social fabrications (Berger and Luckmann, 1967) and that anything that seems to be 'objective' is only so from the perspective of a particular social group.

Likewise, the German sociological tradition, as exemplified in the work of Max Weber, involves reworkings of the Kantian philosophy, in that it sees the 'culture' of a group as 'a finite segment of the meaningless infinity of the world process, a segment on which human beings confer meaning and significance' (cited at Turner, 1996: 5). In other words, culture is what selects from a huge variety of possible phenomena the members of the group could recognise or find important, a finite set upon which their attention dwells. It is in the work of Weber particularly that a transformed Kantianism is mixed with other strains of thought which also fundamentally underpin contemporary sociological thinking. In particular, the Kantianism is wedded with two different accounts of power. The first is Marx's analysis of cultural forms as ideologies, which are expressive of the interests of particular social classes. The second is Nietzsche's (1967) 'genealogy of morals', which sees each cultural form as being the result of, and having embedded within it, the 'will to power' of particular individuals or social groups. In the thought of these two nineteenth-century figures 'culture' is made almost synonymous with 'power'. In Weber's work, this emphasis is retained, and is conjoined with the Kantian notion that culture comprises the selection of phenomena that the group finds meaningful given its particular life conditions. The upshot of all of this is that cultural matters are seen as being thoroughly shot through with social power relations. No cultural form is ever 'innocent', for each is seen to be harbouring some kind of more or less hidden agenda, that is itself rooted in forms of social power.

A further important current in the genesis of modern social science is the stress laid by early nineteenth-century Romantic thinkers on the view that each 'culture' is unique, and that as a result one culture cannot be compared with another (Berlin, 2000). The art of one culture, therefore, could not be compared to the art of another culture. Artistic norms and standards are seen to be wholly internal to each culture. As a result, aesthetic relativism seemed to be the only possible position one could take, for otherwise one would fail to recognise the fact that what was artistically valid in one context was invalid in another (Iggers, 1968). Most contemporary anthropology, and much sociology, works with notions like these, in that it sees each cultural context as being 'valid' in its own right, and comparisons ranking them against each other are based on criteria that can only pretend to be universal in nature (Kuper, 1999). This way of thinking makes its way into modern sociology of culture in the work, for example of Gans (1978 [1966]) and Bourdieu (1992 [1979]), each of whom sees modern, urban cultures as being comprised of a series of different group-based cultures (e.g. upper working-class culture), each of which is internally coherent, and which are not to be measured against the standards of powerful groups like the upper bourgeoisie. Examined in this way, it is clear that contemporary sociology of culture and art owes its aesthetic relativism in large part to its Romantic predecessors.

The ubiquity of power

My argument is that this confluence of ideas – that 'art' is a label put on certain things by certain powerful interested parties, that all cultural values are in the last instance 'arbitrary', and that culture and power are thoroughly interpenetrating, with the latter significantly or thoroughly shaping the former – have become taken-for-granted and mostly unquestioned assumptions in the sociology of art. Indeed one might go so far as to say that the sociology of art is synonymous with these views, which go unquestioned and regarded as 'truth' by those in the sociology of art field. If this is so, then one might take as emblematic of the field as a whole Bourdieu's statement that the sociology of art is fundamentally concerned with the 'barbarous reintegration' of the apparently elevated realm of artistic life with processes of cultural power and mundane activity (Bourdieu, 1992 [1979]: 6). Of course, someone might object to my equating of Bourdieu's position with the entire sociology of art field. Is not Bourdieu's sociology of art a rather extreme case? To this I would respond that while Bourdieu generally states matters more sharply than other sociologists of art, his position is but a strong version of a programme that most, if not all, positions in the sociology of art today subscribe to.

The work of Janet Wolff, one of the key figures in the sociology of art in recent times, does not indulge in the often rather 'extreme' rhetoric that Bourdieu could be accused of voicing. Yet even from her more temperate pen comes an indication of the degree to which the sociology of art subscribes to the views that I have ascribed to it above. In her classic text *The Social Production of Art*, Wolff (1981: 142–43) explicitly avows that the 'sociological study of art does not constitute a denial by exposure of aesthetic enjoyment and aesthetic experience, a denigration of cultural production, or an equalisation of all cultural products...it does so not in any spirit of philistinism or iconoclasm, but from a commitment to its subject matter and with a total sensitivity to its special nature'. Sociology on her view here does not usurp the academic discourses of art history and aesthetics, where judgements of the value of particular artworks are made. Each of these ways of thinking possesses its own form of validity.

Yet in other parts of this book, she characterises the same situation in these terms: 'there is nothing sacred and eternal about the aesthetic, which a sociology of art profanes; on the contrary, sociology demonstrates its very arbitrariness in laying bare its historical construction' (ibid.: 141). One presumably would not wish to trust the 'arbitrary' judgements of a discourse that 'is never innocent of the political and ideological processes' in which it is embedded (ibid.: 143). The 'special nature' of art, whatever that may be, gets lost as the focus shifts to 'political and ideological processes' beyond the realm of 'art' per se. There is a slippage in Wolff's argument, between an attempted acknowledgement of the validity of other approaches to artistic issues, and a sociological critique of these which seems to undermine seriously the claims made within these approaches. All disciplines construct their own 'truths', but it seems that sociology's version of the truth is truer than the others. As Wolff (1993: 29) put it in another context:

> The only thing the social scientist might lack, vis-à-vis the art critic or art historian, is a certain training in the languages of art...Apart from this, art history has no better claim to objectivity in the defence of values than sociology, which at least exposes the origins and interests involved in aesthetic judgements.

This is a very different sort of argument than that which cedes to art history and aesthetics their own criteria of validity. Thus in the same manner as Bourdieu, Wolff is drawn towards imagery which suggests that the deluded high priests of Art are to be challenged by the profaning gaze of the sociologist, which sees what they cannot, namely the thoroughly socio-historical creation of ideas and attitudes that those in the art world, and the parts of the university concerned with 'art', experience as 'natural'.

It is at this point that we encounter an interesting twist to the tale. Surely one might object that such an attitude towards 'art' misses certain of its features, reducing everything to social factors such as the power relations involved in defining something as 'art' or not? Surely there is more to 'art' than 'power' (Crowther, 1994)? From the point of view of the sociologist of art, these objections are not only invalid – for the basic substratum of any human phenomenon is made up of social structures and power relations – but also are indicative of the biases of the person who makes such claims. Arnold Hauser (1985 [1958]: 3–4) expressed the logic of sociological responses to the 'priests of art' in this way: 'requiring the spiritual to be preserved from all contact with the material frequently turns out to be a way of defending a position of privilege'. In other words, criticising the sociology of art as a 'reductionist' enterprise that misses certain features of 'art', is itself the expression of a – semi- or unconscious – desire to defend one's own interests. Those in the art world and its attendant academic departments stand to lose a lot, both psychologically and materially, if sociology reveals the untruths upon which their existences depend. Bourdieu (1993b: 23), as ever, puts the point trenchantly:

> Sociological discourse arouses *resistances* that are quite analogous in their logic and their manifestations to those encountered by psychoanalytical discourse. The people who read that there is a very strong correlation between educational level and museum-going have every likelihood of being museum-goers, of being art lovers ready to die for the love of art, experiencing their encounter with art as a pure love, a love at first sight, and of setting countless systems of defence in the way of scientific objectification. [italics in original]

Thus those who are part of art worlds, or who are staunch defenders of a realm of 'high culture', are just like neurotics who refuse to admit the troubling truths thrown at them by the psychoanalyst. The implication of this stance is that any criticism of Bourdieu's account of all practices of 'artistic' consumption as being based upon the habitus of the upper bourgeoisie, could be dismissed as itself embodying bourgeois biases. To claim that discourses in defence of 'art' are more than merely manifestations of bourgeois cultural power is, according to this logic, unintentionally to reveal one's desire to defend the forms of cultural capital one is endowed with. Criticising the sociology of art reveals not only that one is bourgeois but that one is blind to the sociological reasons for one being the way one is, a particularly reprehensible form of naïvety and ignorance. Criticism of the sociology of art is therefore utterly self-defeating and any apparent victories against it will be Pyrrhic indeed.

Sociological imperialism

When a particular form of thought is so well insulated against its critics, one must pause and consider to what degree one is faced with a self-justifying ideology. In one of the major foundational texts of semiotic cultural studies,

Roland Barthes (1993 [1957]) argues that 'mythical' thought occurs when a particular discourse, the product of the exigencies of a particular set of socio-historical circumstances, passes itself off as commonsense, as a natural and inevitable way of thinking rather than as one discursive possibility among many. My argument here is that the ways of thinking based around the principle of equating 'culture' and 'power' constitute the disciplinary commonsense of sociology today. It is into these ways of thinking that students are inculcated when they take undergraduate and postgraduate degrees in these subjects. Such forms of conceptualising are so ingrained in the world of sociology, that they are, to use Bourdieu's phrase, 'misrecognised' as representing the 'truth' of things in the world, and are taken at face value. This is particularly ironic, given that sociologists tend to be highly suspicious of claims as to 'natural' ways of thinking, and seek to criticise other social groups' commonsensical modes of conceptualisation.

While sociologists like to call into question other people's commonsense views and forms of knowledge, they have been much less keen to carry out the same practice on themselves. Yet if we take seriously the claims of sociology that no claims to truth are ever neutral and free of the interests of certain groups, then it follows that the claims sociologists make about other groups, are *themselves* disguised forms of group interest, in this case the interests of sociologists.

In a classic article on such matters, Phil Strong (1979) argued that when sociologists made claims to understand the particular professional area that they were examining, such as medicine, better than the practitioners in that field themselves, they were exercising a form of power that Strong calls 'socio-logical imperialism'. As Strong (1979: 199) argued, if one looks *in a sociolog-ical manner* at what sociologists do, it follows that 'a sociological critique of medicine [or anything else]...cannot be disinterested for, whatever its inten-tions, it also serves to advance the sociologists' cause'. Once one sees truth claims in the light of the implicit or explicit advancement of the interests of the group making those claims, one can only see that the claims of sociologists are also based around the advancing of sociologists' collective interests.

From this sociological perspective on sociology, sociologists cannot be seen as 'simply detached commentators on medicine [or any other field] but rivals to it. The more the sociological explanations prevail, then the more sociologists' status will increase and that of...other professions diminish' (Strong, 1979: 201). Thus if we see sociologists as one professional group amongst a constel-lation of professional groups, each of which operates within the multiple differentiated spheres of modernity, we see that sociological knowledge exists in a paradoxical fashion. It simultaneously operates around the critique of the knowledge systems of other professional groups, whilst itself being the know-ledge form of a professional group. Moreover, it tends to fail to recognise its own status in this regard, and therefore is guilty of not fully understanding its own nature, and the power relations that are a constitutive part of its social existence. For a discipline oriented around the identification, if not exposure, of the social conditions of possibility of other forms of knowledge, and the forms of power that are involved in them, this is a sad failure indeed.

It is part of the professional occupation known as 'sociologist', argues Strong, 'to be sceptical and they do not feel they have done . . . [their job] properly unless they have been so' during the working day. Without a 'daily toilet of scepticism' the sociologist goes home at night feeling she/he has not carried out his or her professional duties fully (Strong, 1979: 201). A sceptical outlook is encouraged by the professionalised reward system within which university-based sociologists are located. Bringing into severe doubt the knowledge claims of other professional groups is actively rewarded by the academic systems in which sociologists operate, because the sociological game is based around illustrating the social production, and therefore partiality, of particular forms of knowledge. Demonstrating the 'delusions' by which others live is the key to a successful career in sociology.

Given the emphasis of the professional system of sociology on sceptical attitudes towards the knowledges of other groups, it comes as no surprise that scepticism can 'harden into a doctrinaire cynicism' (ibid.). It is all too easy for sociologists to 'formulate themselves as members of some insightful and incorruptible elite and, at the same time, gain considerable pleasure by the exposure and thus potential overthrow of those whom they dislike' (ibid.). Sociologists are trained to think in ways that make them doubt the claims of other academic groups, such as aestheticians, and groups that inhabit art worlds, such as critics and dealers. When on a daily basis you operate inside knowledge systems that insist that culture is always about power, and that no sign system is better than any other, you are almost bound in your professional practice to doubt very much the ideas and attitudes of those who do not share your way of thinking. The knowledges of other groups, both academic and otherwise, will be grist to your sceptical, if not cynical, mill, and you are unlikely to concede to them either much credence or much respect. If you do regard these groups in respectful ways, it will be despite of the dispositions of your professional role, not because of them, and an idiosyncratic and 'personal' response on your own part.

Bourdieu against himself

Beyond the issue of rivalries between different professional groups and their respective forms of knowledge, there lies the sociological question, first formulated explicitly by Max Weber (see Chapter 1) of why certain types of people like certain types of things. Such things can include particular types of thinking or styles of argument. Although such ideas will need at a future point in time to be defended with reference to empirical evidence, I suggest as a series of hypotheses the following claims. We might expect certain types of person, with particular educational and other forms of background, to be attracted towards the sceptical attitudes of sociology towards 'art'. Possible types of person in this regard may include these:

1   those from lower social classes, whose lack of exposure to the things commonly defined as 'art' has made them hostile to such forms of culture;

having been exposed throughout their childhoods to what is defined as 'popular culture', they seek in their adult lives to validate the latter and repudiate the power of the former

2   those from higher social classes who have, for whatever reason, rebelled against the norms of their class; these dissident members of the bourgeoisie may be seeking revenge on their parent class by formulating forms of knowledge that are antagonistic to its social position and apparent cultural hegemony

3   those who are part of the 'new middle classes', groups whose occupations tend to cluster in the so-called 'creative industries' such as media production and advertising; by adopting a sceptical attitude towards what is defined by other groups, whose tastes are seen to be more 'conventional', as 'art', the 'omnivorous' tastes of their own group can be defined by themselves as less 'stuffy' and more 'open' than that of more 'traditional' groups

The reader will notice that this speculative analysis borrows its logic from the ideas of Bourdieu, but turns his ideas against his substantive analyses of class-based cultural tastes. Bourdieu advertised his sociology as one that was thoroughly 'reflexive' in nature in that it cast its critical gaze upon its own practices (Bourdieu and Wacquant, 1996). Moreover, Bourdieu (1990: 36) was of the opinion that 'every sociologist would do well to listen to his adversaries as it is in their interest to see what he [sic] cannot see, to observe the limits of his vision, which by definition are invisible to him'. But this injunction and the reflexive potential in his thinking more generally were not put into practice by Bourdieu in terms of self-critique vis-à-vis his analyses of matters artistic. In this section, I will attempt to realise some of the reflexive promise of his sociology by briefly sketching out what a Bourdieusian analysis of Bourdieu's analysis of art-related issues might entail.

The very taste for sceptical analyses of 'art' mentioned above can itself be seen as the product of the dispositions and interests, tacit or otherwise, of particular social groups. In terms of the first category I outlined, it is interesting that Bourdieu himself came from humble, indeed peasant, origins in provincial France, and freely admitted that despite all the success he enjoyed in the game of French academic life, he still felt like an 'outsider' in the context of elite academic institutions and life among the Parisian upper bourgeoisie (Lane, 1999). Clearly his desire to provide a sceptical account of 'bourgeois' discourse on art derived in part from a feeling that this was a universe of meaning to which he did not fully belong, by background or by education (i.e. training as an anthropologist and sociologist, rather than as, for example, a philosopher of art).

The type of person referred to under the terms of the third category I outlined above may well include some of the students I have taught in my course in the sociology of culture. I have often asked myself why is it that so many of these young people already are suspicious of, and often actively dislike, phenomena that are defined as 'artistic', even before they are exposed to the sceptical accounts of such things offered by sociology and cultural studies. I suspect that this is partly due to social origins, the majority of students in my department hailing from upper working and lower middle-class backgrounds where 'art' generally signifies pretentiousness and pointlessness. However, one must also account for the social trajectories many of these students are engaged in. A substantial number take my course every year because it is about the only one on offer in the sociology Honours programme that seem to offer the possibility of studying things that might be useful in a career in the mass media. Is it the case that a dislike of what 'art' signifies is part of the set of dispositions of the 'new middle classes' that students entering media-related jobs will become part of? If it is, my teaching of sceptical attitudes towards artistic canons and suchlike is fuelling dispositions that were already there. My 'critical' teaching seems to have an 'elective affinity' with a particular sort of middle-class taste culture. This is a possibility which, given that I see myself as a sociologist concerned to criticise the bourgeoisie and all its doings, causes me increasing uneasiness. What is the purpose of 'critical pedagogy' if it is aiding the interests, if not indeed helping to form the worldview, of a newly ascendant class?

We can also utilise Bourdieu's (1988) ideas as to the nature of academic life to begin to think about the often subterranean reasons why particular types of people may be attracted to, and may wish to defend and augment, sceptical attitudes towards 'art'. By drawing a map of the academic field in a given country at a given period in time, we can work out which disciplines and insti- tutions are in positions of relative dominance and relative subordination. Historically, philosophy and art history have enjoyed much more status in academic life in Western countries than more 'vulgar' disciplines such as sociology, especially given the relatively recent arrival of this discipline into the established university curriculum. Just as people hailing from lower social classes may be attracted to sceptical accounts of 'art' because they harbour forms of *ressentiment* against the upper bourgeoisie and its culture, in a similar fashion such accounts may be seen as the revenge of the 'dominated' discipline of sociology over the more 'dominant' disciplines of philosophical aesthetics and art history (Bourdieu and Passeron, 1979). Just as Strong argued that sociological critiques of medicine were connected to struggles between sociologists and medical professionals to gain discursive control over the terrain called 'medicine', so sociological critiques of art may be seen as tacit attempts at usurping the power of those who hitherto have had discursive control in the academy over the terrain of 'art'. Is it too much to see the sociology of culture as an attempted social scientific coup against the cultural power of those in certain types of humanities departments? Is it too much to claim that the sociology of art can be seen as a 'slaves' revolt' against the masters of discourse in art history, aesthetics and other such locales, with Bourdieu as its Spartacus?

Conclusion

In this chapter, I have delineated the outlines of a critique of the critiques of art proffered by sociologists. I have argued that, examined sociologically, the sociology of art's ways of construing the nature of artistic matters are themselves revealed as products of history and social contingency. Yet this is a feature of their outlook upon art that too often goes unacknowledged by sociologists, the standard sociological views as to the ubiquity of power relations generally just being regarded as the 'natural' way of seeing things. I have also set out some hypotheses, which will need to be backed up by further empirical researches, as to some of the personal and professional reasons why sociologists tend to think about art professionally in the ways that they do. I have shown how Bourdieu's sociological categories can be used to identify the reasons why his position on art, and others akin to it, can themselves be explained in terms of socially generated and socially located dispositions and tastes.

The motto of scholars in the sociology of art could well be taken from Rousseau (1933: 141): 'I had come to see that everything was radically connected with politics.' All cultural forms are seen to be 'political' in nature, as they are thoroughly wrapped up in the struggles between more powerful and more powerless social groups. In his critique of Anderson and Nairn's version of the Marxist notion of cultural base and economic superstructure, E.P. Thompson (1978: 86) noted that his complaint

> concerns not what the model purports to explain, but what it does not take into account at all. The preoccupation is with power, and with political analysts this is proper. But all human phenomena cannot be assimilated to the categories of power, nor of class; and yet there appears to be some tendency among Marxists to assume that they can, or ought to be.

The same criticism could be made of sociologists of art. The claim I wish to put forward here is that *it may be the case* that not all 'artistic' phenomena can be *fully* assimilated to categories of power. Yet as it is currently constituted, the sociology of art is configured in ways that allow sociologists to see 'power' and not much else. While the Marxists Thompson writes of see 'class' everywhere, as at the root of all issues and situations, so too do sociologists tend to see 'powerful groups' as ultimately responsible for the form taken by all cultural phenomena.

The sociology of art has indeed shown that naïve celebrations of 'art' and its superiority over other forms of culture cannot be taken at face value. Power relations are endemic in the field of 'art' as in any other social field. Yet this self-consciously 'critical' discipline has as yet been insufficiently critical with itself in such matters. There is a very great difference between a cynical and derogatory approach to artistic matters and the discourses that surround them, and attitudes characterised by a healthily open-minded form of scepticism. Sociologists must avoid lapsing into the former and should embrace the latter. It is never enough just to study art 'sociologically'. At the same instant as one is sociologically comprehending 'artistic' phenomena, one must also question the tacit assumptions embedded in the forms of enquiry one is utilising. In other words, one must sociologically analyse the nature of one's sociological analysis of 'art'. The sociology of art must be reflexive, self-questioning and self-critical, or it will harden into a cynical dogma which fails to recognise its own social conditions of possibility and operation. If the sociology of art makes this necessary 'reflexive turn', narrow forms of derision towards other ways of seeing, and the groups that formulate them, will be avoided. A less dogmatic future is possible in social scientific analyses of art, if sociologists now do to themselves what they have hitherto been doing to 'art' and other academic disciplines, namely relativising, historicising, and laying bare tacit assumptions. In this way sociologists will become more sensitive and appreciative of other modes of perception and other means of knowing, a situation that would encourage a revivification and strengthening of the sociology of art.

Part II
From Theory to Practice: Case Studies in the Sociology of Art

Framing Old Age: Sociological Perspectives on Ageing in Victorian Painting

8

Mike Hepworth

Introduction

One task of the sociological study of art is the analysis of how particular art forms of past societies were viewed, understood and talked about, at or near the time of their creation. The contextualisation of critical and other responses to such artworks can help us understand not only what people of the time thought about particular paintings, novels and so on, it also helps deepen our under-standing of that context itself. This is because what people said about certain artistic forms, and also how they said such things, can help reveal wider facets of the cultural milieu of a particular epoch. As the Victorian critic Leslie Stephenson observed in the July 1875 issue of the *Cornhill* magazine, the 'whole theory of the life and...conduct' of groups of people depends on looking at and seeking to understand the significance of the 'poems which they learn by heart, novels with which they amuse their leisure, the pictures which they hang upon their dwelling rooms' (cited at Macleod, 1996: 351). Quite simply, how people thought about and regarded certain artworks potentially tells us a lot about those people, their ideas and their attitudes.

If this is so as a general principle, then it follows that art which takes as its subject matter a particular theme or phenomenon, can provide us with insights into how at a given historical period a certain group of people – or indeed perhaps a whole society – regarded that theme or phenomenon. We gain such knowledge if we attend to the responses to that art made by, and 'characteristic' of', such people at that time. I intend in this chapter to carry out such an operation with reference to a particular substantive subject matter, namely the representation of old age in British painting during the period 1850–1900. I am not a 'sociologist of art' per se, but rather a sociologist of ageing and life-course processes who is interested in visual and verbal images of ageing in different historical periods. My guiding assumption here is that old age is a biological process deriving its personal and social meanings from visual and verbal imagery (Hepworth, 1995, 2000). My aim here is to set out an argument which suggests that contemporary responses to certain paintings of the Victorian period dealing centrally with ageing, can help us to get access to wider attitudes to this issue characteristic of (certain sectors of) later nineteenth-century British society. I intend to set out the ways in which a sociologist can reconstruct a certain set of attitudes and dispositions towards a particular issue, in this case the meanings associated with old age, by looking not just at artworks themselves but also what people (including the artists themselves) at the time of their creation thought of them and how they responded, intellectually and emotionally, to them.

This chapter, therefore, is about pictures of old age that were displayed in the art exhibitions and 'dwelling rooms' of the time, and what the people who viewed them thought of them, why they liked certain representations and disliked others. The paintings of old age which have been selected are works that were familiar to a wide section of the Victorian public, and which in fact continue to feature prominently in art histories and cultural analyses of British nineteenth-century art. Three paintings by two famous artists have been chosen because they provoked considerable discussion about images of old age in the art criticism and public discourses of the day. As such, I think they particularly help further our understanding of public attitudes towards ageing during the period. The artists are Frederick Walker (1840–75) and Hubert von Herkomer (1849–1914), two men who were highly significant figures in the world of British painting during their own lifetimes.

A further theme running through the chapter, although this time more implicitly, is that my work illustrates some of the issues that arise when a person who is a sociologist by training takes on, to some degree, the mantle of the professional known as the 'art historian'. My argument is that the sociologist can very usefully draw upon art historical work, especially that which seeks to locate particular artworks in socio-cultural context, in building his or her own accounts of particular themes and phenomena. In one way, therefore, this chapter indicates some of the benefits that accrue for sociological research when the sociologist engages with both the artworks of a particular period, and the commentaries of art (and cultural) historians upon them. Yet it is also true that the distinctive contribution of the sociologist can be to take the contextualisation process initialised by art historians in new and potentially more sharply delineated directions than would otherwise have been the case.

Old age and Victorian art history

Before looking more closely at the images of old age created by Walker and Herkomer, it is important to make three general points with regard to recent cultural and art history which analyses the Victorian period and seeks to develop understandings of the contexts in which the art of the period was made and viewed. First, scholars increasingly recognise the diversity of Victorian culture, the tensions and contradictions reflected in 'the instability of Victorian representations' (Shires, 1992: 185) The term 'Victorian' is no longer a byword for unitary repressive respectability, but is becoming a sign of a complex, and often contradictory, series of crosscurrents of beliefs, attitudes and practices (Gay, 1998). Nineteenth-century paintings are now regarded as much more complex (Pointon, 1986), and even subversive (Barrow, 2001), than has often been supposed. Previous interpretations of Victorian paintings are currently under serious scrutiny and much effort is now directed to rescuing this art from the oblivion of dismissive over-generalisation to which it was largely consigned by critics during the decades following the First World War (Wood, 1978, 1988).

Secondly, paintings which include images of old age are not difficult to find during a period which saw an unprecedented expansion in the production and consumption of art. The market for paintings and reproductions of paintings was nothing short of phenomenal.[1] Works in which old age figures in some form or other are found liberally scattered through art history sources, such as catalogues of Victorian art (Morris and Roberts, 1998), studies as widely ranging as Gordon (1988) on paintings of subjects from English novels, Yeldham's (1984) work on women artists, and Lionel Lambourne's magisterial study *Victorian Painting* (1999).[2]

The emergence of feminist art history and criticism has also produced scholarly texts giving some prominence to images of old age and opening up, if often tangentially, lines of further enquiry into Victorian ageing. The work of Casteras (1987), Cherry (1993) and Pointon (1986) is critical in this respect. Art historians concerned with the cultural and socio-economic processes involved in the production and consumption of art (notable examples are Gillett, 1990 and Macleod, 1996) have also provided sociologically grounded research findings which cannot be undervalued for the study of ageing in painting. Amongst these can be included Flint's (2000) superb work on the Victorian visual imagination and Cowling's (1989) definitive study of the influence of physiognomy and phrenology on the representation of moral character in Victorian painting.[3] Indeed, the representation of old age as physiognomic evidence of moral character is a strong theme throughout the period. For example, in his study of rural nostalgia in Scottish painting, Morrison (1989) refers to Gibson and Forbes White's monograph on George Paul Chalmers (1833–78), published in Edinburgh in 1879. Forbes White felt that Chalmers would represent in an aged face 'as far as possible, the history of a life, making it a record of work done and of sorrows felt, and yet a resting place of placid contentment' (1989: 16).

Thirdly, given the popularity and profusion of such paintings, it is not surprising that art historians of the Victorian period from time to time included some focused discussion of images of old age in their analyses. Yet for the most part these references are brief and studies, although essential reading from an art historical point of view, are suggestive rather than substantive sources for the student of old age.

Frederick Walker and *The Harbour of Refuge*

We are now in a position to take a closer look at the first of the three paintings of old age I wish to focus on, namely Frederick Walker's *The Harbour of Refuge*, first exhibited in London at the Royal Academy in 1872. This is Walker's most famous painting and was widely reproduced. Lambourne (1999: 340) recently described it as depicting 'a group of old people sitting in the garden of an almshouse (the Jesus Hospital at Bray), their age being contrasted with a vigorous young reaper, who symbolically wields a scythe'. Lambourne's brief description does not mention the two significant figures to the left foreground of the picture: an older and younger woman walking together. The older woman is supported by the younger, dressed in black and bent with age, her eyes downcast. The young woman is walking tall and upright, her gaze firmly directed towards the young man wielding the scythe.

At one level the message of the painting is clear.[4] Walker depicts ageing in the time-honoured style of a dramatic contrast between youth and age. The old woman is near death, her line of vision confined to the ground immediately before her faltering steps. The young woman's gaze covers a wider field and ultimately comes to rest on the man with the scythe, a figure doubly symbolic of youth and death. In the background of the picture, the group of older people sitting unassumingly around a large statue in the garden remind the viewer that Walker was painting a real place: an almshouse in Bray where poor older people went to spend the remainder of their lives.

This reading reflects two aspects of Walker's claim to fame. He was celebrated during his brief lifetime for his fidelity to 'figurative subjects in domestic or landscape settings' (Newall, 1987). He was also a leading exponent of the 'Idyllist' school. Although he was a painter of scenes from everyday life, he was also, as the term 'Idyllist' indicates, known for his technique of transforming such scenes in his gentle brushwork into a poetic vision. Herkomer, who was influenced by his work, significantly described Walker in the *Magazine of Art* in 1893 as 'the handmaiden of the poet' (Saxon Mills, 1923: 147). In terms of choice of medium and technique Walker is chiefly remembered as a watercolourist, who painted firstly in a fine detail partly erased, in order to give a less defined outline and a more 'dreamlike' effect. This was an effect which Herkomer, as we shall see below, was at pains to avoid in his efforts to achieve a closer correspondence to the harder outlines of 'reality'. As an indication of the tension between 'realism' and the fantasy of the Idyllic school, *Harbour* is included in Lambourne's volume in his chapter on 'social realism'.

Walker's representation of ageing therefore combines social realism with an impulse to soften the harsh 'reality' of old age, so that it is framed within an acceptable and consoling dreamlike vision. The tension here between more 'realist' and 'idealising' aesthetic impulses is expressive of one of the most interesting phenomena associated with ageing as it was understood in Victorian society. There was to some degree an identifiable gulf between artistic practice on the one hand and the 'reality' of everyday experience on the other. Gay (1998) has drawn our attention to the matter-of-fact attitudes of Victorians towards the human body as encountered in everyday life: 'People were born, fell ill, and died at home, in full view of their family ... respectable Victorians – woman as much as men, perhaps even more so – had their faces pushed into real life with all its obtrusive coarseness' (1998: 238). The socioeconomic structure and the level of development of medical science meant that Victorians were inevitably surrounded by the unpleasant aspects of human existence: a dirty and unhealthy environment, the frequency of incurable illness, pain and death, and the teeming, unwashed poor. In Gay's view the Victorians were less sensitive to the problems of the body, including the ageing body, than we may sometimes suppose. This is a view supported by Jalland's (1996) study of the experience of nursing the terminally ill in affluent Victorian families, where the sick, old and dying were looked after at home and often by close (female) relatives in circumstances we would now tend to find intolerable. And, indeed, Jalland's work provides ample evidence of the tension that often existed between the idealised Christian version of the 'good death', when the soul is peacefully released to meet its Maker, and the all-too-painful reality of dying in the absence of the many sources of relief from pain and suffering we now take for granted.

Keeping these background factors in mind, we may say that in one sense Walker's style in *The Harbour of Refuge* comes close to the idealized version of the 'good death' discussed by Jalland. Yet at the same time the dream is not totally divorced from reality. The Jesus Hospital at Bray, as we have seen, did exist and was one source of inspiration for the painting. As a result, we may read *The Harbour of Refuge* not only as an aesthetic form poised between realist and idealist stylistic tendencies, but also as dramatically embodying a central paradox of ageing in Victorian society, a world caught between the often very acute proximity of decaying and dying bodies within the purview of many people on the one hand, and dispositions towards denying or occluding that situation on the other.

Hubert von Herkomer and *The Last Muster*

The tension between the lived reality of ageing and dealing with ageing bodies, and more idealising ideas and dispositions about old age, continues, though in ways more explicitly expressed at the time, in the responses to two of Herkomer's oil paintings of old age: *The Last Muster: Sunday in the Royal Hospital, Chelsea* (1875), and *Eventide: A Scene in Westminster Union* (1878).

Unlike Walker, the aesthetic impulse behind both paintings was deeply and systematically social realist in nature. They were explicitly designed as companion pieces to record two aspects of old age, the one depicting a particular form of 'masculine' ageing and the other illustrating a particular sort of 'feminine' ageing. The public reaction when the paintings were displayed, however, indicated ambiguities in attitudes to representations of ageing, which, I argue, reflected deep-seated distinctions in the perception of the gender and social status of older people. Although Herkomer (originally a native of Bavaria) was strongly influenced by Walker in his early days as a painter living in Britain, they were separated by their country of origin, social class and education. Herkomer's father was a humble craftsman and the painter received little formal education and was proud of his lowly origins. His concern for representing the reality of aspects of the lives of poor people derived from his direct experience of poverty and struggle, and was mediated not only through his acceptance of the value of unremitting hard work, but also his acute awareness of what the market for paintings of his sort would bear.

Again unlike Walker, Herkomer left behind a detailed record in correspondence and also published during his lifetime extensive records of his aspirations and techniques, resources which are very useful for the sociological analyst. *The Last Muster*, a painting of Chelsea Pensioners gathered for Sunday worship in the Chapel of the Royal Hospital, was based upon a wood engraving he contributed to the edition of the illustrated paper the *Graphic* of 18 February 1871. Whilst composing and executing the work, he described its content in these words, which can be taken as indicative of his view of a certain type of 'masculine' old age: 'a mass of old men sitting in their church during service...There are about seventy heads to be seen, and all are literal portraits...It is a grand sight to see these *venerable old warriors* under the influence of divine service' (cited at Saxon Mills, 1923: 87; emphasis added).

The men were painted in his studio following the physiognomic principle widely accepted at the time that external appearance is a guide to internal character and moral worth in later life (Cowling, 1989; Hepworth, 1995). The idea was to record each subtle variation in individuality so that no man would blend indistinguishably into the congregation of old men. Unlike Walker's idyllic technique where individual features are almost indecipherable, the majority of Herkomer's men are precisely delineated and include his own beloved father, dressed as a Chelsea Pensioner.

It is clear that Herkomer's blend of realism was closely in tune with one significant strand of Victorian aesthetic values. As Saxon Mills (1923: 92–3) observes:

> There is no doubt that the circumstances of his life, his lack of brothers and sisters, the perpetual companionship of his parents, the spectacle of their long struggle with unrelenting adversity and his own acquaintance with the harsher aspects of life, had made him old beyond his years and given him a sympathy with toiling and suffering, and especially aged humanity.

Herkomer's valorisation of the 'nobility' of the aged male struck a chord with a public which applauded this positive vision of ageing. We can see this in the fact that *Muster* was an instant popular success and catapulted Herkomer to a fame and fortune that lasted until the end of his life. The *Pall Mall Gazette*, 5 May 1875, noted Herkomer's move away from Walker, who prefered 'idyllic subjects'. In contrast, Herkomer was judged to be characterised by 'naturalistic portraiture without drama', the latter being applauded for its capacity to represent certain positive qualities of the old men depicted in the painting (Morris, 1994: 55, n. 18). The painting was also a success at the Paris Exposition of 1878 where it was commended for what was seen as its explicitly 'English' interpretation of the subject matter. Although a foreigner, Herkomer was regarded at the time as having successfully penetrated the depths of national sentiment. In a letter to his aunt and uncle he observed 'There's hardly another subject that so appeals to English hearts – men who have fought for their country and have come to their last home preparing for their last journey home' (Saxon Mills, 1923: 88).

My argument here is that the positive critical and popular reaction to *Muster* offers a useful insight into Victorian attitudes to old age. As we have seen, Herkomer was commended not because he painted old age as a neutral social realist, but because he intentionally celebrated the heroic old age of individuals who were growing older in one of the few respected institutions for the dependent poor. In the aftermath of the Crimean War, which had become a byword for aristocratic incompetence, former rank-and-file soldiers tended to be perceived by the public as representative of one of the forms of ideal ageing which the Victorians could reproduce and display publicly with equanimity (Hichberger, 1989).

The distinctive scarlet uniforms of the old soldiers indicated a patriotism that had expressed itself actively in combat. Their worn and injured masculine bodies were emphatically *not* taken, or represented, as signs of the wayward self-indulgence or idleness characteristic of the 'undeserving poor', features which it was thought should properly be concealed from view. Rather the old men's bodies were regarded as legitimate subjects for the artist to paint, especially when framed in domestic locations surrounded by several generations of the family and 'living out a prosperous and contented old age' (Hichberger, 1989: 55). As such, the painting could legitimately associate the emotion of pathos with old age. John Ruskin, the influential cultural arbiter commended *Muster* for its 'pathetic' quality: that is, its power to stimulate noble feelings of sympathy, pity and sadness. The success at the time of *Muster* was clearly related to Herkomer's ability not only to reflect, but also to find a visual language to (literally) *embody*, such sentiments.

Hubert von Herkomer and *Eventide: A Scene in the Westminster Union*

Herkomer's representation of a noble form of masculine ageing was a great popular and critical success, a fact that in itself allows us to explore certain attitudes towards the ageing body and person held by the people who adulated this work. But more is revealed about these attitudes and values when we consider the somewhat different reception of his work *Eventide*, publicly exhibited three years later.

The crucial difference between *Muster* and *Eventide* is that whilst the former has normally been described from the time of its creation onwards as a painting about *old age*, the latter has from the start been largely interpreted as a painting about *poverty*. As the subtitle of the painting, *A Scene in*

Westminster Union, indicates, the location is the workhouse, a more realistic terminus for poor people who lived long enough to reach old age than the Royal Hospital, Chelsea depicted in *Muster*. Yet Herkomer himself saw it primarily as a painting of old age. In a letter of 1876 Herkomer informed his uncle in America that he had begun working on a 'companion' picture to *Muster* (Saxon Mills, 1923: 97). *Eventide* was worked up from his double-paged wood engraving *Old Age: A Study in Westminster Union* which appeared in the *Graphic* newspaper on 7 April 1877.

The immediate visual impact of *Eventide* is more muted than *Muster*. The scarlet of the Chelsea Pensioners' uniforms has a warmer effect than that of the black-garbed female workhouse inmates in their white caps. The perspective of the painting is that of a stage sloping downwards towards the viewer, so that the frame of the painting resembles the proscenium arch of a theatre. The whole drab scene is dimly lit by a large uncurtained window at the top left-hand corner; a number of bowed figures whose features are indiscernible are seated in the distance, and two others walk unsteadily in mutual support towards the foreground. Occupying a substantial space in the foreground, and illuminated theatrically from below, are six old women engaged in the conventional feminine pursuits of sewing and reading; their toothless sunken features do not, however, conceal the individuality of their faces, which as we saw was also a feature of *Muster*. The juxtaposition of youth and age as a device for epitomising in static form the fluid passage of time is also evident: at the extreme right hand of the picture a young, attractive woman assists the older women with their sewing. Behind her on the wall hangs a reproduction of Luke Fildes' *Betty*, a painting of a young and beautiful milkmaid, famous in its day and first exhibited at the Royal Academy in 1875.

In composing this 'companion' painting to *Muster*, Herkomer did not intend any explicit gender differential between the old age of men and women. Rather he set out to draw significant parallels between two different experiences of the life of the poor, regarding both as characterised by qualities of heroic struggle. Both the women in the workhouse and the male Chelsea pensioners had 'fought the good fight', and their features bore the marks of their endurance.

Unfortunately for Herkomer, the public did not react with the degree of acclaim that had greeted *Muster* and had established him as one of the most celebrated artists in Victorian Britain, and it is the ambiguity of the public reaction which is of particular interest to students of ageing. The critical reception of *Eventide* at the Royal Academy was less favourable than Herkomer had hoped. The problem was the apparent unacceptability, vis-à-vis thinking of the time, of a representation that was both explicit and sympathetic, of the workhouse as the last resting place for the dispossessed. In this setting, old age was deemed to be a much less acceptable topic for art than it was when it was located in other, more 'savoury' and respectable, locales and contexts such as the Royal Hospital, Chelsea.

But in my opinion the distinct lack of enthusiasm for *Eventide* is not simply a function of the latter being set in that socially stigmatised environ, the workhouse. There is the additional complication of gender factors to be taken into account. Feminist art historians have argued for a closer study of the ambivalence expressed towards women of all ages in Victorian painting (Cherry, 1993). Herkomer's painting of gendered old age is unusual because grandmothers in Victorian paintings in Britain are not normally located amongst the dispossessed of the workhouse. They are usually situated in family settings – the rural cottage is a favourite – where they continue labouring worthily to provide the family support of child-minding, dispensing advice, cooking and sewing. The old soldiers in *Muster* were certainly impoverished and in receipt of charity, but they were regarded by the Victorian public as men who had earned their right to that charity by risking their bodies in patriotic conflict. They were thus regarded as deserving of the sympathy of those who were more fortunate than they. In other words, the bodies of old age were recognised and interpreted according not just to the moral values attributed to specific locations such as workhouses, but also according to certain norms of appropriate gender conduct. Whether Herkomer intended it or not, the setting of the Royal Hospital's Chapel, like that of the family hearth, mediates the perception of old age as a moral process, the consequences of which are physiognomically displayed on the faces of the congregation. And it is the physical *location* of images of old age which reinforces variations in moral interpretations of the physical signs of the ageing process.

Complexities of response

We mentioned earlier the arguments of historians in the present day who claim that what we today call 'Victorian culture' was much more complex and fractured than a stereotypical view of that epoch might suppose. Such arguments are evidenced in the fact that despite the *generally* negative critical and public response in *Eventide*, there were in fact contemporary viewers who found the portrayal of ageing contained within it not only sympathetic, but even that Herkomer had depicted a positive image of contentment in later life.

Some critics of, or near, the time, such as Baldry (1901: 53), detected the 'universal' quality Herkomer had wished to convey in his pictures of old age as 'observations of the ways of modern men' and 'dramatic episodes in human life which are independent of date or period'. From this perspective (1901: 54), the artist had demonstrated a level of sympathy with older people, both male and female, which imparted a

> deeper meaning to such portraits as 'My Father and my Children', and 'The Makers of my House' [other paintings by Herkomer], and to the many studies of aged types that he has painted. He has in all such works shown plainly that his choice of subjects was governed by something more than a love of picturesqueness; and he has distinguished them all with a seal of sentiment that is too fresh and unaffected to be other than persuasive to every one who is susceptible to the purer human influences.

The complexity of possible judgments and responses is here on display. At one level, we have a critical rejection of the 'picturesque', ironically one of the distinctive features accounting for the success of Walker's *Harbour* which, like *Eventide* was also a picture of the last living resting place on earth of a portion of the indigent old. The quality of the 'picturesque' was criticised by Baldry because it glossed over the sharper edges of lived reality. Yet, at a different level, another process is at work. In Baldry's interpretation, 'realism' in painting was justified not as an appeal to a radical re-evaluation of poverty and exclusion and a stimulus to engagement politically with a world of structured injustice and inequality, but as an epitome of graceful ageing as the acceptance of the conventional demands of the preordained social station of each individual. In Baldry's (1901: 54–55) view, Herkomer's figures do not

> protest with dramatic violence against a social system that grinds them down...They suffer and have suffered; but they have accepted their lot with conscious courage, and have fought their fight with no questioning of its rights or wrongs...Their dignity comes from the consciousness that they have done honestly whatever was entrusted to them, and that they have manfully fulfilled the duties, small or great, which were laid upon them as an unavoidable charge by a fate whose workings they could not hope to influence.

Here we have an acceptance of the 'realism' of Herkomer's painting that depends on viewing its 'realist' depiction of the elderly poor not as a protest against social injustice but as a representation of both social acquiescence on behalf of the persons depicted, and the nobility of aged persons who had accepted their, admittedly tough, lot in life. For a person of Baldry's (1901: 55) sensibilities, the artistic depiction of such acceptance was infinitely preferable to 'the sordid excitement of the actual struggle with circumstances'. 'Realistic' depiction of old age could be praiseworthy, but only if it led to conclusions which allowed the viewer to swerve away from difficult questions of social organisation and political responsibility. By attending to critical commentary such as this, we can begin to reconstruct the complex weave of ideas that could be spoken and those that remained unspoken or indeed were unthinkable, within a particular cultural milieu. While Victorian responses to ageing in painting were complex, like any other set of dispositions and orientations, they also had their limitations and points of no return where discursive elaboration could not go.

Conclusion

In this chapter I have looked at a selection of Victorian paintings of old age. I have presented an analysis which has sought to locate them in the cultural milieu of their production and reception. While art historians, sociologists and others have been carrying out similar operations on different types of art for a long time, the specificity of my method of contextualisation has been to attend to how the paintings in question were understood either by their creators, or by the 'general public', or by critics of the period. How all of these sets of social actors thought about and responded to the works in question has, I argue, been revealing of my main object of research, attitudes towards ageing in Britain in the Victorian. This paper has only constituted a brief sketch of what can be done with the materials at my disposal. But I hope to have indicated the ways in which sociologists can both draw on data about particular artworks and artists, as well as on art historical commentaries about these works and figures, in order to begin to gain access to a particular set of attitudes and dispositions characteristic of people long since dead. In particular, I have dwelt upon Hubert von Herkomer's experience of a variable public reaction to his two major paintings of old age, for I believe this case provides some indication of the subtleties of social attitudes towards ageing during the period. While it is no novelty to claim that artworks can afford us privileged insights into the nature of a particular time and place, what I have endeavoured to do in this chapter is to put forward some ways of making this general insight 'work' for the sociologist, namely by emphasising how both artworks 'in themselves' and the contemporary responses to them can afford us certain vistas that otherwise might be difficult to access. At any rate, it is very plausible to claim that the works I have discussed offer us a fascinating pictorial sociology of old age as it was both thought about and lived in the Victorian world.

NOTES

1. A general overview of Victorian painting (Blaikie and Hepworth, 1997) suggests at least five variations in the ways in which ageing is represented in Victorian art: (1) paintings where older people are the focus of attention because they have lived a long time – these include memorial portraits of loved ones who have died; (2) the popular 'ages of life' paintings which depict the life course as a series of ages and stages of moral development terminating in Christian salvation; (3) narrative paintings which 'tell a story' usually with a homely moral lesson; (4) panoramic paintings of, for example, urban life – the work of W.P. Frith is the prime example here; (5) genre paintings or scenes of everyday life, often with a moral message.

2. In the same vein, McKerrow's (1982) biography of the famous Faed brothers, for example, references several of their paintings on themes of ageing, including John Faed's 'Old Age', exhibited in 1867 at the Royal Scottish Academy, and Thomas Faed's 'The Last of The Clan' exhibited at the Royal Academy in 1865. Thomas' painting shows 'the once important clan, now represented by a feeble old man and his grand-daughter, watching with their women folk as John McAlpine releases the hawser to let loose the ship that bears all their young and able-bodied men away' (110–11).

3. As Cowling shows, the work of the highly successful painter W.P. Frith is an interesting example of the Victorian artist's' treatment of ageing as simply one feature that should be included in any 'realistic' panorama of the human landscape. In his *Ramsgate Sands* (1854) 'the old women throughout the painting are particularly well conceived' (Cowling, 1989: 225). According to the *Art Journal*, June 1854,

the older figures in the painting came from '"every part of the wide area between Whitechapel and Paddington"', presenting 'a considerable variety, ranging from the distinctly lower middle class pair to the far left with the newspaper and the telescope, to the distinguished looking couple under the sunshade in the centre of the picture' (Cowling, 1989: 226).

4.   Unfortunately there is an absence of correspondence by the artist concerning his own views of this work but there is evidence that Walker was stimulated by the sight 'one Sunday in church, a group of old bent labourers on a long bench in front of the pulpit, reposing in the gleams of sunlight that lingered in the gloom of the place' (Marks, 1896: 238), and it had occurred to two friends of Walker, Orchardson and Birket Foster 'that here was a scene in which Walker would delight...' (ibid.: 238), observing that the figures seated around the statue 'were very real to Walker' (ibid.: 240). In particular, the little man on the bench in black with his hands on his knees was alleged in *The Magazine of Art* to have been identified with the painter who 'had a whimsical notion that he might himself become just such a little figure in old age' (ibid.: 240). Walker himself wrote of going over to Bray 'to see how things are there' (ibid.: 231) and, according to Marks, in 1884 an old man who remembered Walker was still living at Bray.

The Rise and Fall of the Art (House) Movie

Andrew Tudor

Introduction

Taken at face value the concept 'art movie' is a strange one. In everyday discourse we do not speak of 'art novel', 'art picture' or 'art music': literature, painting, and music are routinely seen as arts in themselves. While their constituent genres may indeed be differentiated by value and by character, distinguished as 'good' and 'bad', 'high' and 'mass', 'serious' and 'popular', they all remain terminologically part of the larger field of the relevant art-form. Not so with film, however, and to inquire as to how that odd usage came about is to raise the much more interesting question of the historical and social constitution of the cinema as an art: the 'seventh art' as its evangelists used to claim. Such a topic immediately brings Bourdieu to mind, for more than any other sociologist he has examined the constitution of fields of art in a variety of contexts (Bourdieu et al., 1990; Bourdieu, 1992 [1979], 1993a, 1996 [1992]; Bourdieu and Darbel, 1991). However, his observations on film are scattered and secondary – he nowhere examines the cinema as such. What follows, therefore, might cautiously be described as a sketch for a Bourdieu-style analysis of the historic constitution of the field of cinematic art.

My account draws, in particular, on Bourdieu's concern with processes of consecration, legitimacy and autonomisation in the construction of cultural products as art (Bourdieu, 1983, 1993a, 1996 [1992]). This is no place to attempt an extended appreciation or critique of Bourdieu's achievements in conceptualising the dynamics of the 'field of art'. But it is necessary to introduce some of his terms, however simplified, as a precursor to the analysis that follows. Fields of cultural production for Bourdieu are always sites of struggle. Such fields are contained within the larger field of power, but they come to develop varying degrees of autonomy from it. What is at issue in these struggles therefore is legitimacy: 'the monopoly of the power to consecrate producers or products' (Bourdieu, 1993a: 42). It is through such consecration that the field's boundaries are defined and agents – who are distinguished by their possession of different forms of symbolic capital, by their occupying of various positions within the field, and by the generalised system of dispositions (*habitus*) that they bring to bear – seek to establish their distinction. Key to this process is the production of the value of a work. 'The producer of the *value of the work of art* is not the artist but the field of production as a universe of belief which produces the value of the work of art as a *fetish* by producing the belief in the creative power of the artist' (Bourdieu, 1996 [1992]: 229). A whole series of agents and institutions are involved in the production of such value, and any sociological understanding of the field must attend to the activities in which they are engaged.

Of course, struggles over legitimacy may be found in all fields. The fields of art are distinguished, however, by the operation of two 'principles of hierarchization'. One of these two – the 'heteronomous principle' – is 'favourable to those who dominate the field economically and politically (e.g. bourgeois art)', while the 'autonomous principle' (often exemplified by Bourdieu as 'art for art's sake') is identified by its advocates 'with a degree of independence from the economy, seeing temporal failure as a sign of election and success as a sign of compromise' (Bourdieu, 1993a: 40). These principles are not immanent to the field. They are historical and social products which, in the fullness of their development in modernity, come to structure the field as if they were inherent. The opposition between art and commerce, then, is an historically specific accomplishment rather than a reflection of aesthetic essence, however much it may appear to be the latter. Bourdieu (1996 [1992]) examines at some length the genesis and institutionalisation of these principles in the field of nineteenth-century French literature. In so doing he uses the distinction between the two as one basic axis for defining the space within which fields of cultural production operate, the other axis of which is degree of consecration. At any given moment works, agents and institutions can be positioned in terms of heteronomy/autonomy and in terms of high or low level of consecration. Over time, positions on this 'map' will alter, specific elements will appear and disappear, but their relations can always be plotted, and, thereby, the 'logic of the field' examined.

It is this kind of project that concerns me here: an attempt to map the emergence of the field of cinematic art in terms of Bourdieu's two principles and the various historically significant institutions of consecration. Since it is primarily this institutional context that is my focus, I shall not be concerned with textual and aesthetic characteristics of the films. It is how people come socially to count certain products as art that is of interest; not those products themselves. Empirically I shall focus primarily on the field of cinematic art as it was constituted in Britain, though there is good reason to believe that similar histories may be found elsewhere. Neale (1981), for example, abstracts a pattern of development from the French, German and Italian experience which, while not directly addressing the issues on which I am focusing, does suggest a certain similarity in historical sequence.

It is heuristically convenient to divide this history into three phases. The first of these, broadly covering the inter-war years, might best be characterised as the period of 'formation' during which the very status of the cinema as art was a central focus for struggle. The second phase, encompassing the 1950s and 1960s, is a period of 'consolidation' and, significantly, the main locus for the rise of a distinctive 'art-movie' genre. In the third phase, from 1970 onward, the constitution of the field undergoes change in a variety of as yet incomplete ways. I shall consider each phase in turn, paying most attention to the crucial first and formative period.

Formation (1918–39)

Locating the main formative locus for film-as-art in the inter-war years should not be taken to mean that the question of film's artistic status was not raised in the period before the First World War. As Bowser (1990: 191–215; 255–72) shows, once feature length films became common in the American industry after 1909 there were growing opportunities to market more 'respectable' subjects for 'an upward striving middle-class audience' (ibid.: 256). The populist roots of the cinema may have belonged in the nickelodeons and with the travelling entertainers, but once multi-reel films and the more luxuriously equipped 'picture palaces' came into being, the temptation to cater for a more 'artistically' oriented audience became irresistible. In this context, Bowser quotes Louis Reeves Harrison writing in the trade periodical *Moving Picture World* in June 1913: 'the making and showing of moving pictures seems to constitute what I have taken the liberty of terming the "New Art"' (ibid.: 255). Two years later his altogether tentative tone was to be overtaken by the rampant evangelicalism of the best known of the early texts in support of film-as-art: Vachel Lindsay's (2000) [1915] *The Art of the Moving Picture*. For Lindsay, film was a 'high art' regardless of its basis in industrial production.

Art, of course, needed artists, and in the American context D.W. Griffith was the first to be thus consecrated. Even before *The Birth of a Nation* appeared in 1915 his skill and technical inventiveness with the new medium had been widely recognised. After that film, his status as the cinema's first major creative figure was assured, initially in America and then, when the film reached Europe, across the avidly film consuming world. In his influential 1939 summing up of the then state of American cinema, Lewis Jacobs (1968 [1939]: 171) was to observe that *The Birth of a Nation* and its successor *Intolerance* (1916) 'earned for the screen its right to the status of an art'. However, it was in post-war Europe that the struggle to establish cinema as art was to find its most powerful expression, partly in an attempt to resist Hollywood's growing economic and cultural domination (cf. Neale, 1981), and partly as a result of the different intellectual and political traditions then prevailing in Europe.

Thus it was that by 1920 in France Ricciotto Canudo had founded the 'Club des Amis du Septième Art', which was followed by the likes of the 'Ciné-Club de France', the 'Tribune Libre du Cinéma', and in due course specialised cinemas of the kind that would later be labelled 'art houses' – most famously, perhaps, the Theatre du Vieux Colombier in Paris. The process began slightly later in Britain. Here it is widely agreed that the key institutional moment is the formation in 1925 of The Film Society and that the key individual was Ivor Montagu. It was the twenty one-year-old Montagu who, following a trip to Germany to report for *The Times* on the German film industry and after a chance encounter with the actor Hugh Miller on the return journey, brought together the group of interested parties who were to form the council of the new organisation (Montagu, 1980 [1932]; Montagu, 1970: 268, 272–81, 319–26; Montagu, 1972; Samson, 1986). They included, as well as Montagu and Miller, two film critics (Iris Barry and Walter Mycroft), Sidney Bernstein (then cinema exhibitor and owner of the Granada chain), the sculptor Frank Dobson, and the film-maker Adrian Brunel.

Clearly, then, their founders were of the middle-class intelligentsia as was their target audience, a social appeal underlined by those of the 'good and great' who were early members: H.G. Wells and George Bernard Shaw; Julian Huxley and J.B.S. Haldane; John Maynard Keynes, Ellen Terry, John Gielgud, Lord David Cecil, and a string of others including a young film-maker called Alfred Hitchcock. Their model was the Stage Society which, because it operated a membership system, was less subject to commercial strictures and safe from the censorious attentions of the Lord Chamberlain. The Film Society, screening on Sunday afternoons in the New Gallery Kinema in Regent Street, had no trouble attracting an audience; presumably a reasonably affluent one given that membership in that first season cost 3 guineas, 2 guineas, or 1 guinea. So popular was it to become that by the middle of the 1928/29 season membership had to be closed since capacity had been reached, and for the next season screenings were transferred to the larger Tivoli Palace in the Strand. Altogether 39 films, both shorts and features, were shown across eight programmes in that first season, including Leni's *Waxworks* (1924) on the opening Sunday, Wiene's *Raskolnikov* (1923), and a hitherto unseen 'full' version of *The Cabinet of Dr Caligari* (1919).

In the programme for the 8th and last screening of the first season, on 11 April 1926, it was noted that the Society had been 'founded in order that work of interest in the study of cinematography, and not yet easily accessible, might be made available to its members' (Film Society, 1972: 32). It was a careful formulation which was to be used in the annual summaries in every succeeding year, making no mention of 'art' or advancing any high-flown claims. And it is true that the Society showed a number of films that were more of a 'scientific' or 'technical' interest than 'artistic'. But their staple material was undoubtedly seen as art, for all Montagu's evident unhappiness with the term. In 1932 he wrote, perhaps disingenuously, that their interest was in the 'unusual' film, adding that 'a good epithet for our quarry is hard to seek. "Artistic" is pretentious; "cultural" bunkum' (Montagu, 1980 [1932]: 105).

To examine the programmes of The Film Society, however, is to see traversed a range of European, Soviet and, occasionally, Japanese cinema which is in style and conception markedly different to the characteristic products of the more commercial cinema of the period. While The Film Society did not advance any distinctive critical line in its programme notes – only occasionally did they offer specific judgements – there seems to be no doubt that their favoured cinema was indeed understood to be a new and formidable art. That they played a key role in consecrating art cinema between 1925 and 1931 is evident from the extraordinary array of films screened in these six years that would continue to be seen as historic instances of film art for decades to come. From *Raskolnikov* (1923) to *Mother* (1926), *Nosferatu* (1922) to *Crossways* (1929), *The Sea-Shell and the Clergyman* (1929) to *Earth* (1930), they introduced many of the films later to be canonised by critical orthodoxy.

What is also clear from examining The Film Society programmes is that by the early 1930s their authority as a leading institution of consecration was waning. Indeed, the Council of the Society was divided from 1930 onwards on whether to continue. In writing of that division, Montagu (1980 [1932]: 107) observed of the Society's state: 'Prosperity, yes. Members, plenty. But when you can see films like *Hauptmann von Koepenick* in the West End, and like *M* and *Turksib* and *Le Million* all over the place, it really is worth asking ourselves whether we have any excuse for being.' In the late 1920s there had been a growth in London cinemas prepared to screen the same kind of material as The Film Society, if under rather more restrictive censorship. Low (1971: 34) lists the Holborn Cinema, the Marble Arch Pavilion, the New Gallery and the Shaftesbury Avenue Pavilion. Then, in 1931, opening with a six week run of French films, came the Academy cinema in Oxford Street, which was to continue in this specialist role for over fifty years. In 1933 it was followed by the Everyman in Hampstead and, a year later, by the Curzon in Park Lane (Low, 1985: 16). The 'art house' cinema had arrived in England.

Meanwhile, inspired by the model of The Film Society in London, film societies were spreading across Britain: in Edinburgh, Glasgow, Billingham, Manchester, Leeds, Ipswich, Southampton, and in many other places. The British Film Institute, founded in 1933, fostered relations with the burgeoning film society movement while also establishing various regional branches (Butler, 1971: 19–23), and the British Federation of Film Societies was formed in 1937. Parallel to this, there also developed more overtly political modes of film exhibition. The London Workers Film Society was founded in 1929, and was followed by Workers' Film Societies throughout the country. Montagu, by now a member of the Communist Party, was deeply involved here also, both with Kino (a left-oriented distribution organisation) and with the Progressive Film Institute (Ryan, 1980, 1983). More openly political and, by the same count, less able to lay claim to 'artistic' justification, the Workers' Film Societies faced many more difficulties with censorship than the more middle-class and respectable non-political societies. But even they faced inconsistency and local problems, a situation which was not resolved until 1939 (Hardy, 1938; Low, 1985: 54–66; Willcox, 1990).

During the 1930s, then, we see the construction of film-as-art in the sense that individual agents, and then institutions, increasingly promote the concept of an artistically distinctive cinema, produced by individual artists, and made available through specialist exhibition outlets. In addition, broad criteria for recognising film art came into common currency. Two of the most important of these criteria – authorship and a degree of autonomy from commercial pressures – are reflected in both the institutions and the critical writings of the period. From the very beginning Film Society programmes routinely attached directors' names to film titles, uncontroversially viewing the director as the true author of the work. Debates about collective versus individual responsibility in film-making are invoked in the literature only to be rebutted in the cause of directorial authority. Almost all would have echoed Spottiswoode's (1935) clarion call in the dedication to his well known book, *A Grammar of the Film*: 'To the Future of the Director's Cinema'.

This ideology of 'authorship' – always central to designating arts in the modern period – was intimately connected with the necessity of demonstrating relative autonomy of artists from commercial constraint, an especially acute problem in an expensive medium like film. In this 'universe of belief', to use Bourdieu's phrase, the true artist is expected to rise above such venal concerns; indeed, it is a condition of their consecration that they are able to do so. The expanding studio system in Hollywood, with its industrialising of the movie-making process, was seen as inimical to the aesthetic potential of the cinema, minimising the possibility of artistic integrity and autonomy. To believe in the art of film, then, was increasingly to be anti-Hollywood, even where there was conflict over what kind of film was to be positively valued. And there was conflict. It should not be thought that the film-as-art camp was unified by its shared concern to promote the seventh art. Even a cursory examination of the books and journals of the time shows that there was nearly as much disagreement within the camp as with those outside it.

From the late 1920s onward there was a marked expansion in the number of publications about the cinema. There had been trade journals since the early days, of course, but they were not on the whole distinguished by their commitment to film-as-art. The first English language voice of that movement was *Close Up* – 'the only magazine devoted to films as an art' as one 1928 cover wrapper put it (Donald et al., 1998: 8). The magazine, published from Switzerland and marketed internationally, appeared from 1927 until 1933, and as Low (1971: 22) suggests, 'its historical importance is very great despite its small circulation'. Certainly it adopted strong views, championing German and Soviet cinema while denigrating the more commercial products of the American and British industries. It also saw itself as promoting the *avant garde*, publishing work by Gertrude Stein and Man Ray (Dusinberre, 1980: 35–7), as well as encouraging independent and experimental film production. In what was no doubt a deliberate echo of 'art for art's sake', its first editorial observed that 'it has to be the film for the film's sake' (Donald et al., 1998: 40).

Close Up ceased publication in 1933, by which time other journals were in place or about to start publishing. *Cinema Quarterly* began in 1932, *Film Art* ('international review of advance-guard cinema') was launched as *Film* in 1933, changing its title for the second issue, and by 1934 the newly formed British Film Institute had taken over *Sight and Sound* and launched its journal of reviews, *Monthly Film Bulletin*. Books on the 'art of film', of which several were published in the 1920s (Low, 1971: 15–31), were to continue to appear in the 1930s. Paul Rotha's (1930) wide-ranging *The Film Till Now* is perhaps the best known, but numerous others emerged during the decade: most notably the volumes by Arnheim (1933) and Spottiswoode (1935). Without entering into details here – which space precludes – it should be apparent that by the late 1930s there were widespread voices raised in support of film's claims to artistic status. These voices were not always in accord, of course, and they often sought to consecrate different film-makers and films in the cause of demonstrating the legitimacy of their claims. But, whatever the character of those disagreements, the consecration of both artists and works was crucial to the process as was the demonstration that some degree of autonomy was both possible and essential in the creation of film art.

Let me now try to map, albeit impressionistically, some of the agents, works and institutions that constitute the field of film art in the formative period.

The basic terms of this figure derive from Bourdieu (1993a: 49, 1996 [1992]: 113–40). The horizontal axis distinguishes the degree to which a mapped component is dependent upon other fields, notably those of political power and the economy. The process that Bourdieu refers to as autonomisation

High Consecration

Charismatic consecration

Intellectual audience

Institutional consecration

Bourgeois audience

Respectable and

---------------------------------The Film Society------------------------- 'serious' US

--------   and UK cinema

Soviet Cinema

French & German   D.W. Griffith

Cinema

Film Society movement

BFI, *Sight & Sound*, etc.

Close Up   'Art House' Cinemas

Workers' Film Societies

Film Art   Documentary

movement

General

Avant-garde   Hollywood

cinema   Product

Sectarian audience   Mass audience

Low Consecration

Autonomy   Heteronomy

Figure I   The Field of Cinematic Art 1918–39

involves a move, as it were, from right to left on the figure, from heteronomy to autonomy, and is a central feature of the constitution of arts in the modern period. The vertical axis reflects degree of consecration in the field as a whole. Like all such distinctions, this one is relational. Thus, for what I have here termed the 'sectarian audience' the latest avant-garde work may well be viewed as highly consecrated, but in the field overall it remains beyond the pale of artistic acceptability. In due course, avant-garde work may, and often does, move up the figure into the realm of charismatic consecration. This was the fate, for example, of *Entr'acte* which attracted abuse and violent disagreement at its Film Society screening on 17 January 1926. As Montagu (1970: 334–35) recalled it: 'some started to boo, others to scream and cheer, people got up and shouted, others shook their fists and even their neighbours – I have never seen an English audience so passionate.' In a very few years, however, it had become one of the staples of accepted cinema art.

Of the four ideal-typical audiences placed at the corners of the figure, the 'bourgeois audience' was probably the least important in this phase. A significant class fraction of the bourgeois intelligentsia was involved with The Film Society of course, but for the broader reaches of the middle and upper-middle classes the cinema remained an inferior popular form mainly associated with the (proletarian) mass audience. At this stage there is relatively little institutional consecration of film or film-makers reflecting the tastes and the striving for distinction of those controlling the fields of power and the economy. Cinema had not yet attained the degree of artistic and social acceptability necessary to make it a worth-while focus for bourgeois cultural appropriation. Indeed, one aspect of the struggle to constitute film as an art involved persuading established authority of the medium's aesthetic significance, a process in which The Film Society played a key foundational role later to be carried further by the more establishment oriented British Film Institute. For that history, however, we must turn to the post-war period.

Consolidation (1950–70)

It is in the nature of consolidation that its processes are far less dramatic than those typically found when an artistic field is in the course of formation. By the 1950s, although evangelising on behalf of the art of film remained real enough, the main terms in which film-as-art would be understood were in place. A canon had been formed, an aesthetic history constructed, a pantheon of artists distinguished. Institutional corollaries of this universe of belief were now firmly established. The Film Society movement grew rapidly, from approximately 250 societies in the mid-1950s, up to 400 at the end of the decade, 500 in the early 1960s, and 750 or so by 1970 (Butler, 1971: 178–80; BFFS, 2001), publishing its own journal, *Film*, from 1954. The British Film Institute also prospered. Whereas the major objective of the BFI at its founding in 1933 was defined as 'the use and development of the cinematograph as a means of entertainment and instruction' (Butler, 1971: 17), by the time of the 1948 Radcliffe Report, which redefined the Institute's functions, it was expected to 'encourage the development of the art of film' (ibid.: 28). To that end an exhibition outlet was an obvious requirement, and, having retained the cinema built for the Festival of Britain as a National Film Theatre in 1952, the NFT proper opened five years later. Membership boomed in the wake of this innovation, rising from 2266 in 1950 to 7739 full members and 32,390 associate members by 1958 (ibid.: 28–9).

This growing audience for films not normally to be found in the more commercially oriented exhibition circuits of the 1950s and 1960s was also reflected in a rise in the number of art-house cinemas, programming a repertory mixture of older favourites, foreign language 'art' films, and anything that could be marketed as sexually explicit. By 1963 the *International Film Guide* was listing sixteen such 'specialist cinemas' in the London area (Cowie, 1963: 233), with most larger cities also supporting at least one. The Classic Cinemas circuit, for example, maintained ten repertory cinemas outside London in the early 1960s. In addition, small distributors who specialised in importing foreign language films (Connoisseur and Contemporary were among the best known) developed to meet the steady increase in demand. This was the heyday of the art-house and its characteristic product: the art-movie.

In some part the rise of the art-movie was a consequence of European attempts to resurrect national film industries after the Second World War and, in so doing, to resist Hollywood domination. In France, Germany and Italy, for example, state intervention of various kinds fostered national cinemas which were distinctive in comparison with the typical Hollywood productions of the period (Neale, 1981). Rather than compete with the American cinema on its own terms (the doomed strategy adopted by the British film industry) European industries sought niche markets, both nationally and internationally. In Britain where, with occasional exceptions, there was no domestic art-movie production, imports from Europe in effect came to constitute a genre: a distinctive category of cinema, founded in certain expectations about 'seriousness' and 'profundity' and formal 'artistic' invention which had been established as part of film-as-art doctrine in the inter-war years. However diverse were the films sheltering beneath this generic art-movie umbrella – and the works of Antonioni, Bergman, Bunuel, Fellini, Godard, Resnais, Truffaut, Wajda, and the rest of the directors thus charismatically consecrated, were indeed diverse – they were presumed to share a certain autonomy from commercial constraint and a certain seriousness of moral and aesthetic purpose. They were the inheritors of the cinematic forms that The Film Society had nurtured, and the art-house cinemas were their home.

Socially, of course, this preference remained predominantly middle-class and relatively highly educated, one of the ways in which distinction could be demonstrated by class fractions whose tastes had been significantly formed in the post-war expansion of education. The few empirical studies of art-house audiences – of the Illini Theatre in Champaign-Urbana in 1951–52 (Smythe et al., 1953), for example, or, rather later, of the British RFTs of the 1980s (Docherty et al., 1987) – confirm that extensive education is a significant characteristic of art-house audiences. Unsurprisingly, then, this educated and growing audience was also supported by a considerable expansion in cinema book publication and an array of increasingly 'serious' film magazines, with *Sight and Sound* joined by the somewhat less esoteric *Films and Filming* in the mainstream market, and a changing population of variously deviant 'little magazines' developing particular critical lines: from *Sequence* in the early 1950s to *Movie* in the late 1960s. By then, however, fractures would be appearing in the traditional film-as-art position as a new generation of critics and film-makers sought to re-evaluate the artistic credentials of Hollywood cinema. That shift in what was to count as the art of film would spell the end of the art-movie era. But before moving on to that, let me try to map the consolidation phase in the same somewhat impressionistic terms as before.

As before, authorship and autonomy are crucial constituents in defining the art of film, and the ideal-typical audiences located at the corners of the figure constitute taste sub-cultures revolving around their own preferred cinema. For the intellectual audience the art-movie provides the major organising category

High Consecration

Charismatic consecration   Institutional consecration

Intellectual audience   Bourgeois audience

Antonioni,   'Classic' cinema

Resnais,   ---------------------- Art movies -------------------- + 'respectable'

Bergman,   --------   US/UK film e.g.
                                                        Lean, Kubrick,
Et al   etc.

A   Sight and Sound   H
u   e
t   NFT   Art House Cinemas   t
o   e
n   'Little   Film   r
o   o
m   magazines'   Societies   British 'New Wave'   n
y   o
                                            Films and Filming   m
                                                                      y
         Hollywood 'auteurs'

         Film-makers' Co-ops

                          Picturegoer, Picture Show, etc.

         Avant-garde/   General
         independent   Hollywood and
         cinema   UK Product

Sectarian audience   Mass audience

Low Consecration

Figure 2   The Field of Cinematic Art 1950–70

for consecrating films and film-makers, with its attendant institutional apparatus of critical appreciation and specialist exhibition. The bourgeois audience now has at its disposal a received view of film history and film art which both identifies 'classics' and expects a certain order of 'seriousness' in contemporary films. The kind of film which, to borrow Sarris' (1968: 22) mocking characterisation of it, 'would deal Realistically with a Problem in Adult Terms, or employ the Materials of the Medium in a Creative Manner.' In this we can see the seeds of what might better be termed the 'middlebrow audience' which was to come into its own in the 1980s. There are still sectarian audiences, of course, as always viewing their favoured work as being at the forefront of innovation. Increasingly, such *avant garde* concerns are linked to the rise of independent film-makers' movements in the USA and in Britain. The London Film-makers' Co-op was founded in 1966, followed by similar organisations elsewhere (Blanchard and Harvey, 1983). And there remains the mass audience, for whom film is still a significant if declining entertainment medium unsullied by the considerations of art and distinction that, in their different ways, so concern the other three audiences. All this was to change, however, in the course of the 1970s.

Fragmentation (1970–2000)

In seeking to constitute film-as-art, institutions and agents had, necessarily, drawn upon conceptions already established in other fields. To construct a field of art requires that it is rendered legitimate within the larger culture, and by the twentieth century legitimacy of arts in European societies had, minimally, come to depend upon the presence of consecrated authors and on the capacity to demonstrate their relative autonomy from commercial constraint. The economic exigencies of film production had made this a particularly acute problem for film-art evangelists, who had therefore promoted a somewhat Manichaean view of Hollywood – the most industrially elaborated form of film production – as the negative pole against which film art was constituted. By the 1960s, however, the logic of the field had become such that agents and groups seeking a new basis for establishing distinction had little choice but to find some alternative to the existing consecrated forms: art-movies, classical/respectable cinema, or the various *avant gardes*. In consequence, and in part influenced by the 'politique des auteurs' as that had emerged in somewhat similar circumstances among the *Cahiers* group of critics and film-makers in France, a new generation sought to re-evaluate the American cinema. For them, the inherited view of film-as-art represented orthodoxy and tradition. If they were to establish their own forms of distinction and symbolic capital, where better than in the hitherto condemned ghetto of American commercial film?

So it was that the boundaries of film-art were shifted by the rhetoric of auteurism in the American cinema. Artists were discovered where none were previously known, and the cinema once condemned as the commercially polluted province of the mass audience was quarried for overlooked gems. This shift was to have significant ramifications, in due course changing the shape of the field and, in the process, precipitating the decline of the art-movie. By the 1980s, art-houses, film societies, magazines, and most other institutions of consecration (including the growing apparatus of film education) were to embrace this restructuring. Not, it must be said, immediately or without conflict. The 1970s, in particular, were years in which the constitution of film art once more became a focus for struggles internal to the field. For example, in the later 1960s the BFI had begun establishing a chain of Regional Film Theatres, and by 1970 there were thirty-six of them aiming, as the Chair of the BFI governors put it at that year's stormy AGM, to 'show film programmes which would otherwise not be available, to the maximum number of people' (Butler, 1971: 51) – in effect, the Film Society and Art House model. As the decade progressed, however, this policy became an issue of much debate, with marked divisions between those adopting a broadly traditional art-house posture, those opposing them in the name of cultural radicalism and the rediscovered American commercial cinema, and those increasingly oriented to the newly expanding independent production sector (cf. McArthur, 2001).

Independent production, too, had an important impact, especially via the funding and organisational initiatives of the late 1970s and 1980s. The BFI's Production Board changed its policy in favour of funding feature length films, the National Film Finance Corporation re-oriented itself toward a kind of art cinema, and, from the early 1980s, television played a growing role in film production (and, of course, exhibition) through the activities of Channel 4. As Hill (2000) argues, these institutional developments for the first time generated work which might plausibly be termed British art-movies, of which the likes of *Radio On* (1979) and *The Draughtsman's Contract* (1982) were early examples. However, while these films clearly shared certain textual characteristics with earlier foreign language art-movies, the subsequent emergence of so-called 'heritage cinema', with its dependence on already respected literary sources or 'serious' historical subjects, contributed to an expansion of the 'art-movie' category to encompass almost any film that did not clearly fall into the commercial mainstream (ibid.: 24).

These organisational and aesthetic developments (along with changes in the character of film consumption, both theatrical and home-based) profoundly altered the topology of the field. That history is not yet complete, and I cannot hope to encompass all its ramifications here. Suffice to say that by the late 1980s the map of film-art had been redrawn, and the institutional apparatus of exhibition and consecration had changed radically. The film society movement was shrinking and the traditional art-house cinema had gone into decline – by the 1990s even the Academy Cinema had closed – partly because the social corollaries of the system of distinction on which the art-houses were founded no longer prevailed, and partly because the spread of video and of multiplex cinemas changed the pattern of cinema-going.

In many ways the multiplex stands as a useful emblem for the new state of the field. Whatever the reality, multiplex cinemas present themselves as containing diversity, blurring previously established lines of distinction between different films and their audiences, bringing all together into a consumer oriented world of pluralist entertainment. Eclecticism is the order of the day, with all genres (including aspiring art-movies) treated as aesthetically equal. In this world, the art-house, with its presumption of a socially distinct, educated audience responding to an artistically superior product, has no place. And where there are still art-houses, they tend to be smaller versions of the multiplex phenomenon: multi-screen cinemas offering mixed programming that balances foreign language or more exotic films with precisely the same commercial products that can be found in their bigger multiplex kin.

It will be clear, then, that the late century field of film art is fragmentary and shifting, for which reason it is particularly difficult to map. I shall make an attempt here for the sake of completeness, but it should be borne in mind that this is very tentative.

High Consecration

Charismatic consecration   Institutional consecration

Intellectual audience   Middlebrow audience

Esoterica, foreign film,   Respectable cinema e.g.
new 'art movies', etc.   'heritage' films, literary
                                                      adaptations, classics, etc.

Sight & Sound, BFI, etc.

------------------------------ Multiplex art-houses -----------------------------

A   Channel 4/Film Four   H
u   e
t   ----------------------------- Multiplex Cinemas ------------------   t
o   e
n   Mid-range magazines (eg *Empire*)   r
o   o
m   TV movie channels   n
y   o
                                                                                  m
                                                                                  y
Independents,   Mainstream
'cult films',   Hollywood
'fans'   Video
underground   Celebrity magazines   TV film
video

Sectarian audience   Mass audience

Low Consecration

Figure 3   The Field of Cinematic Art 1970–2000

Note that the 'bourgeois audience' is here renamed the 'middlebrow audience' – a reflection both of the changing significance of class structure in the late twentieth century as well as the growth of a distinctive taste sub-culture. The preferred films of this audience now cross a range from literary adaptations like *A Room with a View* (1985) to sentimental feel-good movies such as *Billy Elliot* (2000), from mainstream foreign language films like *Jean de Florette* (1986) to 'serious' American work such as *The Shawshank Redemption* (1994). This is an audience much prized by the art-house multiplexes. Although there is still a small 'intellectual audience' whose members seek to maintain their distinction as the cognoscenti of film art, there are much larger numbers who – unlike their bourgeois predecessors – now consider the cinema to be an entirely acceptable art-form, even if they would be unlikely to discuss it in such terms. They still maintain their distinction from the mass audience and popular cinema (although increasingly individual films and film-makers may straddle both sectors of the field) by laying claim to greater selectivity and 'good taste'. They are, in effect, the product of the successful institutional consecration of film-as-art.

Meanwhile, there has been a proliferation of sectarian audiences. What was once primarily the domain of the artistic *avant garde* now hosts cult movies, the 'fans' who cluster around, for example, video distributed horror or semi-pornographic material to which they attribute aesthetic, moral, or social radicalism, as well as the kind of independent cinema familiar in earlier periods. There has been a pluralisation of the field, as there has been in many areas of culture in the late modern period. If the pattern continues, it seems likely that the high autonomy area will fragment even more, leaving the middlebrow audience to dominate consecration in company with an ever-shifting assembly of sectarian audiences each struggling to sustain its own basis for distinction.

Conclusion

What of that strange concept with which I began, the art-movie? As I hope to have shown, drawing upon Bourdieu's analysis of fields of cultural production, the art-movie was a product of the logic of the field, a conjoint consequence of the ineradicably commercial character of the cinema and the then established view of 'art' as grounded in relative autonomy from commercial pressures. In such difficult circumstances, the status of film-as-art was always going to be precarious, always open to the accusation of mercenary motives. To constitute a genre of 'art-movies', then, was to mark out an area of the field which could be defended as relatively immune from such pollution and utilised as a basis for establishing distinction and symbolic capital. Now, however, that space is no longer available, for with late modern fragmentation the structuring opposition between art and commerce is not the force that it once was. In a multiplex culture, art *is* commerce, and the art-movie has become yet another niche product on the shelves of the cultural supermarket.

Opera, Modernity and Cultural Fields

Alan Swingewood

10

Introduction

One of the main postulates in recent developments in the sociology of music is that society is not something external to music but lies within musical organisation and structure itself. An emphasis on purely internal analysis of the formal autonomous structures of music, as Kerman (1985: 73) notes, 'removes the bare score from its context in order to examine it as an autonomous organism, the analyst removes the organism from the ecology that sustains it', situating it within an historical and cultural vacuum. Today musicologists argue that to grasp music adequately it becomes essential to situate it in its historical and cultural context and in recent years there has been a growing interest in analysing opera in terms of historical, social and cultural contexts by focusing on politics (Rostand, 1991; Arblaster, 1992; Tambling, 1996; Bokina, 1997), cultural history (Lindenberger, 1984, 1998; Robinson, 1985) and gender studies (Clement, 1988; McClary, 1989). Many of these works raise important conceptual questions concerning the appropriate methods for studying opera contextually as well as substantive issues concerning the relation of opera as an aesthetic form and practice, as an ongoing set of practices which contribute to the making of its socio-cultural context and ideology.

Clement (1988), for example, has argued that operatic heroines from Carmen to Butterfly constitute strangers, or 'others', within their specific contexts, their role as martyred heroines reflecting the status of women in patriarchal cultures. Exploring the relation of opera to history, culture and society, Lindenberger (1984, 1998) has argued that while all art can be related to particular contexts, opera, unlike literature, is the product of the workings of diverse elements and a 'variety of social and aesthetic entanglements', including the financial powers of the state or private patronage, the distinctive class composition of the audience, advances in technology, nationalism and popular culture. He draws attention to the ways in which opera has always been imbricated in power relations: Wagner's *Tannhauser* and *Die Meistersinger* expressed a concept of national history rooted in the impending unification of Germany, while in *Nabucco* and *Don Carlos*, Verdi took on the public role of Italy's national dramatist affirming his commitment to the ideals of the *risorgimento* and opposition to the Austrian domination of Italy.

While operatic studies have increasingly explored the relation between social context and musical text, they have failed to develop both conceptual tools for exploring this relation and a substantive theory of operatic development. And although a theory of opera has been attempted by such diverse thinkers as Adorno (1999), Kerman (1985) and Dahlhaus (1989), the contribution of sociology to the current debate on the social and cultural role of opera has restricted itself to establishing the relationships between the musical work and the wider social context, effectively restricting sociological scrutiny to the analysis of external determinants of musical form such as the social background of composers, the different publics for opera, the relation between opera and nationalism, and opera as a symbol in class domination. Questions of aesthetic value are ignored within this general analytical framework.

Fundamentally, the sociology of opera raises the problem of the ways in which the external socio-cultural context becomes a constituting element in poetic and aesthetic construction, inscribed within the work as a dynamic element in the process of poetic and aesthetic production. In this way the social nature of art is revealed: the social not as a passive datum existing within an art work waiting to be revealed and interpreted, a reflection of particular contexts, but rather as an active shaping force. As Adorno noted, the logic of music must be made to speak sociologically. To reduce music to mediated social content is to marginalise the problem of aesthetic autonomy, the processes which differentiate 'art' from 'non-art'. There is a tendency in cultural studies to define the social context as social background made up of various elements which are then loosely linked with the aesthetic work. But such studies suffer from a failure to deal with the often complex relations between opera and other cultural and social forms, as well as raising difficult problems of the potential autonomy of the work itself. How is it that aesthetic forms such as opera, while rooted in a specific social context, become increasingly independent of that context? How does the socio-cultural context become part of the internal aesthetic structure of opera? Thus the question is raised of a sociologically oriented aesthetics, a subject largely neglected by modern sociology.

In this chapter I will argue that from its origins in seventeenth-century Italy the history of opera has been characterised by an ongoing tension between its roles as public entertainment and its striving for aesthetic autonomy. It was Monteverdi (1567–1643), the first major opera composer, who used the term 'modernity' to describe his break from the prevailing Italian musical tradition: it is this newness that is a crucial part of opera history and which is inscribed in those works which strive for aesthetic autonomy. This chapter examines some decisive moments in the history of opera in which this concept of aesthetic modernity is bound up with a wider sociological notion of modernity as involving processes and contexts characterised by social differentiation and cultural autonomy.

Modernity, operatic discourse and power

The relationship between music and society is perhaps at its clearest in opera. Although opera originated in a socially exclusive context – the aristocratic milieu of Renaissance Florence in which opera was presented as entertainment during the carnival season for members of the Court – the opera house opened its doors to a wider audience especially when the first commercial opera houses became established in republican Venice. By the eighteenth century, opera had spread to all the major European countries especially France and Germany, and was understood and appreciated both by the notables of the European courts as well as a broad cross section of the urban population. This more inclusive public greeted new operas with great enthusiasm with both composers and especially singers showered with the adulation usually associated with modern pop stars.

From its beginnings, opera – 'the spectacle of princes' – was closely imbricated in power relations, with displays of splendour constituting a major function of court opera. Combined with official court rituals and ceremonies, opera helped to legitimise political authority. In the mid-seventeenth century, the family box was not only hereditary but the place where political intrigue and issues of state power were discussed. Lindenberger (1984: 239–40) notes how the Naples opera house, the San Carlo, built in 1737 to glorify the Bourbon dynasty, was erected next to the royal palace, the juxtaposition of the two house symbolising the union of art and power. Opera houses in Italy, France and Germany frequently occupied important, conspicuous sites in the major cities, archaeological statements of aristocratic power over the new middle classes. With the growth of public opera and a paying middle class audience, opera increasingly became divided between *opera buffa* or comic opera built around ordinary life, national culture and local dialects, and *opera seria* with its heroic, mythical subject matter drawn from more 'universal' cultural forms. Composers were often the servants of power. Neapolitan composers, Scarlatti and Cimarosa were assured of financial support as employees of the royal chapel; Haydn and Diddersdorf accepted their servile status as servants to the nobility, the majority of Haydn's operas, for example, being composed for and performed by the Esterhazy court.

Within the aristocracy, music and especially opera functioned as modes of social distinction with patronage, the exemplar of political and cultural power. In seventeenth-century France, operas were performed within the King's apartments. As the official court composer, Lully provided opera as spectacular displays of festival and triumphant processions effectively turning it into an instrument of the state. Similarly, during the French revolutionary period, French opera sought to glorify the Revolution by presenting implicitly topical works through the right kind of *mise-en-scene* and in co-opting revolutionary sentiments. Throughout its history opera has frequently enjoyed the support of arbitrary political authority with Napoleon championing the music and operas of Spontini; and conversely opera composers have sometimes actively legitimised totalitarian power, as with the Italian composer Casella whose opera *The Conquest of the Desert* (1937) directly transposed the values of Fascism in its depiction of Mussolini's conquest of Ethiopia.

In recent years, however, cultural critics have focused on the ways in which music and especially opera signify power relations in less direct and subtle ways through the 'politics of representation'. Thus McClary has argued that while seventeenth-century opera was largely under the patronage and control of wealthy aristocrats 'the works themselves often appear...to undercut assumed social hierarchies and call into question the authority of patriarchy and nobility' (McClary, 1989: 207). During the first half of the seventeenth century, humanist discourses centred on patriarchical domination, gradually gave way to more complex operatic discourses in which women were represented as controlling and dominating the lives of the male protagonists. While early court opera, through stage spectacle and pomp, reproduced aristocratic and thus patriarchical interests, close textual analysis suggests a more nuanced set of discourses at work, subverting traditional modes of authority and questioning the legitimacy of the dominant institutions.

This concept of operatic discourses in terms of the potential subversive power of representation is echoed in Edward's Said's (1993) analysis of *Aida*. Said suggests that Verdi's opera, 'is a hybrid, radically impure work that belongs equally to the history of culture and the historical experience of overseas domination'. It is not so much '*about* but *of* imperial domination' representing an 'orientalised' Eygpt in which the voices of the others (the native people) are drowned by the dominant imperialist discourse. However, the orientalism and imperialism inscribed in *Aida* (and further represented in other nineteenth-century operas including Meyerbeer's *L'Africaine*, Delibes' *Lakme*, and Massenet's *Le Roi de Lahore*) does not imply a monolithic discourse, for as a 'hybrid' form, *Aida* is 'built around disparities and discrepancies', requiring what Said calls 'contrapuntal interpretation' to bring out all the tensions within it, 'a simultaneous awareness' of the ways a dominant discourse acts against 'other histories' or other discourses. Said makes the point that *Aida* eventually becomes an autonomous aesthetic work free of its contexts but nevertheless redolent of them. Contrapuntal interpretation brings to light the individual characters and musical structure of the opera, as well as revealing the external forces that shaped it: the building and opening of the Suez Canal, and the imperial authority expressed by the 1867 Paris International Exhibition, for example. Through the power of representation, notably the ways in which European art depicted female oriental eroticism, European society enhanced its cultural supremacy over the oriental 'others'. *Aida* embodies 'the authority of Europe's version of Egypt at a moment in its nineteenth century history', contrapuntal analysis revealing 'a web of affiliations, connections, decisions, and collaborations...' (Said, 1993: 137–51).

While Said's method reveals the potentially open and polyphonic nature of operatic discourse, it focuses on the controlling power of the dominant voice or discourse. It is an approach to cultural analysis based in a specific concept of modernity as the expression of the European Enlightenment. Modernity is theorised as the supremacy of European science, technology and political and cultural values over modern society, and the development of national unity through a centralising and powerful state. Modernity comes to mean the drowning of the voices of the marginalised social groups, those living on the fringes of society, minority ethnic groups with their own distinctive culture and language. In a similar vein, Tambling (1996) describes the development of nineteenth and early twentieth-century opera as a struggle between discourses of modernism and those of monologism: modernism, as the aesthetic mode of modernity is rich with ambiguity and irony while monologism assumes a single voice and a homogeneity of values.

Thus Verdi's early operas (those written in the 1840s and 1850s) were expressive of a more 'modernist' sensibility, while the later works (those written in the 1880s and 1890s such as *Otello*) coincided with the more authoritarian nation state that Italy was becoming under Crispi, and thus should be seen as forms 'whose late nineteenth century expression permitted little self-reflexivity or no more than local irony, smoothing things over in favour of monologism'. In Tambling's view it is as though Verdi turns his back on modernity with his work fitting 'the dominant discourses of the 1890s, both as it was and as it wished to be' (Tambling, 1996: 112). Tambling concludes by arguing that through the indeterminate nature of values characteristic of modernity, modern opera can both be linked to the culture of fascism (for example, the operas of Wagner, Strauss, and Pfitzner), and also be seen as having been transformed into a 'dead' museum culture, the endless recycling of canonical forms, with its successor, the musical, emerging as a tool of late capitalist domination.

Tambling's is a narrowly conceived concept of modernity as a closing down of discursive possibilities. Conversely, modernity can be theorised as a cultural process involving the emancipation of the artist within a growing civil society and the developing autonomy of cultural institutions and practices. It is this modernity which provides the possibility for the artist to establish freedom from *both* patronage and the commercial pressures of the capitalist market, to take control both of their own work and in some cases, its production and reception (as with Wagner and the building of his Bayreuth festival opera house). Said's contrapuntal interpretation, while stressing the inner and the outer determinants of aesthetic form, misses the subversive elements implicit in modernity, that while opera may reflect and express dominant political and cultural ideologies, it can also challenge and criticise these assumptions.

Theorising modernity

While many musicologists, literary theorists and cultural historians have drawn attention to the multiple forms of discourse that characterise the development of the operatic form stressing the 'polyphonic' multiplicity of meanings this generates (notably Lindenberger, 1984, 1998; Elmie, 1993) there has been a general failure both to explore the social grounding of this aesthetic pluralism and to provide an adequate concept of modernity both as an historical, sociological and aesthetic category. There is no substantive theory of modernity as a specific historical and cultural process, a theory which would generate the concepts necessary for sociological analysis.

A key substantive sociological theory of modernity, one which to date has not played as major role in cultural theory as it perhaps should, is Weber's thesis on Enlightenment reason and science as forming the bedrock of the modern world. The increasing rationality of society and culture, the break-up of the pre-modern world of stable world views (as expressed in religion for example) and the emergence of differentiated 'value spheres' (the economic, political, aesthetic) with their corresponding body of 'specialists' inevitably produced a modern world dominated by pluralism, scepticism, relativism and dehumanisation, overall described by Weber's image of an iron cage constituted of a narrowly conceived practical reason.

Extending Weber's concept to modern culture, Adorno deepens its pessimism by identifying rationality and science with the historical development of art: rationality produces differentiation within culture, between its 'higher spheres' which maintain a critical perspective and refusal to accept conventional values (as with aesthetic modernism) and the 'lower spheres', commercialised and commodified cultural products which follow the capitalist law of economic exchange, what Adorno (1990) terms the products of the 'culture industry'.

Adorno's thesis is that modernity produces both the potential autonomy of culture and its opposite, the 'culture industry'. Modernism, with its basic concept of the autonomy of the art work, develops as a direct critique of mass culture. In describing the dark side of modernity as the fate of the modern world, what I will call the Weber–Adorno thesis weakens the emancipatory potential of the modernity project, a standpoint criticised trenchantly by Habermas (1985: 9):

> The project of modernity, formulated in the eighteenth century by the philosophers of the Enlightenment consisted of their efforts to develop objective science, universal morality and law, and autonomous art according to their inner logic. At the same time, this project intended to release the cognitive potential of each of these domains from their esoteric forms. The Enlightenment philosophers wanting to utilise this accumulation of special-ised culture for the enrichment of everyday life – that is to say, for the rational organisation of everyday social life.

However, the emancipatory core of modernity which informs both the internal and external determinations of opera must be further developed as a useful sociological concept, raising questions about the nature and complexity of opera enabling the researcher to explore the links between the aesthetic content and the social and historical context. The problem lies in grounding the concept of modernity in specific institutional structures rather than conceiving it, as Weber does, as a rather abstract broad histor-ical process. Modernity must be adequately contextualised in order to articulate its numerous, varied and complex relations with culture and aesthetics. Adorno and Habermas provide no adequate conceptual tools for this task. I suggest that a critical application of Bourdieu's theory of fields will open up the possibility of an historical and sociological analysis of modernity.

Aesthetics and cultural fields

Drawing on Weber's theory of social differentiation, Bourdieu has redefined 'value spheres' as fields, as networks of objective positions which individuals occupy through possessing different forms of capital – economic (material skills, wealth), cultural (knowledge, intellectual skills) and symbolic (accumulated prestige and sense of honour). Fields are socially structured spaces characterised by internal differentiation and hierarchisation, such as education, religion and culture, each with their own distinctive logics, principles and body of specialists. As the products of modernity, fields become increasingly autonomised over time. The development of modernity therefore involves often slow and piecemeal processes of the augmentation of the relative autonomy of each field. In each field, those who occupy dominant positions adopt 'conservation strategies' to preserve their status while newcomers develop 'subversion strategies' to overthrow the dominant orthodoxies (Bourdieu, 1991). Thus fields are always open and unfinished, developing through conflict, struggle, opposition and, although never entirely autonomous – the capitalist market always exerts a significant external effect – they become increasingly separated from, and independent of, the centralised economic and political institutions of the modern nation state.

For Bourdieu, it was not a question of isolating a social group and linking it directly with cultural production, but rather one of analysing the complex set of relations existing between social groups, artists and society. Artistic production does not take place in isolation from other forms of cultural activity, but is imbricated in a whole network and field of artistic production as a whole. Focusing on the social group as a source of creative activity fails to specify the complex play of forces at work within 'the universe of artistic production', with its particular traditions and laws regulating its workings, recruitment and history. The autonomy of art is no more than the relative autonomy of this structure, or field, which is unfinished and open, characterised by specific practices and reflexive agents.

The value of the concept of cultural field for the sociology of opera lies in focussing attention on the specificity of the context and the complex play of different forces at work within it. Opera, as a hybrid form, necessarily involves a variety of practices for its realisation: music, literature, theatrical and design expertise. Moreover, the field enables research into the making of operatic discourse as the product of struggles between rival composers and intellectual groups for cultural domination. Thus it is important to have an artistic language which establishes the autonomous definition of artistic value, that is, ways of speaking about 'art' and making judgments on the individual style of composers. The development of fields is a lengthy historical process involving the practical mastery of the specific knowledge inscribed in past works, recorded, codified and canonised by an entire body of professional experts. The contents of a field thus accumulate as an irreversible process. New opera composers must situate themselves reflexively vis-a-vis the history of the opera field itself, to knowledge of past opera and performance history, musical orthodoxy and tradition.

While cultural fields can be traced to pre-industrial societies, their structure in such societies was characterised by only partial autonomisation. Thus the opera field as a sub-field of the wider field of cultural production remained dominated by religious and political patronage until the end of the eighteenth century. But many of the features of both the wider cultural production field and the opera sub-field were present in playing a significant role in aesthetic production and laying the basis for later developments in opera form. One of Bourdieu's most valuable insights is that cultural fields develop through conflict and struggle over such aesthetic issues as the status of a 'classic' and the dominant canons in musical performance. Furthermore, the precondition for entering and participating in any field is the recognition of the 'values at stake' (what Bourdieu calls the 'spirit of the game') which effectively circumscribes the limits to criticism. Hence all internal struggles within fields lead to 'partial' and not total revolutions, in action which destroys an existing hierarchy 'but not the game itself'. A revolution in the artistic field, for example, will challenge established definitions and practices in the name of a purer art, film, literature, music or opera, 'shaking up' the structure of the field while leaving its legitimacy intact (Bourdieu, 1993a: 134). The remainder of this chapter will suggest ways of applying the concepts and substantive theory of modernity and cultural fields outlined above to specific forms of opera.

Modernity and Venetian opera

Until the end of the eighteenth century, opera constituted an aesthetic form produced for aristocratic rulers and wealthy patrons given on special festival occasions mounted with no expense spared. From its origins at the beginning of the sixteenth-century opera was tied to court patronage, its social function to display the splendour of the court and the noble status of its members. Its subject matter was drawn from mythology and antiquity represented in stereotyped conflicts about love and honour, themes close to the hearts of the aristocracy. Yet although opera had been invented by a group of Florentine intellectuals around 1600, with an emphasis on chamber forms employing a limited range of musical effects and highly sophisticated in feeling and declamation, by the middle of the century it had been transformed into an early example of 'mass culture', a public, not private, spectacle supported by the wealthy middle classes and box-office receipts.

The paying opera first appeared in Venice in 1637 at the theatre of San Cassiano, followed shortly after by London in 1639 and Paris in 1669. While opera in its origins represented aristocratic and courtly power its historical development exemplifies the tensions within it, between an aesthetic form striving to achieve some degree of aesthetic autonomy and the aesthetic taste of its court and bourgeois audience.

Adorno (1999) has emphasised the distinction between Court and Bourgeois opera, with the former as a private institution played before an invited audience or guests appealing to aristocratic tastes. In contrast, the 350 operas performed in Venice between 1637 and the end of the seventeenth century were performed before socially mixed audiences (Grout, 1988: 87). The Venetian public opera system constituted the only competitive system in the seventeenth century and for the first time opera was structured through an embryonic cultural field. Mid-seventeenth-century republican Venice constituted a society in which a burgeoning cultural field was dominated by economic forces restricting its development towards autonomy: the opera theatres repeated performances of particular operas, regular seasons were instituted, a subscription system was introduced, and as a business enterprise seeking high profits, there was a high turnover of operas. Although there was little sense of a field in the modern sense Venetian opera was structured hierarchically and featured struggles between rival groups of composers (Monteverdi, Cesti, Cavalli) for supremacy over the field. In contrast to Venetian public opera, Court opera constituted a closed form, as there was little competition between composers and no real sense of the boundaries between specifically 'operatic' and political institutions.

While Court opera derived its characters from mythology, virtually all forms of Venetian public opera were based on recognisable human figures with ordinary feelings and passions, drawn from history but contemporised. Action defined their dramatic and musical identity as complex human beings. In his Venetian operas, Monteverdi radically departed from the prevailing orthodox aesthetic norms employing the concept of 'modernity' to refer to what he called *seconda prattico*, a musical practice opposing the orthodox forms derived from the sixteenth-century madrigals. Monteverdi, who had come to Venice from employment in the Mantuan Court became the leader in a type of new operatic discourse which emphasised music and drama over vocal display. In his *The Return of Ullyses* (1640) and *The Coronation of Poppea* (1643), he sought the 'true way of imitation', in which music does more than imitate words but evokes actions and feelings, generating dramatic tension and the emotional distances between individuals. For Monteverdi music became both the expression of character and the means of dramatic action, a unity new to operatic discourse. In *The Coronation of Poppea*, for example, Seneca's acceptance of death, and the sensual passions of Nero and Poppea, are given depth and meaning through the music rather than simply through dramatic action, thus achieving a balance between drama and music (Rostand, 1992).

McClary (1989) makes the valuable point that the new Venetian opera subverted the formal patterns of traditional operatic discourse, critically questioning the traditional hierarchies of authority. Employing Bakhtin's (1984) notion of carnival she grounds her analysis in the ways these operas subverted authority to focus on an evolving conflict between 'official' and 'unofficial' musical cultures. With contemporary reality as its main subject, Venetian opera sought to grasp historical change as an open-ended, not finished process expressing a new world in the making. There was a real sense of struggle between two opposing modes of operatic discourse, between opera seeking canonical status working within the traditional categories of the official culture and new opera, which through its musical language and dramatic imagery, represented modernity. Monteverdi's 'partial revolution' was to make music the equal partner of the text while Cesti made the composer the dominant voice over the dramatist. Cesti's work was performed, for example, at the royal festivals of Louis X1V at Versailles, while Rossi's *Orfeo* (the exemplary work of official culture striving for canonical status), faithful to its original myth, was given in Paris in 1647 to a libretto weighed down by irrelevant episodes which mixed serious and comic scenes, and intermingled with ballets. The result was diminution of specifically 'operatic' discourse and 'autonomous' operatic values.

Court opera, based on ritual and ceremony had been challenged by the new forms of Venetian opera, especially Monteverdi's 'unofficial' modernity. But it was the official culture which, maintaining continuity with musical orthodoxy and rejecting the new forms, succeeded in establishing its dominance. Although Monteverdi had made one of the most striking developments in opera, his work disappeared from operatic history only to be rediscovered as an uncannily 'modern' composer in the early years of the twentieth century. In his synthesis of drama and music, and in his depiction of historical characters as complex beings whose identities are not fixed once and for all but are constantly developing through action and interaction with others, Monteverdi absorbed the 'modernity' of the Venice of his times, and transformed this social experience into new aesthetic categories of operatic discourse and practice.

Court opera and bourgeois opera

Before the nineteenth century there was little distinction between high/elite and popular culture, but by breaking the monopoly of aristocratic court opera, bourgeois/commercial opera became an early form of 'mass culture'. The rise of mass culture is typically traced to the development of nineteenth-century mass production extended to the realm of culture. However, one of the origins of mass culture was the development of public concerts during the second half of the eighteenth century which gradually replaced the private concerts first established in courtly and aristocratic milieu.

This 'democratisation' of music is closely linked with the growth of music publishing, which transformed music from a semi-feudal craft serving church, town and court, into a free enterprise profession linked with bourgeois markets. During the last quarter of the eighteenth-century patronage declined sharply and commercial developments in music distribution such as copying, engraving and printing enabled composers to become increasingly independent of traditional modes of patronage. With the expansion of printing and music publishing, the organisation of commercial networks, with music becoming a business enterprise geared to profit, and with the broadening of public interest, an autonomous field of music was opening up. In the early part of the eighteenth century, the personal relationship between performer and patron had formed the basis of the social order with success hinging on maintaining and not expanding the social relations of locally based groups. During the seventeenth century, public festivals provided free concerts to the population; in France musical performances in public places were open to everyone on festive occasions. But with the growth of population and expansion of civil society in urbanism and city culture, the relationship between musicians and the growing public became increasingly impersonal, the unique quality of the musical event disappearing (Weber, 1977: 5–22).

In the largest European cities – London, Paris and Vienna – composers wrote for a growing musical culture partly free of traditional forms of patronage. While Monteverdi had been the dominant figure in the origins of musical modernity, it was now Mozart whose music and operas came to embody a more complex notion of 'newness'. Mozart's life straddles the end of patronage and the beginning of the independent artist, a process Elias (1993) describes as a transition from 'craftsmen's to artist's art', to a market of 'anonymous buyers mediated by agencies such as art dealers, music publishers, impresarios etcetera'. Like Haydn, Mozart was treated as a servant, regarded as inferior to his aristocratic employers, remaining an outsider in court society and 'nurturing towards this world an increasing antagonism and rebelliousness that manifested itself...in the notably anti-aristocratic *Don Giovanni*' (Elias, 1993: 95, 136–37).

Unlike France, which had developed a centralised court system, the German lands were mostly fragmented into a variety of courts and here opera enjoyed the highest status for musical works: from the age of twelve Mozart began composing operas (*La Finta Semplice*, 1768) working within the orthodox musical style of the court appealing to the tastes of the aristocratic audience. Mozart's music could not develop within the restricted culture of the Salzburg court, which demanded traditional forms of music making producing marches, sonatas, and masses to order. He left the Salzburg court for Vienna but when the *Die Entfuhrung aus dem Serail* (1782) was given before the reforming Emperor Joseph II elicited the comment that it contained 'too many notes', a clear indication that even working within the existing forms, Mozart's music was going beyond orthodoxy. The earlier *opera seria Idomeneo* (1781) was not a new starting point but the last example of a declining form. In *The Marriage of Figaro*, *Don Giovanni* and *Cosi fan tutte*, composed during the 1780s, Mozart's synthesis of music and drama take as their subject contemporary reality, not the closed classical world of *Idomeneo*, depicting individuals as highly complex beings whose feelings, emotions and identities are changed in response to action. In *The Marriage of Figaro*, Mozart sharpened criticism and social comment by turning the two worlds of aristocracy and servants upside down, dissolving the boundaries between them and collapsing the hierarchical structures. In Mozart's world nothing is fixed or permanent: there is no dominant discourse present here as with more traditional operatic forms. This aesthetic modernity is further highlighted in *Cosi fan tutte* when Fiordiligi sings longingly for her absent lover while the music slyly suggests her attraction to another, a reflexive element both musically and dramatically.

The complex, multiple discourses which are Mozart's innovations in music drama can be attributed to an evolving cultural field and an increasingly developed sense of the 'modern' which was developing among sections of cultural producers at this time. Mozart enjoyed the freedom of Vienna, with its free market in theatre and opera, and its public sphere of self-regulating institutions separate from state structures. Vienna had a large number of upwardly mobile lower aristocracy, recently ennobled court officials who indulged in private entertainments such as musical performances.

A contrast can be drawn between the Viennese situation and the case of early nineteenth-century French opera, which at that time was becoming an increasingly commercialised part of a burgeoning 'culture industry'. After the 1830 Revolution, the Paris opera was transformed from a court to an entrepreneurial, capitalist system in which the box office and state subsidy combined: the court system which had commissioned Rossini to write *Il viaggo a Reims* (1825) for the coronation of Charles X, now became bourgeois grand opera dominated by composers such as Auber, Halevy, and Meyerbeer. Opera was now a fully-fledged capitalist business. Adorno (1999) in his essay on Bourgeois and Court Opera, notes how in Weber's *Der Freischutz* (1821), the original tragic ending was replaced by a happy one to satisfy a growing German bourgeois public, thus anticipating one of the major elements of 'culture industry' production. But it is the rapid expansion of commercialised French opera which inaugurated the transformation of the operatic field. 'High culture' was defined as entertainment, and French grand opera displayed this with large choral ensembles, ballets, five acts dealing with heroic events, subjects derived not from antiquity (as with Lully) but from medieval and modern history. It was staged spectacle on a massive scale, with Vesuvius erupting in Auber's *La Muette de Portici* (1828), the heroine burnt in boiling oil in Halevy's *La Juive* (1835), and a massacre in Meyerbeer's *Les Hugenots* (1836) in which chorus and massive crowd scenes dominated: opera became Hollywood before Hollywood.

The bourgeois government of Louis Philippe (1830–48) had abandoned aristocratic opera underpinned by state finance and demanded that opera be placed on 'efficient' capitalist lines. French grand opera was the product of bourgeois entrepreneurship, a commercial enterprise built around popular operas and singers appealing to the *haute bourgeoisie* of Paris and facilitated by the development of specific technical and social conditions (a middle class paying public, advanced lighting, complex stage machinery) all of which made music and especially opera 'an appropriate field upon which the cultural battles of the nineteenth century could be fought' (Lindenberger, 1984: 228). The opera house became the meeting place for the dominant classes to flaunt their wealth, status and taste, the pivotal element in an artistic field wedded to the old, traditional and the hierarchical, in which opera was closely bound to a social order that its works maintained. Grand opera was an aesthetics of 'finished' or 'fixed' forms functioning within a cultural apparatus that sought to communicate a socially acceptable and hierarchical meaning through works structured in explicit rules and codified principles. Thus composers such as Berlioz, who rejected this commercialised and closed culture, were outsiders. His penultimate opera, *Les Troyens* (1860), based on Vergil's *Aeneid*, is one of the longest operas in the repertory. A dramatic epic dealing with the fate of nations, it was never performed in his lifetime. Although sharing many of the features of grand opera (five acts, ballet scenes, the central role of the chorus) *Les Troyens* marks a decisive shift away from the static, unmotivated dramaturgy built around an artificial engineering of tension, towards a 'natural' dramatic narrative based on the inevitable logic of historical fate and destiny.

Bourgeois grand opera had the power to seduce composers who craved artistic success in the French operatic field. Wagner, for example, for all his radical ideas on the need to reform nineteenth-century opera, had sought fame and fortune in Paris with his version of grand opera, *Tannhauser* (1861) cultivating the company of grand opera composers such as Meyerbeer and Rossini. His failure to conquer Paris (*Tannhauser* was not successful) found its expression in his vast corpus of writings on opera in which he contrasted his own concept of opera as music drama with the passive, consumerist entertainment of grand opera. In an interesting echo of the writings of Adorno on the culture industry, Wagner describes mid-nineteenth-century French opera exemplified by Meyerbeer and Halevy as eroding all genuine dramatic possibilities for operatic discourse. In Wagner's view, Meyerbeer's craftsmanship failed to penetrate below the skins of his characters to see the world through their eyes; the music is pictorial and illustrative, portraying but not expressing emotions. Meyerbeer, argued Wagner, was not interested in complex human situations but in large scale monumentalism, 'effects without causes'. Opera was at its most empty, he claimed, when it aimed only to provide spectacle, tunes and vocal display. It should aspire to the ideals of Greek art, notably tragedy, which aimed to integrate drama, poetry, music and song, costume, mime within a myth embracing the whole of a nation.

With the opera controlled by bankers, musicians were tied to the established musical order through a system of prizes which rewarded conservatism. Although many of the more innovative composers (Berlioz, Bizet, Debussy) were initiated into the musical field through this institution, they went on to challenge musical orthodoxy. Bizet was roundly criticised for transgressing the aesthetic norms of the operatic field when in *Carmen* (1875), he portrayed proletarian figures and outsiders as flesh and blood individuals who refuse to reform themselves in terms of bourgeois respectability; there is a strong sense of sexual freedom and the autonomy of the self. Bizet's opera, unsuccessful at its premiere at the less prestigious Opera Comique, challenged the prevailing distinction between grand opera (serious, heroic, declamatory) and comic opera (ordinary everyday life, non-serious, conversation) with its drama of the everyday, given complex aesthetic form by multiple levels of Otherness: Carmen the gypsy as racial, proletarian and female Other.

Thus one of the most significant cultural battles of the nineteenth-century lay between those composers aspiring to remain within the traditional and orthodox forms, and those striving to revolutionise opera. By the end of the nineteenth century the French opera field constituted part of one of the most advanced and complex cultural fields in Europe. It was a cultural field which had achieved a high level of partial autonomy within its various sub-fields although each developed unevenly at its own specific tempo. Put more broadly a dualism emerged between those striving for 'artistic art' and those who remained committed to orthodox commercialised forms. Debussy is the key figure here. Bizet had worked within the conventions of the operatic field until *Carmen*, but by 1900 when Debussy's *Pelleas and Melisande* was produced, the operatic field was structured such that it enabled composers to innovate. This is a process of partial autonomisation of cultural fields, paralleled within visual art (Manet) and literature (Flaubert): Manet, for example, overthrew the social structures of the French academic apparatus in the 1860s (Bourdieu, 1993a) in the same way that Debussy revolutionised and overthrew the commercialised mass culture in French opera at the end of the nineteenth century, without becoming marginalised by being regarded as an 'outrageous' avant-gardist.

The French cultural field, like all other fields, is historically specific in its social forms, differing sharply from the German, English and Italian fields. Debussy's operatic revolution lay in redefining operatic discourse as non-representational so that in *Pelleas and Melisande*, the language, images and musical structure are anti-mimetic, producing their own reality and meaning: a dream world inhabited by mythic characters, yet a recognisably a modern world dominated by love, jealousy, violence and murder, a world dominated by fear and cruelty. In the quiet reserved dialogue close to natural declamation and the subtle, understated relations between the characters, *Pelleas and Melisande* constitutes a new operatic form – 'artistic art' – clearly distinct from the products of grand opera and those contemporary composers such as Massenet, whose operas were produced at the opposite, heteronomous, commercial and 'culture industry' pole of the cultural field.

Operatic canon and modern opera

By the beginning of the twentieth century, the operatic field had become firmly established, notably in France, Germany and Italy in hierarchical and dualistic forms, and less so in England and America, where opera was becoming canonised as museum art. One of the striking features of twentieth-century opera was the formation of a canon of operatic works and the founding of a core repertory for opera houses. Unlike in the eighteenth and nineteenth century, new operas failed to achieve public popularity, surviving in the margins of the opera field and no longer offering new additions to the canon. Only a relative few modern operas, including Puccini's *Turandot* (1926), Britten's *Peter Grimes* (1945), and Stravinsky's *The Rakes Progress* (1951), joined the established repertoire.

Increasingly through the twentieth century, the operatic field became dominated by those institutions and social groups who consolidated and reproduced a narrow operatic canon of works performed regularly in the world's opera houses by an internationally mobile elite of singers, a process facilitated by ease of travel and communication media. Adorno (1976: 77–84) describes this situation as involving a restriction of the operatic repertory, and as a failure of opera to engage with modernity, so that increasingly opera houses became museums of culture, recycling the old with mere gestures to the new. As a result, opera came to be in a permanent crisis, with producers aiming to modernise and make 'relevant' past operatic forms. The power of subscription and an audience which identifies opera with social status means that the aesthetic object becomes severely diminished.

However, Adorno's views seem to me rather outdated, for alongside this development, the operatic field has further evolved in the twentieth century in two highly significant ways. First, the emergence of a cadre of opera specialists, promoting heightened awareness of past operatic works not as museum pieces but as living modern music drama. For example, research into the seventeenth and eighteenth century has led to the recovery of lost works and reinterpretations of Baroque forms. In 1911, the French composer and musicologist D'Indy produced the first performing version of *Orfeo* since the sixteenth century; while in England, Germany and Italy, other Monteverdi operas were rediscovered, restored and given public performances. The growth of the number of dedicated musical specialists, made possible by the evolution of a partly autonomous musical and operatic field, opens the way to the production of knowledge, debate, criticism and communication, in a manner reminiscent of Habermas's account of the emancipatory potential of modernity.

Secondly, far from being characterisable only as a museum for an exhausted genre dominated by tradition and a narrowly conceived notion of the canon, the operatic field has during the past thirty years become the site of social and political engagements. The dualistic structure of the field remains, but in new interpretations of specific canonised as well as non-canonised works, opera producers have generated new modes of reception in which the inherent aesthetic modernity of specific operas becomes integrated with interpretations of contemporary reality, as for example in Scottish Opera's 1980s production of *Les Troyens*, and Patrice Chereau's 1976 Bayreuth production of Wagner's *Ring Cycle*.

Until the twentieth century, with a few exceptions (notably Monteverdi and Mozart) operatic composition had been dominated by the needs of singers, such as in the case of the seventeenth-century castrati. In the work of Puccini and Richard Strauss, this domination was hardly challenged. Traditionally, for many opera producers theatrical and dramatic values were secondary (and indeed in England until quite recently, the operatic field was dominated by producers who paid only lip-service to dramatic theatrical values). Yet today, producers routinely emphasise the value of dramatic effects in the pursuit of operatic 'truth'.

Modern opera also has retained the power to shock. For example, John Adams's *The Death of Klinghoffer* (1991) deals with the highly topical subject of terrorism, through the portrayal of the real-life highjacking of a cruise liner by Palestinian commandos and the subsequent killing of a Jewish passenger. Glyndebourne Opera, which had co-commissioned the work, refused to stage it, and the opera has rarely been staged, not surprising given its provocative opening chorus of exiled Palestinians:

> My father's house was razed
> in nineteen forty eight
> When the Israelis passed
> Over our street

Adams's opera is, however, a dense, complex and challenging work which refuses to embody a singular dominant discourse. It is in many ways an exemplar of the complexities of late modernity, given its expression of multiple discourses, such as the competing claims of terrorism versus the Jewish family; and the conflict between the Palestinians and the Israeli state. Such a work demands highly active rather than passive reception and illustrates in a characteristically 'late modern' way Tom Sutcliffe's (1996: 3) point that 'opera is not a sport. The purpose of performing opera is to bring the work to life, to make its meaning tell, to help the audience believe in the truth and vitality of its message. Every serious attempt to perform an opera adds to the richness and depth of that process.'

Conclusion

In this chapter I have argued for a sociologically informed account of artistic forms grounded in the concepts of cultural field and an emancipatory notion of modernity. The theory of cultural fields opens up a new perspective in the history of opera by rigorously contextualising its varied forms, its relations with class and power, the tension between commercial market forces and the demands for artistic autonomy. The concept of modernity further deepens this analysis by focusing on the ways in which artistic forms strive to emancipate themselves from direct economic and political forces, a process made possible by the increasing autonomy of the cultural field itself. Modernity signifies that the relative autonomy of artistic forms is made possible by the developing autonomy of the cultural field itself, as it is no longer wholly determined by economic, political and other external forces, but by its own internal dynamic and laws.

Although opera is often denigrated as an elitist art form supported by a small elite minority, it remains a significant presence within modern culture, with the form constantly renewing itself through new, challenging works and the subversive strategies of modern stage production. Such 'revolutions' in the operatic field challenge established definitions and practices, shaking up the structure of the field while leaving its legitimacy intact. Linking opera with an emancipatory notion of modernity within the framework of field theory goes beyond conventional approaches to the sociology of artistic forms by focusing on the collective nature of cultural production involving a whole range of institutions and practices. In this way cultural sociology can avoid what Bourdieu calls 'the short-circuit effect' in which the genesis of artistic forms become linked directly to the world view, ideology or the patronage of specific social groups or classes, an 'external' mode of analysis which fails to take account of the complex set of relations that characterise cultural production, a process involving among others 'creators' and interpreters as well as new generations who seek to overthrow the established artistic forms bound up with old hierarchies of power and status.

The sociological analysis of opera places it firmly within the broader sociological study of culture and art. Opera is more than elitist entertainment but an artistic form that throughout its history has engaged with many of the fundamental problems of modern, pluralist culture. Its relevance for those involved in developing a sociology of art lies both in its centrality to modern culture and in its rich and complex history.

'World Music' and the Globalization of Sound

David Inglis and Roland Robertson

Music is certainly the most global aspect of our 'global village'.
– Robert Burnett

World Music is the 'new aesthetic form of the global imagination'.
– Erlmann, 1996: 467

Introduction

In the present day it is increasingly recognised that the discipline of sociology is being transformed by the need for it to comprehend processes and phenomena that traverse and exist in certain ways beyond the boundaries of nation-states (Urry, 2000). It follows that the specialist field of the sociology of art and culture must likewise seek to rework its inherited analytic frameworks and heuristic devices in order to be able to grasp artistic and cultural phenomena which are 'global' in scope and/or have certain 'global' elements, facets and qualities. In this chapter we will take the example of 'world music' to illustrate both what a particular 'global' cultural form looks like, and to show what sociology can usefully say about it. As we will see, the 'world music' phenomenon is both very complex and also often very controversial, for how various different authors have construed it has constituted a field of discourse that is best characterized as a 'politicized, polemicized zone' (Feld, 1994: 270).

Despite the difficulties involved in negotiating one's way through this political and aesthetic minefield, it is the case that world music raises various interesting questions for the sociologist, from the more general problem of how sociology should seek to grasp 'global' aesthetic forms, to the more specific issues involved in unravelling the relations that pertain today between music and ethnicity/identity on the one hand, and music and geographical space on the other (Guilbault, 1997: 41). As we will see, world music can be seen as

reflective of, and actively contributing to, the transformation of these relations, such that the world of music is now truly a world that is 'global' in
nature. Such developments challenge the sociologist to think about how best
to grasp fundamental alterations in musical life specifically, and aesthetic/
cultural life more generally. The aims of this chapter are therefore (1) to delineate and make sense of the complex phenomenon of world music; (2) to illustrate possible ways in which the sociology of art and culture can make the
'global turn' that the rest of the discipline is undergoing.

We shall first consider the controversies involved in defining what the genre
includes and does not include, and what sorts of music can be included under
this heading. We will then consider how world music has been socially organised by record producers, musicians, commercial record outlets and others.
Next we will reflect upon how best to understand the relations between world
music and processes of globalization. Our argument is that attending to the
details of world music's creation, distribution, consumption and discursive
elaboration compels the sociologist to recognise the ambivalent nature of the
whole phenomenon, an ambivalence that may well be characteristic of other
aesthetic and cultural phenomena that are global in scope.

The nature of 'world music'

Answering the apparently simple question 'what is world music?' actually
leads us into a very complex realm. In one way, 'world music' is not a new
phenomenon, in that its modern manifestations have a long pre-history that
stretches back over many hundreds of years. This is because music is one of
the most geographically portable of all artistic and cultural forms, and it
seems to be particularly prone to syncretisms and fusions of different styles.
As Lipsitz (1994: 126) puts it, 'musical syncretisms disclose the dynamics of
cultural syncretisms basic to the processes of immigration, assimilation and
acculturation', processes that themselves have a long history. For example,
both Jewish and Christian musics have accompanied particular groups of
people on their travels across the globe in the last two millennia (Pahlen,
1949: 17, 27). Indeed, given their long-term global travels, and the various
localised mutations they have undergone in the process, there is good reason
for understanding forms of Jewish music such as klezmer as truly 'global' in
nature (Slobin, 2003: 290). Another musical form tied up with historical processes of travel, migration and the mixing of different cultural milieux is
tango, which originated in Argentina, spread across many regions of the world
in the early twentieth century, and was subsequently appropriated in places as
'unlikely' as Japan and Turkey (Born and Hesmondhalgh, 2000: 25; Stokes,
2003: 298).[1] In the same vein, 'black' musical forms developed in North America
and the Caribbean are clearly musics produced by, and in many ways
expressive of, the socio-cultural conditions of diaspora. One might argue, on
the basis of the centrality of black music in the creation of what is now called
the Anglo-American rock and pop mainstream, that 'the compulsory diaspora
of Africans . . . has had a much greater impact on popular music history than

even the cultural imperialism of the Anglo-American entertainment industry' (Hatch, 1989: 72; also Stokes, 2003: 307). Thus even the mainstream music of the 'white' Anglo-American world, which ironically is often the *bete noire* of musical standardisation against which many present-day 'world musicians' rebel, can be seen to be a fusion of both European and African influences, and thus in its very nature a cultural hybrid.

It would be a mistake, therefore, to claim that what we today call 'world music' appeared suddenly out of the blue in the last few decades with no historical antecedents. However, the cultural, social, political and economic conditions of possibility for the contemporary 'world music' phenomenon resulted from the globalising tendencies of the second half of the twentieth century (Bohlman, 2002b: xvi). From a situation where particular musical cultures had hitherto been relatively (but not absolutely) separated, there has arisen a situation where all (or almost all) the musics of the world have come into some form of inter-connection and dialogue with each other (Wiora, 1965). Hitherto existing interconnections between many musical cultures, and trans-national networks of individuals making, selling and listening to music, became in the late twentieth century more extended, dense and complicated (Taylor, 1997: 197). It is this density and complication that both reflects, and has made possible, what we today call 'world music', a constellation of musical forms which seem particularly to flourish in large-scale, multi cultural cities like London, Paris and New York (Nettl, 1985), although there are also important recording centres for certain world music styles located outside of these metropolitan centres, Kingston in Jamaica being a good example (Guilbault, 2001: 190).

Apart from its historical location, the one thing that can be said with confidence as to the nature of 'world music' is that definitions of it are always controversial and open to contestation, with different academic authors, and different interest groups in the music industry, favouring differing identifications of what world music 'is', and which sorts of music can legitimately be referred to under this heading (Guilbault, 2001: 176). For some, the category of 'world music' is a 'utopic all-embracing term', while for others it involves 'a restrictive ghettoisation' of particular musics and musicians, relegating them to a category that they would be better unassociated with (Fairley, 2001: 286).

The ambiguities involved in defining what 'world music' is can be seen clearly when one considers the sheer heterogeneity of different musical forms that are habitually referred to under this heading by both cultural commentators and those involved in the production, marketing and distribution of such forms. Writing critically of the world music genre, the musician David Byrne stresses the unfettered multiplicity of musical styles that tend to be sold under the umbrella term of world music. For Byrne (1999) the world music category is

> a catchall that commonly refers to non-Western music of any and all sorts, popular music, traditional music and even classical music...a name for a bin in the record store signifying stuff that doesn't belong anywhere else in the store. What's in that bin ranges from the most blatantly commercial music produced by a country, like Hindi film

music...to the ultra-sophisticated, super-cosmopolitan art-pop of Brazil...from the somewhat bizarre and surreal concept of a former Bulgarian state-run folkloric choir...(Le Mystére des Voix Bulgares) to Norteno songs from Texas and northern Mexico glorifying the exploits of drug dealers...Albums by Selena, Ricky Martin and Los Del Rio (the Macarena kings), artists who sell millions of records in the United States alone, are racked next to field recordings of Thai hill tribes. Equating apples and oranges, indeed.

Thus lurking beneath the generic heading of 'world music', there seems to exist a morass of musical and cultural opposites and contradictions, for existing within the world music 'genre' (or more accurately, 'meta-genre') are musics that are 'popular' and 'obscure', 'pop' and 'traditional', 'commercial' and (relatively) 'non-commercial' and so on. This theme of extreme eclecticism is made explicit in the Introduction to the most well-known and influential of encyclopaedic guides to the world music field in the English language, *World Music: The Rough Guide* (Broughton et al., 1999a,b). The editors of the guide introduce their 1400 page, two-volume set of analyses of various world music genres by noting that their publication 'deals with the oldest and newest music in the world – from centuries-old traditions to contemporary fusions. It includes the most sacred and profound music and the most frivolous and risqué, music of healing, music of protest, the loudest music you'll ever hear, the softest and most intimate' (Broughton et al., 1999a: ix).

From all this emphasis on heterogeneity, it would be tempting to conclude that the 'world of world music has no boundaries' at all (Bohlman, 2002b: xi), and that the term 'world music' is ultimately 'unfixable' (Guilbault, 2001: 191) and characterised by great instability (Taylor, 1997: 14). While this is true to some extent, nonetheless to regard the label 'world music' as a wholly meaningless cipher would to ignore the fact that there exist certain patterns and regularities in 'world music', as this is understood both by academic commentators, and, more importantly in this context, by the groups of people who make, distribute and listen to such music. It is relatively safe to say that 'world music' is defined more by what it is *not* than by what it *is*. To a large extent it is what is not 'mainstream' in any given musical environment (Guilbault, 2001: 191). In the Western world, as evidenced in record company catalogues and promotional materials, in magazines and other publications dedicated to 'world music', and on record shop shelves, we see that 'world music' is, very generally speaking, made up of musics that are not part of the Western rock and pop 'mainstream' (Shuker, 1998: 311–12). Moreover, again very generally speaking, although not necessarily so, in Anglophone countries world music tends not to be sung in English, although certain Anglophone 'roots' and 'folk' recordings sometimes get labelled as world music (Guilbault, 2001: 177). Local, indigenous versions of the Western rock and pop mainstream (e.g. Hungarian rock) may or may not be defined as 'world music'; such borderline cases illustrate the importance of examining which particular groups are doing the defining of 'world music' in particular socio-cultural contexts. Thus, for example, Far Eastern genres like Japanese karaoke and

Chinese pop tend to be defined by Westerners as being too 'pop' to be 'real' world music, although pop from other countries, such as those in the Middle East, is often included within the world music category (Taylor, 1997: 9). As such, we can see that while in the English-speaking West 'world music' tends to be made up of forms that are not Anglophone rock and pop, it is still relatively contingent on particular circumstances which musical forms are allowed into the world music stable.

Does this mean that for a music to be a 'world music' form it has to be non-Western in origin? Some commentators argue that the vast majority of what is taken in the West to be 'world music' does indeed derive from cultural traditions that are outside of the Western world (Pacini, 1993; Guilbault, 1997: 31). However, the term world music today 'covers American, Asian and European musics, albeit those of minority groups within these geographical areas'. Thus music from Western countries can be defined (by particular interested parties) as world music if it 'is the product of aggrieved populations' such as French Canadians or Catalans (Guilbault, 2001: 176). It should be noted, however, that if one were to claim that 'world music' and the musics produced by musicians hailing from, or claiming to represent, 'oppressed minorities', were synonymous, then one would have to conclude that musical forms like jazz and rap originally developed by black Americans were world musics too. What is sold as 'world music' is therefore always to some degree an arbitrary matter, decided by the fiat of music companies and commercial outlets. In a sense, what counts as 'world music' in a given time and place may tell us more about the people who decide what lies inside and outside the category than the music itself (Guilbault, 1996). It is not too much of a generalisation to say that the term almost always refers to music made (at least apparently) by an exotic 'Other'. What counts as 'world music' clearly depends on which part of the world you are in; the term is relational through and through.

Categories of world music

Now that we have looked at the complexities of which musical forms get included under the heading of world music or not, we will now turn to examine the subtleties of nomenclature within the term itself as it is understood in the West. The term 'world music' derives from two main sources of classification. In the first case, the term is of academic provenance. It was coined from the 1960s onwards by (primarily liberal and leftist) ethnomusicological scholars sensitive to debates about imperialism and post-colonialism in order to describe their objects of study, namely all the musics of the world. The aim of scholars from the 1960s onwards was to replace older views and classifications of 'traditional non-Western musics' with their elitist and colonialist overtones (Rice, 2000: 224), in favour of a non-hierarchical celebration of musical diversity which refused to regard Western musical forms as the norm against which all others should be measured (Feld, 1994: 266; Bohlman, 2002a: 13, 16; Feld, 2000).

In the second case, 'world music' as a term has its genesis in the world of the capitalist culture industries. In this sense, 'world music' was primarily a marketing category, devised by music companies and distributors 'as a label applied to popular music originating outside the Anglo-American nexus' (Shuker, 1998: 311). Quite simply, the label 'world music' was a way of selling musics that hitherto had not been as exploited for commercial purposes as fully as they might. The term was meant not just to identify a particular genre (or meta-genre) but also, as we will see below, was created as a marker of a new musical marketing strategy, intended to reach a certain sort of clientele.

Within this commercial categorisation, 'world music' refers to a further two major types of music. In the first case, the term refers to 'ethnic music', that is, music that is taken to be in some way representative or indicative of a particular identifiable 'culture', 'people', 'nation' and so on. A particular, specific 'world music' is seen as the cultural expression of a particular ethnic group. On this view, a particular musical genre reflects a 'geographical space...consisting of stable, bounded territories', with musicians seen as expressing in sounds the 'spirit' of the ethnic group of which they are a part (Guilbault, 2001: 178). Particular musical styles that are regarded as being in certain ways 'expressive' of the ethnic groups that the musicians who create and perform them hail from, are reggae (Jamaica), cajun and zydeco (creole culture in Lousiana and environs), polka (several central European countries), salsa (various Caribbean countries), tango (Argentina), juju and highlife (Nigeria), räi (Algeria), conjunto (Mexico and southern Texas) and flamenco (southern Spain) (Feld, 1994: 264).

In the second case, and by contrast to such a focus on the nation, the commercial category of 'world music' also refers to musical forms that have resulted from 'fusions' of two or more, hitherto geographically and/or soni-cally distinct, musical forms. Such musics are generally referred to as 'fusions', 'hybrids', 'creolizations', 'syncretisms' and 'cross-fertilisations' (Pacini, 1993: 48), terms that also have come to the fore in much academic writing about globalized cultural forms in the last decade or so. The mixings of styles in fusion music could take the form of either an admixture of particular 'ethnic musics' with each other, or a combination of 'ethnic music' with a Western musical form, such as pop or electronica (Frith, 1989: viii; Guilbault, 2001: 177; Loosely, 2003: 50). Examples of the latter would include the American singer-songwriter Paul Simon's collaboration with the South African group Ladysmith Black Mambazo on the album 'Graceland' and the American composer-player Ry Cooder's work with Cuban, Indian and Malian musi-cians (Fairley, 2001). The 'fusion' version of 'world music' could thus be described as resulting from processes of 'mixing of styles and borrowing elements from the available global encyclopaedia of musical styles' (Rutten, 1996: 67). A whole series of fusion sub-genres have emerged, such as 'world ambient', 'tribal music', 'ethnic fusion', 'ethno-techno', 'techno-tribal', 'New Age' and many others (Taylor, 1997: 4). These tend to involve reworking of particular ethnic musics, often those with some expressly 'spiritual' component – e.g. Buddhist chant, Islamic hymns – with Western electronic beats and rhythms. Such fusions can then be sold to Western listeners as embodying both 'pop' and 'spiritual' elements, ideal for meditating or relaxing with (Heelas, 1996).

Whereas in certain world music circles, the greatest accolade one can give to an 'ethnic music' is to praise its 'authenticity', the 'fusion' version of world music implicitly or explicitly involves a rejection of authenticity in favour of a validation and celebration of 'mixing, syncretic hybridization, blending, fusion, creolization, collaboration across gulfs' (Feld, 1994: 265). Here we have one of the major faultlines in evaluations of world music by those involved in its production, distribution, and consumption. Should one advocate and defend the (alleged) 'purity' of a singular cultural tradition, or should one promote and eulogise the (alleged) 'vibrancy' of new fusions of hitherto distinct styles of music? This is the specifically musical dramatisation of a wider dilemma that faces everyone in a globalizing world: should one seek to hold on to (what one perceives as) particular cultural traditions and heritages, or should one embrace the consequences of the trans-border social and cultural crossings, convergences and blendings that are concomitant with a globalizing condition?

The social organisation of world music

As Guilbault (2001: 177) notes, while world music at the level of epistemological reflection 'remains elusive as a genre or category', nevertheless it does indeed have its own social existence, in that it 'has its own sections in record stores, and is the focus of its own magazines, recording labels and advertisements, its own festivals, radio and television programmes, and so on' (also Goodwin and Gore, 1990). Indeed, the development of the commercial label 'world music' can be seen as involving from the 1980s onwards 'a major reconfiguration of how the musical globe was being curated, recorded, marketed, advertised and promoted' (Feld, 2000: 151). One task of the sociology of culture must be to identify the ways in which a particular cultural form, in this case 'world music', is socially organised, a task we will now turn to briefly.

In the first instance, we must recognise that without the efforts of certain music industry entrepreneurs, the history of world music would be very different from the way it actually developed. The development of world music in particular Western countries should be seen as in large part resulting from the efforts of networks of festival organisers, record producers, distributors, and magazine editors (Fairley, 2001: 275). In the UK, for example, the commercial world music category began to take on a life of its own in 1987, when a group of eleven independent record companies joined forces to develop the marketing of this new musical category. Their explicit aims were, first, to find a way to sell otherwise unclassifiable – and thus unsellable – recordings (Fairley, 2001: 277), and second, to promote such music to what they saw as a more sophisticated and mature audience than that for mainstream rock and pop, an audience comprised of people who prized musical 'authenticity' and who had a sense of themselves as non-mainstream music connoisseurs (Frith, 2000: 305–306). The extent of sales success was measured from the late 1980s onwards in dedicated music charts, such as the World Music Charts Europe and *Billboard* magazine's World Music Chart (Fairley, 2001: 280). The American National Academy of Recording Arts and Sciences created a new Grammy award for world music in the early 1990s. The award has proven controversial in certain circles, as critics have argued that it favours certain styles and artists over others, with recordings that are obviously Western pop-influenced tending to win the favour of the judges (Taylor, 1997: 9–10).

Throughout the late 1980s and on throughout the 1990s, the world music industry in many Western countries began to flourish. Festivals like Peter Gabriel's UK-based WOMAD (World of Music, Arts and Dance), although important sites for the promotional marketing of new artists and musical styles, were also presented as politically progressive events. As Gabriel described it, WOMAD 'allowed many different audiences to gain an insight into cultures other than their own through the enjoyment of music. Music is a universal language, it draws people together and proves as well as anything, the stupidity of racism' (Henery, 2004). In more explicitly commercial terms, dedicated record stores, websites and catalogues emerged, and world music sections began to appear in major music shops like Virgin, HMV and Tower Records (Feld, 2000: 150). Magazines devoted to world music such as *Rhythm Music, World Music,* and *Songlines* appeared to service the new genre, and act as advertising locales for the record companies, both large and small, which were increasingly keen to get into the world music market (Born and Hesmondhalgh, 2000: 26).

In the same vein, book guides to world music began to emerge. These, and magazine editorials too, tended to promote the view that an interest in world music allowed entry into a hitherto occluded Aladdin's Cave of musical treasures. As one of the editors of the *Rough Guide* mentioned above put it, 'part of the joy of the World Music phenomenon is the way in which barely known, but wonderful, music regularly emerges from relative obscurity' (Broughton, 2000: viii). However, despite claims that 'great music' can speak to the listener and move and excite him or her in direct and unmediated ways, regardless of how far the apparent cultural distance between musicians and listeners, world music recordings and guides also tended to rely on 'displayed expertise', with both the sleevenotes to particular recordings and also writings about particular musical 'traditions', often involving popularised versions of academic ethnomusicological writings. More often than not in the case of ethnic musics, such writings would assert the 'authenticity' of the music the purchaser was listening to, musicians being presented as 'uncorrupted' exponents of age-old traditions (Taylor, 1997: 16; Frith, 2000: 307). Here we see an interesting commingling of academic (or quasi-academic) 'expertise' and the commercial requirements of finding means to promote particular musical forms.

Alongside discourses of 'authenticity' the world music scene also thrived on the basis of a displayed and often quite self-conscious eclecticism. Radio programmes on both commercial and State-funded stations, for example, were hosted by DJs whose publicly displayed tastes ran the gamut from French *chanson* to Buddhist chanting. Such programmes, and the concomitant emergence of certain DJs as world music 'experts' – e.g. in Britain figures such as Andy Kershaw and Charlie Gillett – are interesting insofar as they embodied certain socio-cultural processes that helped to give world music an institutional shape of its own. Such programmes not only helped to shape world music listening communities within particular nation-states, but also over time began to exercise a certain amount of power to popularise particular artists and recordings, and to define certain recordings as bona fide 'world music' rather than 'mere' mainstream rock and pop (Fairley, 2001: 280–281). Partly through the gatekeeping activities of DJs, magazine journalists and so on, a recognisable pantheon of world music 'stars' emerged in the 1990s, such as the Cuban musicians associated with Ry Cooder in the Buena Vista Social Club project, the Cape Verdean singer Cesaria Evora, the Pakistani *qawwali* singer Nusrat Fateh Ali Khan and many others. The emergence in the 1990s of world music as a meta-genre with recognisable artists and musical styles was due in no small measure to specific networks of music industry professionals, who have had to find a way of negotiating a path between their often genuine liking of particular musics and the requirements of the record industry system to find ways of constantly selling records.

World music and globalization

If world music is both produced by, and expressive of, the globalizing cultural conditions of the present day, how should we more precisely comprehend the relations between such music and 'globalization'? It is certainly the case that the world music scene today involves two related processes of musical appropriation. On the one hand, 'local' musicians appropriate 'global' musical styles (e.g. musicians in Mali appropriating Western pop styles and combining them with 'indigenous' musical forms). On the other hand, 'global' musicians in turn appropriate 'local' sounds (e.g. Western rock musicians taking inspiration from the music of Mali) (Fairley, 2001: 273). Beyond that empirical identification of musical processes, however, we find ourselves within more polemical terrain, where judgements made by commentators both academic and non-academic as to the relations between world music and globalization, are informed by their views as to whether world music specifically, and the processes of cultural (and social, political and economic) globalization more generally, are phenomena to be welcomed or condemned. To a certain extent, whether one praises or attacks world music is dependent upon whether one feels more positive or more negative about the impact of globalization processes on cultural life.

Certain authors stress the 'trans-national' character of both globalization and world music, and regard both of these in a positive light. In this 'democratic and liberal vision', there is an emphasis on unfettered flows between different musics and cultures (Feld, 2000: 167). For Loosely (2003: 53), world music is reflective of the multicultural reality of modern Western societies. For Robinson et al. (1991: 228, 276), globalization processes such as migrations, diasporas, trans-border economic transactions and so on bring 'people everywhere into direct contact with each other and each other's music', leading to a 'new social order of music where national boundaries no longer separate musics, musicians and audiences' (see also Bohlman, 2002a: 1; Erlmann, 1993). Frith (1989: viii) argues that there are no culturally 'pure' sounds any more, because 'all countries' popular musics are shaped these days by international influences and institutions, by multinational capital and technology, by global pop norms and values' (Frith, 1989: 2; also Feld, 2000: 145). The upshot of this, he argues, is a great tendency towards constant musical revolution: 'everywhere, at an accelerating pace, conventions are challenged, new styles emerge, and innovations appear, spurred on by urbanisation, migration, international mass communications [and so on]' (Frith, 1989: viii). The globalization of music, therefore, does not signal the 'death-knell of musical variety in the world'; indeed, in quite a converse fashion, one might argue that globalization encourages rather than hinders musical diversity (Nettl, 1985: 3, 165). For Frith, even 'nationalistic' musics are today self-conscious responses to the perceived threat to national traditions posed by cultural, social, political and economic globalization.

In positive analyses of world music, the genuinely trans-national character of music-making today is seen to bring great benefits for both audiences and musicians (Feld, 1994: 270). In the case of the former, cross-border collaborations between musicians and producers is regarded as having the benefit of discovering new musics for Western audiences to enjoy (Feld, 1994: 271). Such listeners can then be dazzled by 'daring, novel combinations hitherto never imagined or thought possible' (Guilbault, 1997: 36; Jowers, 1993: 69). Fears of world music fusions reducing the 'authenticity' of particular musical traditions can be countered by arguing that hybridity has been the central quality of most musical production in most parts of the world for many centuries, and thus 'authenticity' cannot be lost, for there never was such a thing in the first place (Frith, 2000: 312).

The conditions of production of world music can also be represented as being of great benefit to artists too (Barlow and Eyre, 1995: vii). Musicians can be freed from what are seen as the shackles of the musical traditions in which they have grown up. As the Senegalese musician Youssou N'Dour, who has worked with Western stars such as David Byrne and Neneh Cherry, puts it, 'now, Africans aren't just the bearers of that traditional music which kind of represents the image people have of them from the outside; but they also have a new music fed by urban trends like rap or funk. This is what we're discovering and it has a lot of potential' (quoted in Loosely, 2003: 54).

For those writing in a more negative vein about world music, the above arguments often seem to function as apologetics for the practices of Western recording companies. For these critics, the very term 'world music' itself is 'today's dominant signifier of a triumphant industrialization of global sonic representation', a very dubious development indeed (Feld, 2000: 146). From this perspective, the 'world music' category is mostly a convenient euphemism for musics from Third World countries, which hides the imbalances and uneven power relations implicit in the so-called 'dialogue' between different musical cultures (Taylor, 1997: 6). The category of world music in fact simply promotes 'an old binary of "the west" and "the rest", putting hugely diverse bodies of musics into the same box' in record stores (Taylor, 1997: 14). The marketing of world music presents an Other that is exotic, sensual, mystical and attractive (Perna, 1996: 105; Guilbault, 2001: 178), yet such marketing is informed by a neo-colonial sensibility that is only apparently embracing of Otherness (Loosely, 2003: 53). The bottom-line involves profit margins, and so whilst world music marketing creates an exotic Other, it also seeks to render that exoticism domesticated and safe for Western consumption (Byrne, 1999). The result is 'consumer-friendly multiculturalism' (Feld, 2000: 168), which actually involves the exploitative use of the cultures of oppressed minorities for 'the nourishment and enrichment of an entrenched Anglo-centric power base' (Mitchell, 1993: 325).

For critics of world music, the 'rough edges' that Western listeners might discern in certain 'ethnic musics' could jeopardise sales potential, and thus the 'subtleties and complexities of indigenous musics have to be neutered to fit the regular pulse of pop and appeal to the jaded Western appetites which the majors [record companies] and FM radio have produced' (Loosely, 2003: 53; also Hesmondhalgh, 1998: 171; Guilbault, 1993). Consequently, musical 'authenticity' is 'reduced to packaged exoticism for musical tourists' (Feld, 2000: 152; Loosely, 2003: 53). In particular, world music fusion projects can be as seen as encouraging the loss of distinctive ethno-musical identities, thus contributing not to dynamic new musical forms but actually towards a decline in musical diversity across the world (Gardinier, 1991).

In the same vein, instead of being beneficial to non-Western artists, the world music industry could be seen as actually working against their interests. Western stars and record companies can exploit the labours of non-Western musicians, failing to pay them at full rates or not giving them full acknowledgement and copyright entitlements on recordings (Meintjes, 1994; Horner and Swiss, 2003: 231). Although some critics of world music fear the loss of musical 'authenticity', others regard it as a discursive trope that is used by that industry to enforce a certain conformity on musicians. A Western desire for musical 'authenticity' can be forced upon Third World musicians, with both the record industry and world music audiences demanding they 'keep it real' and stick to 'indigenous' musical forms only (Byrne, 1999). This was indeed the fate of Youssou N'Dour, whose album with Peter Gabriel was seen by music critics and audiences as 'too Westernized' and he was dropped by the Virgin record label as a result soon after (Broughton, 2000: 133).

The ambivalences of world music

Beyond these rather polarised positions as to the alleged beneficence or perfidiousness of the world music phenomenon, sociological analysis would, we argue, be more productively focused on the ambivalences – musical, cultural, social, economic, and political – inherent in the condition of world music today. We must recognise that world music is a thoroughly contradictory entity, attended by debates and polemics where 'assertions of altruism and generosity appear as frequently as accusations of [cultural] cannibalism and colonialism' (Feld, 1994: 271) and where simultaneously 'tropes of anxiety and celebration' are to be found, creating a discursive field where the idea of 'the diversity of world music – its promise' coexists with 'the spectre of one world music – its antithesis' (Feld, 2000: 153, 154). Only by concentrating on the ambiguities within the whole socio-cultural-economic complex that is 'world music' can the nuances of the relations between world music and globalization really be discerned.

It is indeed the case that one must look at world music as a sub-system within the wider system of music recording and distribution. When looked at in this macro-level way, we see that the vast majority (more than 90% in 1994) of gross world-wide sales of recorded music come from albums, singles and videos owned or distributed by six multinational corporations: Philips, Sony, Matsushita, Thorn-EMI, Bertelsmann and Time-Warner (the slogan of the latter corporation is, fittingly enough, 'The world is our audience'). The music industry is therefore characterised by the commercial dominance of American, East Asian and European corporations (Hesmondhalgh, 1998: 172–73) Thus records made by United States artists account for more than 50% of world-wide sales each year (Burnett, 1996: 2, 4).

However, the specific case of world music cannot simply be interpreted as an instance of 'cultural imperialism', whereby one region's culture, musical or otherwise, comes to dominate particular 'local cultures' (Tomlinson, 1997). This is because although large corporations and their subsidiaries have sought to promote both particular 'ethnic musics' and 'fusions', they do not fully control the world music market. To a certain extent, the main players in the world music sub-system are smaller, independent recording companies, primarily although not exclusively based in metropolitan centres like London, Paris and New York (Stokes, 2003). These companies are often owned and run by people with left-liberal sympathies, who are acutely aware of the problems of cultural imperialism and exploitation involved in making world music. Although they have to conform to what are perceived as the demands of the market (the need for 'exoticism' and 'authenticity') to some degree, they also often seek to struggle against these tendencies, attempting to produce styles of music that are what they would see as culturally sensitive and non-imperialistic (Hesmondhalgh, 2000). Thus we are not always dealing simply with producers hell bent on commodifying any and all musics at any price, for oftentimes those running world music labels are acutely reflexively aware of the musical and more general cultural dilemmas that face them as they seek to reconcile the potentially contradictory desiderata of making money and cultivating musics they them-selves appreciate and admire. Moreover, as we noted above there are also recording companies based in certain Third World locales like Jamaica and they have some input into what styles of music are recorded and distributed in wider trans-national networks (Stokes, 2003: 301). As a result, world music is not *wholly* based around a centre-periphery, West-Third World, exploiter-exploited structure, and thus its products cannot simply be evaluated as expressions solely of Western power.

Moreover, as Goodwin and Gore (1990) note, while the production of world music is structured around the hegemony of Western production companies, the results of that production are not themselves *necessarily* hegemonic too. The overall phenomenon of world music production, distribution and consumption is too complex for any outcomes to be guaranteed in advance. In terms of the activities of particular musicians, while some may be regarded as 'selling out' by accepting contracts from Western companies, it may also be the case that in so doing they both contribute towards changing what is regarded as 'mainstream' Western music (Guilbault, 2001: 178) and get to promote anti-hegemonic political messages, about Third World debt and other issues, in front of Western audiences (Lipsitz, 1994: 14). Moreover, while world music production might eventually consign certain genres to the museum of music, it also involves not only the creation of new hybrid forms but also the revitalisation of certain genres hitherto neglected in their places of origin (Guilbault, 2001: 280).

In terms of audiences, while more empirical work needs to be done on the reception of world music forms by particular social groups, it seems to be the case that there are ambivalent features, in this case of listening practices, present here too. In one way, we are clearly dealing with a case of 'sonic tourism' (Taylor, 1997: 19; Frith, 2000: 308), whereby (primarily) middle class, well-educated, politically liberal and leftist, well-travelled, middle aged people with relatively high levels of economic and cultural capital get to revel in a form of global musical eclecticism and bricolage (Taylor, 1997: 202). They are each in search of a special identity for themselves achieved by displaying 'non-mainstream...eclectic or unusual tastes' (Taylor, 1997: 20). As Fock (Cited in Ling, 2003) puts it, world music can be seen as 'the middle-aged, middle class harmless flirtation with the strange' (also Ling, 2003; Hesmondhalgh, 1998: 175). Such people can be construed of as 'jaded Westerners' (Lipsitz, 1994: 11) who are in search of 'new' sounds that seem less tired or corrupted than standard Western forms (Taylor, 1997: 20). Such people seek in music a sense of 'community' that their own highly indvidualized existences lack, and project their desires onto other places and cultures, deemed to be more 'alive', 'spontaneous', 'spiritual' and so on (Fairley, 2001: 274).

Yet at the same time, the existence of world music, and its popularity amongst certain strata in Western societies, is irreducible to forms of status and distinction. It is also the case that world music is both expressive of, and has helped to constitute, new groups of listeners 'who are receptive to culturally different genres' in ways that their parents and grandparents were not (Robinson et al., 1991: 272). If we examine the cultural preferences of these people, we see that their listening habits are no longer reflective of an organic cultural totality, for their tastes are too 'global' and eclectic to be expressive of a particular delimited national community any more (Erlmann, 1993: 12; Fairley, 2001: 282). The artists and audiences associated with world music cannot fully be defined by national boundaries What the sociology of culture has to engage with when dealing with world music is 'the often powerful attraction people feel for music that they did not grow up with or to which they have no direct sense of connection through "heritage"' (Slobin, 1994: 247). Why such attractions arise, and how they are made possible, is what must be investigated. It may well be the case that coexisting with the use of world music as a cultural distinction strategy to delineate one's superior musical knowledge and aesthetic tastes, is a certain consciousness of the whole of humankind being part of a totality brought about in part by processes of globalization. World music may be fostering among certain social groups, in no doubt somewhat fragmentary and hesitant ways, a sense of a 'global community' (Pacini, 1993) of artists and audiences united in a love of certain sounds and the sentiments they embody. This is a sensibility that encourages to some degree a cosmopolitan 'planetary identity' (Leymarie, 1991) where the individual is made aware through musical means of the ties that bind them to people in far-off parts of the world.

Quite simply, then, whereas world music might be made in conditions characterised more (but not exclusively) by exploitation and First World power, the *effects* it has in different parts of the world, including in the West, are not necessarily understandable in those terms alone. The methodological lesson to be drawn here is that one can only understand the nuances of this particular realm of cultural endeavour if one examines in detail both the 'production' and 'consumption' of world music and the interrelations between them; what happens in the one sphere does not necessarily indicate what occurs in the other.

Conclusion

In this chapter we have sought to outline certain ways in which the sociology of art and culture can seek to 'go global' in terms of its analytic reach. By taking the example of world music, and by examining its history and pre-history, its modes of social organisation, the polemics that have been waged over it, and the ambivalences that we take to be at its heart, we have intended to demonstrate some ways in which a 'global sociology' of art and culture might develop. The key elements that we suggest such a programme might involve are: (1) an awareness of 'trans-national' cultural processes in historical periods prior to modernity, thus avoiding naïve presentist judgements which assert that 'global' phenomena are strictly of very recent provenance; (2) a commitment to analysing the complex interconnections that pertain at any particular point in time between 'global', 'local' and 'glocal' (and 'hybrid' and 'creole') aesthetic and cultural phenomena and forces on the one hand, and social, political and economic networks and systems of worldwide, regional and national reach on the other (Robertson, 1995); (3) an analytic orientation that desists from over-hasty polemical judgements about the 'goodness' or 'badness' of certain phenomena, in favour of a desire to tease out the complexities and nuances that we take to be characteristic of a globalizing world.

Given that this general modus operandi has informed our delineation and analysis of the world music arena, we can conclude that the latter is both reflective of, has been constituted by, and has in turn helped to constitute, wider processes of globalization in their various cultural, social, political and economic manifestations. World music is emblematic of the current global condition as it is quite 'as complicated as the rest of contemporary cultural life', if not more so (Lipsitz, 1994: 16). The world music phenomenon is indicative of both cultural homogenisation (Nettl, 1985: 85, 164–65) and heterogenisation (Robinson et al., 1991: 4, 227, 237, 248). As Robinson et al. (1991: 276) phrase it, one of the central paradoxes of this thoroughly paradoxical realm is that in the present day, 'music has become increasingly experimental and fragmented while at the same time its once diverse and exotic elements are becoming more widely familiar, more accepted and more predictable'. If sociology is not to betray the empirical phenomena characteristic of a globalizing world condition, it must seek to be as alive and as sensitive as possible to the ambiguities and ambivalences that are at the core of that state of affairs.

NOTE

1. Beyond the realms of 'popular music', Western 'art music' also has a 'global history'. As Ling (2003: 236) argues, Western classical music was a sort of 'world music for Europeans in the eighteenth century, as the same operas and concertos were performed all across the continent'. Western classical forms spread all across the world, either directly through imperial expansion or by more indirect means, taking especially strong root in countries such as China and Japan (Kraus, 1989).

'High Arts' and the Market: An Uneasy Partnership in the Transnational World of Ballet

Helena Wulff

> When I first got into the company, people said:
> 'Oh, its Friday! Payday!!'
> It used to shock me –
> I just didn't connect art with money!

Introduction

In the ballet world, the market tends to be regarded with ambivalence. Ballet people are disturbed by the belief that the market wants to buy other 'commodities' than they are prepared to sell, that is, unforgettable experiences of ballet art. For the audience, on the other hand, the milieux of gilded opera foyers and the opportunity to rub shoulders with famous people in the intermission may be what matters.

This chapter discusses the market in the ballet world by applying a transnational perspective which uncovers both homogenizing and heterogenizing cultural processes produced by similarities in work practices and differences in funding systems. One centre and periphery structure in the ballet world follows transnational economic domination patterns through American corporate sponsoring, but there is also a separate structure of old and new ballet centres, which negates much rhetoric about globalization, especially in terms of an American domination of cultural life.

This chapter is based on material from an anthropological study of career and culture of the transnational world of ballet (see Wulff, 1998). It was conducted by way of participant observation and interviews over almost two years between 1993 and 1996 mainly with three national classical ballet companies: the Royal Swedish Ballet in Stockholm, the Royal Ballet in London, the American Ballet Theatre in New York, and also the contemporary company Ballett Frankfurt in Franfurt-am-Main. For discussion of the methodological issues that arose in this study (see Wulff, 2000).

The emergence of the transnational ballet world – politics, mentors, patrons[1]

Ballet came about in the fourteenth century at Italian courts, as a pastime for the entertainment of noble families. They took part in a dance form which combined peasant folk dancing and court processions. In the sixteenth century, the Florentine Catherine de Medici was married to the French Crown Prince Henry. Because of de Medici's interest in lavish entertainment, and her position at the court in Paris, she invited and supported Italian musicians and dance teachers, among them Balthasar de Beaujoyeux, who created what has come to be regarded as the first ballet production, *Ballet Comique de la Reine*. But it was King Louis XIV, an ardent ballet lover and dancer who began a professionalization of ballet by organizing training academies and commercial theatres. The eighteenth century saw ballet companies in other European countries as well. Yet it was in Paris in the early nineteenth century that classical ballet was set into the particular form of etherealness by which it is still often characterized. This happened when Swedish-Italian Marie Taglioni danced *La Sylphide* on pointe in 1832 to great acclaim, dressed in a delicate bell-shaped tutu. Taglioni had a Danish partner, August Bournonville, who was to develop a particular ballet style in Copenhagen. Meanwhile in St Petersburg, the French dancer Marius Petipa choreographed classics such as *The Sleeping Beauty, Swan Lake* (in collaboration with Lev Ivanov), and some of *The Nutcracker*.

In the beginning of the twentieth century, Russian culture did not attract any particular interest in Europe, but French art and lifestyle were greatly admired in Russia. As France and Russia were becoming political allies against Germany, artistic exchange between the two countries was encouraged and funded by both governments. It was during this time that Sergei Diaghilev set up the Ballets Russes, which gave annual seasons in Paris and went on tours mostly to London and New York. Because of the revolution in 1917, Diaghilev never went back to Russia. George Balanchine, who worked as a choreographer with Ballets Russes, was approached by Lincoln Kirstein, an American writer from a wealthy family, about setting up the School of American Ballet in New York, which they did together, as well as the New York City Ballet in the 1940s. By then the American Ballet Theatre had already been operating in New York for about a decade. One of the Ballets Russes dancers, Anglo-Irish Ninette de Valois, was to found a national ballet company in Britain, which became the Royal Ballet in London in the 1950s. Thereby the five old ballet centres – Paris, Copenhagen, St Petersburg, New York, and London – were established. They all acquired transnational reputations based on their different schools, which have been conceptualized in terms of 'national ballet styles' seemingly expressing the essence of the national characters, as it were. There are thus the 'chic' French, the 'cute' Danish, the 'dramatic' Russian, the 'athletic' American, and the 'reserved' British ballet styles. There was also an Italian ballet style coming out of Milan, but it has never been identified as a national ballet style, possibly because Italy is still not really united as nation.

World politics, financial patrons and impressarios such as Diaghilev and Kirstein who were driven by a passion for ballet, and artistic mentors who tend to be forceful individuals and choreographers, have thus built and structured ballet since its inception. Many of the influential figures in the ballet world have been foreigners working abroad, sometimes in political exile, a circumstance which seems to have released a creative energy which they probably would not have had the opportunity to cultivate in their native countries. This also applies to those contemporary choreographers who have come to establish new centres for ballet and dance. There are thus, for example, Americans John Neumeier in Hamburg and William Forsythe in Frankfurt-am-Main, the Czech Jiri Kylián in the Hague, as well as French Maurice Béjart who has worked in Brussels and Lausanne.

The historical association of ballet with court life and the upper classes is still being nurtured in the world of national classical ballet where the companies have patrons and trustees, often drawn from royal families and the nobility. There are also ballet societies and friendship circles with a base in the upper classes that have been important for building audiences, and still often contribute financial support, as well.

Market, ballet and distrust

Dancers are hardly unique among artists for regarding the market with unease and distrust. In the art world, the market is often regarded as a threat to genuine artistic quality, since artists who are aiming towards getting a reputation feel that they have to make accommodations to the market, which they would rather not do. Bensman (1983: 27) traces 'the familiar devils of economics' in the arts back to the church, the aristocracy, the dynastic and national states and their religious, political and national ambitions. The development of the performing arts in the nineteenth century can be attributed both to mass audiences and national and municipal governments states. During the latter half of the twentieth century, the performing arts have become dependent on the welfare state, which, however, as Bensman says, may produce crises if such support is discontinued. Bourdieu (1993a) notes that with the emergence of an art market, artists did get rid of the demands of patrons, but found themselves having to negotiate with commercial interests. Ballet 'art' versus the market was a common topic of conversation in the ballet world during my fieldwork, usually in terms of an opposition: ballet *against* market.

A part of the dancers' distrust of the market included their own marketing and press departments. The dancers more often than not criticized the marketing of their company for being inefficient. At one point in Stockholm, the dancers asked the head of the marketing department at the Opera House to come to a meeting and explain why she did not market them more. She had then defended herself by saying that 'ballet doesn't need any marketing. It sells itself'. This obviously angered the dancers who then formed their own press group aiming to give advice to the marketing department about how to market ballet. But the tension remained. To me, the marketing lady confessed in private that 'ballet is difficult to sell' referring to the shortage of money and staff, and that only a fraction of all the press releases that are sent out are published.

The dancers wanted to open up the company and back-stage life to the world outside the theatre, so as to attract a wider audience. Other strategies in this vein included the broadcasting of trailers of upcoming performances on television, the selling of cheap tickets at hotels, and giving performances in schools. Most of the companies in my study had done parts or all of this at some point. In order to reach new audiences, it also happened that the marketing departments wanted dancers to perform in shopping malls, department stores, on cruises, as well as outdoors on open air stages in parks in the summer. During my fieldwork, the English Royal Ballet and Covent Garden got a lot of bad press. This was before the renovation of the opera house had began, and the battles over power and funding were intense, as was the criticism of Covent Garden as 'elitist'. As a way to mellow the criticism, a BBC team was allowed to make a backstage television documentary, *The House*, which revealed mismanagement and animosities between people in key positions at the opera house. Such embarrassing revelations did, however, I was told by one of the ballet producers, only increase the ticket sales.

Although dancers have a basic distrust of marketing, they understand that it is unavoidable. They do need to be prepared, however, especially when there is media involved. This is not always the case such as one grey January morning when a television crew, with their huge bags and bulky equipment stumbled into the class of the American Ballet Theatre. If the dancers had been informed in advance they would had the time to put on nicer practice clothes and perhaps some make up, some of them would probably even have stayed away since they were out of shape after the Christmas holiday. Now they were moaning quietly, trying not to show their discomfort with the strong spotlights and the camera men zooming in on one dancer at a time who in turn struggled to look good.

One important explanation as to why dancers have a problem with marketing is thus that it is more often than not done through the media which rarely convey pictures, video or text about ballet or ballet culture in ways that dancers recognize: 'Watching themselves on video, dancers note that the dancing does not look from the outside like it feels from the inside while doing it' (Wulff, 1998: 9). They rarely think that they are at their best on pictures or on film. Many times, dancers pointed out to me that something gets lost in mediated ballet. Even though photography, film, video, text and Internet materials on dance may be imaginative and interesting pieces of art in themselves, they cannot represent or create the vibrating closeness including a certain amount of unpredictability of a live performance. So much can happen in a live performance, not only can things go wrong and mistakes be made, but inspired by the presence of a receptive audience, unimaginable ballet art might be born on stage.

The marketing department at the American Ballet Theatre claims to be the first company to have been doing 'aggressive marketing'. This included both illustrated newspaper articles and advertisements, posters in town, features on television and radio at the beginning of a new season, or a tour and gimmicks like famous dancers dancing on paint on a canvas which was then sold as a piece of art. On a tour to Chicago, dancers were dancing a section from Swan Lake at 8 a.m. at the zoo with real swans in the background, which was filmed and broadcast on local television. The alleged 'aggressiveness' of the American Ballet Theatre was to a great deal a product of the competition and conflict with the other major New York company, the New York City Ballet. This tension runs especially high once a year, in the spring when the American Ballet Theatre has its eight weeks 'Met Season' at the Metropolitan Opera House next door to the State Theatre of the New York City Ballet at Lincoln Center. There was, however, a certain regret at the marketing department of the American Ballet Theatre, over the good times during the 1970s. This was during the height of the 'dance boom' and people who did not have a special interest in dance or ballet went to ballet performances. New York was called 'the Mecca of dance', attracting dance and ballet people from all over the world. Some of these people, such as Mikhail Baryshnikov came from the Soviet Union and defected, which meant a huge media coverage and thereby publicity for ballet. This also happened, although to a lesser extent, in Paris and London. The most famous ballet defector to Paris is undoubtedly Rudolf Nureyev who became a permanent guest artist with the Royal Ballet and eventually artistic director of the Paris Opéra Ballet.

It was Nureyev who discovered Sylvie Guillem when she was a young corps de ballet dancer, gave her the opportunity to do solo parts and made her an 'étoile' at age nineteen. Now a principal guest artist with the Royal Ballet for a long time, Sylvie Guillem has certainly established a name for herself, quite independently of the companies she has worked with. She is a good example of individual marketing by contrast with marketing of the whole company, which are different and often conflicting endeavours. In a widespread advertisement for Rolex watches, Guillem does her celebrated routine of raising her leg straight up almost above her head, illustrating 'six o'clock'. Famous dancers have agents who arrange guest performances for them, often abroad, given that they are skilled enough at negotiating about time off from their company schedule. Agents also look for openings in other companies for dancers, which can be used in negotiations for higher salary or more performances in the company a dancer is in. This primarily applies to those who have transnational fame, some of whom develop quite sophisticated marketing strategies by nurturing the media (including critics) through free tickets, invitations to dress rehearsals, parties, even weddings and other more private functions. Some dancers would not mind launching themselves on this kind of 'celebrity' market, but they prefer to keep a low profile because they do not feel particularly comfortable at rock concerts or fashion shows. They may also be reluctant to announce that they are gay, which is a circumstance which is likely to be revealed were they to join the glitterati circuit.

There are slightly different markets for ballet dancers depending on whether they have an intellectual inclination such as Sylvie Guillem and Deborah Bull, or celebrity capital such as Darcey Bussell, all acclaimed ballerinas with the Royal Ballet. Sylvie Guillem has arranged her own video titled evidentia, which was originally made for television. In this video she introduces five new dance pieces, some of them by major contemporary choreographers, by dancing a short section of alternative choreography and talking about life and dance. Both Deborah Bull (1999) and Darcey Bussell (1998) have published autobiographies, although the one by Bussell is said to be 'with Judith Mackrell', a London dance critic. Bussell's book is a rather conventional ballet autobiography about the ups and downs of a prominent ballet career including an account of when she had a wax model made of her at Madame Tussauds and her subsequent shock when she learnt that the model (herself, in a sense) would only be kept in case her career was going well. If not, it would be melted down! Bull's (1999) autobiography is a more outspoken diary of one of the recent turbulent years at Covent Garden, from which she also read some extracts on BBC radio.

Otherwise the marketing of ballet companies is predictably done according to casting. Dancers the management want to promote or keep on top, get to do leading roles and are then offered to journalists for interviews for advance features in the press (daily newspapers, dance magazines) and on chat shows on television and radio. It is likely that this focussing on one dancer at a time and his or her personal biography, just like the marketing done by famous individual dancers outside the company, is more efficient when it comes to attracting a new audience to ballet than when companies are presented as one collective, but more anonymous, entity. One way to cultivate a sense of community in the ballet companies is the policy to post positive reviews and feature articles about the company on noticeboards backstage, but not articles about one dancer only.

When Darcey Bussell appeared in a headshot with a diamond in her mouth in The Tatler, she was doing it in her capacity as a celebrity promoting herself primarily and ballet in general secondarily, but not really her company. It is not unusual that dancers, both men and women do modelling, but often they do it anonymously. Occasionally, dancers are asked to take part in regular advertisements promoting all kind of products from mineral water to credit cards and airlines, as well as sports wear often displaying a characteristic ballet step which most people cannot perform, or just jumping upwards like Swedish dancer Anneli Alhanko did in an advertisement saying 'milk makes your legs strong'. In the 1970s, Anneli Alhanko and her partner Per Arthur Segerström had their picture on a Swedish stamp, since Alhanko especially was hailed as an outstanding ballerina. To some extent Alhanko's recognition should be seen in the context of the new transnational awareness of ballet and dance which the dance boom in London and New York at the time had created.

Besides the crucial ballet performance, there are a number of smaller commodities, or cultural artefacts, that circulate in the ballet marketplace, and contribute to 'selling' ballet in general, a particular company, a certain tour, or a star dancer. These are commercial videos, CD records, books, postcards, t-shirts, cups, umbrellas, posters, even jewellery and other souvenirs that are for sale at box offices, stalls in the theatres, and ballet wear and book shops. They also display point shoes, an object of great fetishism in the ballet world, worn and signed by famous dancers (cf. Wulff, 2002). There are ballet and dance CD-ROMs such as William Forsythe's *Improvisation Technologies or Self Meant to Govern*, an 'installation' from 1994, which is both an art work and an introduction to Forsythe's choreographic ballet style, at the same time as it promotes Forsythe as a choreographer (cf. Wulff, 2003 on dance and technology).

The greatest dancer: Nureyev and his market

Even after their death dancers can be major agents on the ballet market. Those who have really made it as choreographers have their ballets held in trusts such as the Balanchine Trust, although the leading dancers on whom a choreography was first made, may inherit the performance rights (see Wulff, 1998). When Rudolf Nureyev died in 1993 a number of European and American foundations were established from his enormous fortune, also aiming to provide funding for young dancers, a museum in Paris, and to support dancers with AIDS. Born a poor Tartar boy in Stalinist Russia, Nureyev had, against all possible odds, not only a brillant career in the West, but he also amassed a vast amount of wealth. At a Christie's auction in New York, art works and furnishings from his New York flat, as well as jewellery and costumes he had worn were sold at $7,945,910, which was regarded as extraordinary by the chairman of Christie's America. The record sale was explained by 'Nureyev's personal magnetism and with Christie's ability to market him' (Gladstone, 1995: 21). This transnational event took place in Park Avenue in two halls where art collectors, dancers and fans had gathered. A jacket from the ballet *Don Quixote* was sold for $32,000. One pair of pink worn out ballet shoes was sold for $8000. 'Amazing – for sombody else's', i.e. used ballet shoes, the lady next to me, an ex-dancer, commented.

Much has been written in the press and in popular biographies about Nureyev, his life and his fortune. Dance and theatre writer Otis Stuart (1995) devotes a chapter to 'The Nureyev Industry', mentioning the fact that Nureyev had seven homes including an island. Nureyev was excellent at marketing himself both in the ballet world, and outside, which importantly reflected back on his position in the ballet world, increasing his prestige there. Stuart points at the impact of Nureyev's two advisors: one impressario on career matters and one financial advisor on business matters. Dance anthropologists such as Judith Lynne Hanna (1988: 143) have commented how the flamboyant Rudolf Nureyev captured ballet audiences and made 'big bucks' thereby earning respect, as well as improving the status of the male dancer. Writing about another Soviet defector who also has made a lot of money, Mikhail Baryshnikov, dance historian Joan Cass (1993) describes how Baryshnikov came to New York in the mid-1970s, and I would add was to acquire celebrity capital, not least by acting in films and on Broadway, and even promoting a line of perfume and cosmetics.

Marketing is one area of heterogeneity in the transnational ballet world. The Royal Swedish Ballet at the Opera House in Stockholm had been instructed to democratize the audience as a part of a governmental agenda to 'make culture accessible for all citizens irrespective of age, home locality, income or social position'. Written in 1974, during the aftermath of the 1960s radical political ideology, but before the commercial boom of the 1980s and subsequent conservative turn, this resolution of the Swedish Parliament stated that 'commercial considerations were not to control what was being offered' (Sandström, 1993: 2). This was before corporate sponsoring was accepted at the Stockholm Opera.

In line with Bourdieu's (1993a) reasoning, the marketing departments at the Royal Swedish Ballet, as well as at the American Ballet Theatre, were working to remove ballet from its field of 'restricted production', which is that of the cultural elite, and towards a field of large-scale production. The latter is less prestigious and succumbs to market forces, but such commercial art can, as Becker (1984) has pointed out in fact foster a versatile craftmanship in order to meet all kinds of demands. The field of restricted production is also connected to a market, but of a different, smaller kind. So is the experimental alternative contemporary work of William Forsythe, taking place within yet another field of restricted production although at the same time linked to the exclusivity of classical ballet, since Forsythe's pieces are danced by classical dancers at many opera houses, among them Covent Garden and the Stockholm Opera.

The exchange: Ballet and business

Private, corporate and foundation sponsorship of ballet is well established in New York and London where it follows the pattern in other art forms. It is not at all as prominent in Frankfurt, and rather marginal in Stockholm at least compared to the hundreds of sponsors and donors in New York and London. Tours, guest performances, new productions and revivals, awards including scholarships for young dancers to train and work with renowned teachers and choreographers abroad, are taking place because of sponsoring mostly from business corporations. They produce various commodities such as cigarettes, liqueur and matches, automobiles, but also cosmetics, designer fashion and even pharmaceutical appliances. Breweries and banks have moreover provided tax-reducible support. Some of these corporations, an American cigarette corporation, for example, operate transnationally both in their business and in their ballet sponsoring. Importantly, this means that representatives of an American cigarette corporation have an impact on the social organization of the transnational ballet world in terms of the distribution of awards and scholarships, as well as what companies will come on tour to the United States and their choice of repertory. By sponsoring ballet, this cigarrette corporation can also be said to try to compensate, gain morally as it were, for the fact that it is making a product that is dangerous to people's health.

As a part of the exchange between sponsors and the ballet world, sponsors also appropriate some cultural capital. Sponsorship is one way to legitimate wealth. A circumstance that tends to be left out in social anaysis of ballet is the paradox that many dancers do not possess very much cultural capital from their upbringings, and that backstage the ballet world is far from an upper class institution. In fact, dancers often feel trapped between cultural capital and the market, out of place in both of them.

One element in the exchange between sponsors and the ballet world, is that corporations and private donors are invited to dress rehearsals, premieres, receptions and dinners where they get the opportunity to meet the dancers. The latter, on the other hand, tend to be rather uncomfortable about these encounters. Post-performance banquets take place when the dancers are exhausted from dancing and acting for three hours. They often feel that they put on an act when they have to answer well-meaning but uninformed questions about their dancing, diet and career, especially why they started to dance, over and over again. Expensively dressed donors and their guests make conversations to the dancers, who often find themselves embarrassed by the fact that they do not remember these people who behave as if they have met before which they most likely have, at a previous banquet. This polite 'acting' of the dancers at marketing occasions like this, is talked about in the ballet world in terms of 'spielen' or 'it's all theatre, anyway'. Private donors who the dancers and the management get acquainted with are often respected, even liked, but this is not necessarily the case when it comes to representatives of corporations who can be the target of ridicule, especially by a dancer, a choreographer or even a ballet director who has just made an effort to charm them. As Ostrower (1995: 135) points out, wealthy donors tend to have a commitment to the organizations they give large sums of money, but that they 'do keep their distance, and remain apart', which confirms my observations of dancers' experience of meeting those kinds of people.

In general, established dancers or those who were on their way upwards in their career were more favourably inclined to marketing than those who felt that they were in a bad patch, or even realized that they would not get any further than they were now, which usually meant downhill to minor roles, corps work for soloists, and so-called 'walking roles' i.e. kings and queens who hardly dance at all. George Balanchine, the Russian choreographer in New York, expressed his sense that marketing ballet was important, yet a nuisance, by saying: 'you have to go everywhere, give interviews, attend receptions. It's all terrible and tiring. And then you think: after all, it's for the theater, that means it's important, it's good' (Volkov, 1986: 59).

It is significant that the very apex of the donors are on boards of ballet companies and opera houses, and thus have a say about ballet politics in terms of repertory, casting, tours and appointments. It is common that donors and corporations that have given large sums of money to a ballet company, in some cases over the course of many years, have certain seats and boxes reserved for them at every performance. There are special lists and advertisments of names of private, corporate and foundation sponsors in the ballet programmes, including the piece of information that a certain number 'wish to remain anonymous'. Those who have donated most substantially get their names engraved on brass plates that are exhibited in the foyers of theatres and opera houses. Ballet sponsoring also involves anecdotes like the one about the wealthy Chicago lady, Mrs Becky D'Angelo who commissioned the Joffrey ballet to do the ballet titled *Birthday Variations* as a birthday present for her husband (Drell, 1995).

Ballet needs marketing structures to survive and develop, and there is, again, no doubt that the importance of marketing is recognized in the ballet world. Nevertheless the unease with ballet on the market remains. Stuart Plattner (1996: 197) has suggested with reference to painters: 'high-art producers live in a value system that is conflicted, not to say schizophrenic, about the importance of selling work'. This was most pronounced in Sweden with its traditionally large public sector spending on education, health care and indeed the arts. The Royal Swedish Ballet is primarily state-subsidized. It happened that the unease with ballet on the market came up at the contemporary Ballett Frankfurt which also relies mostly on state-subsidy, but almost never at the Royal Ballet where sponsorship is much more developed, and hardly ever at the American Ballet Theatre, the only company which was funded by sponsorship except for a very small percentage. Although dancers are anxious to widen the audience and include all classes, they are reluctant to become a part of the artistic field of large-scale production (Bourdieu, 1993a) because of the alleged impact of commercial forces there. Ballet companies are sometimes concerned that they are linked to business corporations that are accused of 'polluting the environment, making unhealthy products or exploiting their employees' (Wulff, 1998: 54). The crux of the matter for ballet companies is that they would not be able to survive without sponsoring. This is so even for those companies that are mostly state-subsidized, since that funding is not enough.

Conclusion: Ballet in the global marketplace

Although the ballet world has been transnational since Catherine de Medici invited Italian musicians and dance teachers to Paris, the amount and density of communication between ballet centres such as London, New York and Frankfurt-am-Main and peripheries such as Stockholm, have escalated through intensified touring and guest performances, but also through ballet competitions, festivals, and the fact that dancers go abroad to train and work for a few years with other companies. Ballet in media such as video, photography, television, the Internet, CD-ROMs, as well as international press and dance magazines are important for transnational connectivity in the ballet world (Wulff, 1998).

This article has discussed ballet in the global marketplace, both ballet and its market being Western systems that operate globally even outside the scope of Euro-America. Although I have used the concept 'the market' in singular here in order to signify a transnational entity, it is moored to certain places: old national and new choreographic ballet centres and peripheries. The ballet world is generically transnational with 'a consciousness of the world as a whole' (Robertson, 1992: 8) coming up on a daily basis backstage. Yet my research goes against the idea that globalization and transnationality neces-sarily necessarily imply total deterritorialization. It is noteworthy that the transnational ballet market in fact consists of multiple interrelated markets, that are distinguished in the first place by different *national* funding systems and *national* ballet cultures, that in their turn are composed of a vast number of other markets. Those individual actors, famous dancers such as Rudolf Nureyev and Sylvie Guillem, who learn how to create their own markets, do in fact also increase the demand for ballet in the global marketplace.

Contrary to much rhetoric about globalization, the ballet world is not controlled from America. Ballet came about in Europe, and Paris and London are still influential ballet centres, as is Frankfurt-am-Main. Yet, as I have argued, when it comes to the market, the American ballet companies are the most 'aggressive'. While the European companies in this study are more or less state-subsidized, the American Ballet Theatre gets almost all its funding from corporate and private sponsors. This does not only mean that business repre-sentatives and private donors have an impact on repertory, appointments, and tours at the American Ballet Theatre, but since American corporations also contribute to European ballet in the form of awards and support of tours, there is a certain American *influence* on European ballet but not outright domination.

Despite the unease with ballet in the marketplace, from the ballet world's point of view, ballet people develop strategies to relate to the market, to perform promotion, sometimes with regret, sometimes with triumph, feeling that they can manage the market for their purposes, rather than having passively to submit to its demands. Dancers distrust the market primarily because there is a disagreement over the definition of how the commodity, such as a single performance, should be defined. For the dancers it is the quality of the performance that matters, they want the audience to be 'mesmerized' and 'to go home and really remember', while the audience may well appreciate the performance, but it may be in the theatre for additional reasons other than watching ballet. A great part of the audience, including private and corporate sponsors and donors, buy ballet in order to legitimate economic capital with cultural capital. In her study of the special case of elite philanthropy in the United States, Ostrower (1995: 12) found that such donors explain their giving in terms of 'an obligation that is part of their privileged position', but that they engage in it mindful of the prestige it can win them in the eyes of their peers.

At the heart of this situation is the fundamental difference which dancers perceive between an experience of ballet 'art' and the mechanisms of the market. Dancers realize that an experience of ballet art will not happen to the audience, nor the dancers, without the market, neither will it happen during every performance or throughout one performance. Since such exceptional moments cannot be ordered – they happen unexpectedly and irregularly – it is impossible to buy them in advance. Finally, it is interesting to note, in view of dancers' unease with the market, that Jacques Maquet (1979: 9) in his discussion of when an object becomes an art object, concludes that: 'In our society a first criterion, crude but fairly accurate, of art is access to the art market. Objects belonging to that network are art objects'. This is to say that ballet companies, stars, and performances, that are in demand in the global marketplace do have capacities to move and to touch audiences, but these capacities are to a large degree mediated through, and made possible by, market mechanisms.

NOTE

1. See mostly Wulff (1998), but also Cass (1993), and in a few instances Robertson and Hutera (1990), as well as Sorell (1981).

Reconstructing the Centre: Sociological Approaches to the Rebuilding of Berlin

13

Janet Stewart

Introduction

Throughout the 1990s, Berlin has been a city obsessed with architectural and planning issues. There has been a myriad of publications, exhibitions, radio broadcasts, television programmes and films on the 'New Berlin', many of which focus on the reconstruction of the area around the renovated Reichstag and of Potsdamer Platz. Architects, architectural historians, urban planners, cultural historians, sociologists and others have been drawn to Berlin, fascinated by the chance to experience at first hand the massive reconstruction of a European capital city for the twenty-first century, itself a consequence of the dramatic events of 1989, which were signified most poignantly by the fall of the Berlin wall. Although the symbolic re-ordering of space taking place in Berlin is still an 'unfinished project', the architecture of 'New Berlin' has come to be seen as a test case for the role and nature of architecture at the millennium and beyond. As Davey (1999a: 28) puts it:

> For all its problems, Berlin is the world's most potent crucible of thought about the nature of cities. With vast expenditure of wealth, the richest nation in Europe has generated projects designed to knit the fractured metropolis together [...]. They have much to teach.

The caution expressed in this passage, however, turns into pessimism at the hand of Andreas Huyssen (1997: 59), who suggests that:

> Berlin may be the place to study how this new emphasis on the city as cultural sign, combined with its role as capital and the pressures of

large-scale developments, prevent creative alternatives and thus represents a false start into the twenty-first century.

In contrast to the pessimism of cultural critics such as Huyssen, Berlin's city fathers have not been slow to recognise and act upon the opportunities for tourism offered by the city as cultural sign. Accordingly, in 1999, in co-operation with the Chamber of Architects in Berlin, and the Federal Ministry for Transport, Building and Housing, and under contract to the Senate of Berlin, the Berliner Festspiele put together a publication presenting the city of Berlin itself as an exhibition. In *Berlin: Open City* (Enke et al., 1999), ten separate routes through different parts of the city – East and West, centre and periphery – are described in architectural detail. In the catalogue/guidebook to the exhibition, the entry for each building is prefaced with the names of its architect(s). There then follows a short description of the object, in which due attention is paid to aesthetic, technical and, to a lesser extent, historical considerations. As far as possible, then, each individual building is listed under the 'authorship' of a named architect or firm of architects. This, together with their very inclusion in the *Berlin: Open City* exhibition, means that the architectural objects on display here have all been deemed to possess what Walter Benjamin (1992: 218) termed 'exhibition value'; they are being presented as art objects to be gazed upon, which makes them an ideal focus for this chapter.

Each of the ten tours described in *Berlin: Open City* guides the visitor through a particular area of the city, and each tour is structured around a distinct narrative, which aims to establish the distinctive character of each area. There are, however, also a number of ways in which the individual tours are connected. The most obvious of these is that in each tour, the city is conceived as an extended space for the display of architecture. Simultaneously, however, many of the tours also demonstrate a fascination with the architecture of display. In locations such as the Spandauer Vorstadt (Route 2), the Kulturforum (Route 3), the East End of the Friedrichstadt (Route 4), the Info-Box on Leipziger Platz (Route 4), die Neue Mitte (Route 5), the Märkisches Museum and the German Architecture Centre (Route 6), Savigny-Platz (Route 7), the East Side Gallery (Route 9), and the Kulturbrauerei (Route 10), the main function of the exhibited objects is to house exhibitions. The two architectural objects that form the focus of this chapter, Daniel Libeskind's Jewish Museum and the Kunsthaus (Arts Centre) Tacheles, are both prime examples of the architecture of display contained in *Berlin: Open City*. They are representative of architecture as both an aesthetic idea and as a place in which aesthetic ideas are housed, displayed, created and stored.

Investigating these objects and the architectural dynamics of present-day Berlin more generally, will allow us to reflect on the complex relationship between architecture, sociology and art. The argument of this paper is that sociology should seek, more than it has hitherto endeavoured, not just to comprehend the social significance of architecture, but also to explicate the ways and means by which certain architectural forms may or may not be viewed as 'art'. A straightforward 'sociology of architecture' approach is useful but is not on its own up to this task. Instead sociologists must seek to treat architecture and architectural discourses not just as objects of study but as themselves critical resources to be deployed in the understanding of aesthetic phenomena.

Formalism vs Functionalism

Libeskind's Jewish Museum, conceived as an extension to the existing Berlin Museum on the Lindenstrasse, is to be found on Route 4 of the *Berlin: Open City* exhibition, which takes the visitor through the old Friedrichstadt. The Jewish Museum is described in the catalogue/guidebook as 'one of the most spectacular new buildings in Berlin since the Second World War' (Enke et al., 1999: 110). Libeskind first presented his ideas for the design of the building in 1989, and it was opened to the public a decade later. The aim of his project, which he called 'Between the Lines', is to 'give form to the broken relation between German and Jewish culture' (Heynen, 1999: 200). The museum's ground plan is laid out in a zig-zag pattern, which can be seen as a deconstructed Star of David, and was arrived at through the complicated plotting of points of historical interest on a map of the city, which were then connected to form the final shape of the structure (Libeskind, 1992). The building's interior consists of five 'voids', only one of which can actually be entered. According to Libeskind (Enke et al., 1999: 110), these voids are the tangible expression of the absence of Jewish life in Berlin and symbolise the 'presence of the absence' in the museum. Indeed, 'absence' is a key word here, since although the building was opened to the public in 1999, the first exhibition was not installed until September 2001. At least up until this point, the building and the tale of its reception would seem to represent a triumph of form over function.

In contrast, the Kunsthaus Tacheles could be argued to demonstrate the primacy of function over form. The building is to be found on Route 2 of the *Berlin: Open City* exhibition, which takes the visitor through the Spandauer Vorstadt and Prenzlauer Berg, the site of artistic resistance in the former East Berlin. Now home to numerous art galleries, cafés and bars, the area has played on and transcended its former neglected appearance (due, in no small part, to the East German government's suspicion of 'bourgeois architecture') to become a definitive location of culture in 'New Berlin'. In *Berlin: Open City*, the description of the Kunsthaus Tacheles opens with the comment that 'in 1990, young artists occupied the ruined shell of the former department store, which was threatened with demolition, and established the Kunsthaus Tacheles' (Enke et al., 1999: 50). The architect of the building, however, is listed as Franz Ahrens, who designed the original shopping arcade that was completed in 1909. As an arcade built towards the end of the first decade of the twentieth century, the Friedrichstrassen-Passage, as the building was then known, was in some sense a ruin before it was completed, part of the prehistory of modernity before it could assert its own modernity. It was a type of building already on the brink of extinction – indeed, it had the dubious distinction of being the last arcade built in Europe – but at the same time, in its construction, Ahrens used entirely modern technical innovations both for the structure and for the organisation of the circulation of money in the interior.

The building enjoyed a chequered history before it finally became the Kunsthaus Tacheles in the early 1990s:[1] After an unsuccessful career as a department store/arcade, it was purchased by the electric company AEG, who styled it as a 'House of Technology' that would function as a permanent exhibition space for the 'New Berlin' being created by modernist architects such as Peter Behrens. Following the rise to power of the National Socialists, AEG abandoned the building, although it was in constant use during the Second World War. In GDR times, it was denigrated as an example of bourgeois architecture and its fabric was more or less left to rot. At the same time, however, its cinema was still in use, showing alternative art films which would not have appeared in mainstream programmes. As early as 1977, a demolition order had been served on the building which lay in the path of a planned four-lane feeder road. However, the wheels of demolition turned slowly in the GDR. The building's imposing glass dome was destroyed in a controlled explosion in 1981, but its facade was still standing when the Berlin wall came down in 1989. Because of its prime location in the middle of the newly reunited city, the ruined shell of the former shopping arcade was then seized upon by young artists and by the mid-1990s, had become the flourishing centre of Berlin's alternative culture scene.

Both Libeskind's Jewish Museum and the Kunsthaus Tacheles are prime locations of culture in the 'New Berlin', and yet there appears to be a fundamental distinction between the two buildings. The former is a carefully composed structure that would seem to demand formal analysis, while the latter, the result of a century of decomposition, would seem best analysed in terms of social function. In other words, it would appear that the Kunsthaus Tacheles would be a prime candidate for a sociological approach to architecture, while an investigation into Libeskind's Jewish Museum would be best carried out in terms of architectural discourse. This is entirely concomitant with Neil Leach's (1997: xiv) observation that 'traditionally, architectural discourse has been largely a discourse of form'. To that, we could add that sociological discourse has been mainly concerned with social function.

Architectural discourse and sociological discourse

This distinction would seem to be mirrored by the way in which, in architectural discourse, a distinction is often drawn between architecture and art. In a lecture on the nature of architecture, delivered in Berlin in 1910, the Viennese architect, Adolf Loos (1982: 101), polemically claimed that 'only a really small part of architecture belongs to art: the gravestone and the monument. Everything else that serves a purpose is to be excluded from the realm of art.' Similarly, Nicholas Pevsner (1945: xvi) began his appreciation of European architecture by asserting that 'a bicycle shed is a building; Lincoln Cathedral is a piece of architecture.' Pevsner and Loos differ in their use of terminology; while Loos used the term 'architecture' to refer to the tectonic, Pevsner used it to signify the aesthetic. Both, however, were essentially making the same point, which is that there is a distinction to be made between the use value and the exhibition value of an architectural object, and that only when the latter is of significance can the object be regarded as art. Postmodern architectural theory, however, sought to undercut this neat distinction. Venturi et al. (1992) devoted Part II of *Learning from Las Vegas*, to 'Ugly and Ordinary Architecture, or the Decorated Shed'. Generalising from their analysis of urban sprawl, they seek to show how the binary opposition employed by Pevsner can be deconstructed. However, other contemporary theorists question the postmodern approach. For example, Hilde Heynen (1999: 22) reiterates Loos's distinction, arguing that because most architecture does have use value, 'it is intolerable for it to be critical and negative in the same way as modern art and literature.'

Sociological approaches that would want to reject the assumption that a clear distinction can be made between architecture and art might seem to demonstrate an affinity with the postmodern paradigm. However, a conventional sociological analysis would approach the problem from the opposite angle, arguing that even in the creation of 'monuments', other questions can be asked of architecture, and that in such cases, it is especially important not to lose sight of what Jameson (1997: 240) has termed architecture's 'virtually unmediated relationship' with the economic. Indeed, in studying canonical architectural objects, the sociology of architecture might seem as though it would want to bracket out (or at least play down) the aesthetic in favour of an emphasis on the economic and/or the social. Particularly in the case of large-scale monumental projects, sociology would set out to question the cult of genius, with its emphasis on 'authorship' based on an 'ideology of the aesthetic', seeking to penetrate the facade and lay bare the muddied reality of large-scale architectural projects. In order to investigate the relations of artistic production in this way, it would be necessary to employ insights based on a Marxist approach or to follow Howard Becker (1984), who used symbolic interactionism to great effect in his seminal study of the relations of production in the world of art.

Alternatively, or indeed, simultaneously, the sociologist of architecture might focus on the reception of the canonical architectural object. Approaches which could productively be employed here include semiotics, Foucauldian approaches focusing, in particular, on the interplay between space and power, or theories derived from the work of De Certeau (1988) and looking at the way in which 'ordinary practitioners' inhabit the city, gaze upon monumental buildings and utilise the spaces associated with them. In other words, it would seem that while conventional architectural discourse might seek to embrace the formal aesthetic attributes of a monument, and postmodern architectural discourse would set out to demonstrate that the shed can also be considered to be art, a sociological approach would seek to lay bare the social dimensions in the production and reception of both the monument and the shed.

Towards dialectics

This definition, however, denies the actual complexity of the relationship between architectural discourse and sociological discourse, which is influenced by the interplay between exhibition value, exchange value and use value that characterises any given architectural object. Acknowledging this complexity, Lawrence Scaff (1995: 81) argues that in the twentieth century there was a convergence between the two discourses – 'one devoted to an analysis and diagnosis of the social world, and the other oriented toward a shaping of the built environment in thought and practice.' Above all, both are shaped by an interest in the complex relationship between stability and flux, permanence and transience, tradition and modernity that shapes people's experience of the world. In his reflections on the contemporary architect and theorist, Peter Eisenmann, Andrew Benjamin (1997: 293) suggests that '[architecture] is always in the process of becoming, of changing, while it is also establishing, institutionalising.' In other words, in order to understand both architectural and sociological discourse, it is necessary to be able to think dialectically.

When considering the architecture of display in 'New Berlin', the most obvious example of the dialectical nature of modern architecture is the 'Info-Box' on Leipziger Platz, which was designed by the German architects, Schneider and Schuhmacher, as a temporary space in which information about the symbolic reordering of space taking place through the creation of 'New Berlin' could be exhibited. The description of this architectural object contained in the catalogue/guidebook for the *Berlin: Open City* exhibition opens by informing us that 'the red Info-Box is a temporary building...' (Enke et al., 1999: 91), but this is a temporary building whose prime function is to provide information about permanent changes being made to the landscape of Berlin. Moreover, it is also a building which has been designed so that it can be easily re-erected in another location once it has lost its place on Leipziger Platz to more straightforwardly permanent structures (Enke et al., 1999: 92).

Equally, a dialectic of transience and permanence can be discerned in the two architectural objects that form the centrepiece of this investigation. One of the central structuring principles of Libeskind's Jewish Museum is the dialectic of transience and permanence of Berlin's Jewish community, expressed, above all, in the way in which, as an aesthetic idea, the building's voids symbolise the absence of Jewish culture, while the building itself is also a place in which the presence of that absence is exhibited. In the case of the Kunsthaus Tacheles, the dialectic of transience and permanence manifests itself in the squatters' desire to celebrate the provisionality of the building as a ruin, which, as Claudia Wahjudi (1999: 213) argues, 'functions as a signifier of the identity of post-Wende Berlin, of a time in which revolution was everything'. The credo of the squatters was: 'Our ideals lie in ruins – let's save the ruin' (Rost et al., 1992: n.p.). The irony here is that there was a move to make provisionality permanent, and indeed, in order to ensure the preservation of the provisionality of the building, the squatters enlisted the help of the heritage authorities, and had a preservation order placed on the ruined façade (Clewing, 1993).

German sociologists investigating the relationship between architecture and modernity have been drawn to the dialectic of transience and permanence upon which modern architecture is predicated. In his analysis of the buildings erected to house the 1895 Berlin Trade Exhibition, Georg Simmel (1997: 256) points out that their unique character was attributable to the 'entirely new proportion between permanence and transience [which] not only predominates in the hidden structure but also in the aesthetic criteria.' Walter Benjamin's treatment of architecture in his *Arcades Project*, is based on a similar thematic. His claim that 'all collective architecture of the nineteenth century provides the home of the dreaming collective' (Benjamin, 1982: 1012), is based on his reading of the Parisian arcades as architectural objects functioning both as a permanent visual and tactile link to the prehistory of modernity, and, as a result of the run-down state in which they found themselves by the second decade of the twentieth century, as a signifier of the transience of past dreams. In 'Farewell to the Linden Arcade', Siegfried Kracauer expands on this point, dwelling on the way that the arcade, a form of bourgeois architecture whose 'time has run out' (Kracauer, 1995: 338), became a location which 'by disavowing a form of existence to which it still belonged, gained the power to bear witness to transience' (342).

Simmel, Benjamin and Kracauer, together with other German social theorists such as Ernst Bloch and Theodor Adorno, present insightful work on architecture, in which they set out to explore the relationship between modernity, dwelling and architecture (Heynen, 1999). In so doing, each of these theorists specifically sets out to take into account the aesthetic dimension of architecture and in particular, the critical or disruptive possibilities offered thereby. There are, however, differences in approach and in the conclusions drawn by these various theorists. Benjamin argues that modern architecture, in its concern to create spaces that have no fixed character, takes the crisis of experience that is modernity into account. These spaces, he argues, embody an impetus for change, responsive to the requirements of a new society (Heynen, 1999: 5). In contrast, Ernst Bloch, writing at the same time as Benjamin, was critical of the 'poverty' of modern architecture, which he saw as part of bourgeois capitalism. This being the case, he was unable to identify any utopian dimension to modern architecture (Heynen, 1999: 121). After the caesura of the Second World War, Adorno revisits the relationship between architecture and critical theory, art and modernity. In *Aesthetic Theory*, Adorno (1999: 118–35) explains how because of its essentially 'enigmatic' character, art lends itself to interpretation rather than straightforward understanding. As Habermas (1997: 231) points out, he draws an important distinction between the work of art as a use-object 'functioning for exterior purposes' and as an object which 'functions within itself'. It is only the latter from which art's disruptive and resistant potential can be divined. Adorno therefore regards architecture to be both affirmative and constitutive of the systems that characterise modernity, and also to be an art form that contains within itself the possibility of radical autonomy.

The key to understanding Adorno's view of art is to engage with his theory of language, and in particular, to understand his critique of the false distinction between theoretical language and art (Heynen, 1999: 178–79). This, Adorno and Horkheimer (1972: 17–18) argue, has come about through a separation of what Benjamin (1972: 478) terms the 'mimetic' and the 'semiotic' dimensions of language. Following Benjamin, Adorno and Horkheimer argue that it is imperative that both theory and art 'confront the fissure between sign and image, and [...] attempt to bridge the gap' (Heynen, 1999: 185). In the specific case of architecture, it would appear that, at least from the theoretical direction, overtures are being made towards 'confronting the fissure'. In *Architecture as Metaphor*, the Japanese Professor of Literature, Kojin Karatani (1995: 4) bases his whole argument on the observation that 'Western thought is marked by a will to architecture'. This view echoes Andrew Benjamin's (1997: 286) contention that 'philosophy can never be free of architecture', and is also the point of departure for Elizabeth Grosz's (2001) extended discussion of points of connection between philosophy and architecture.

A similar claim could be made for sociology; we need only mention the influence of structuralist and poststructuralist thought, structural function-alism, and systems theory to illustrate this point, but it is also striking that the use of architectural metaphors abounds throughout the history of sociology to the present day. While a recent sociology textbook bears the title, *Sociology: Exploring the Architecture of Everyday Life* (Newman, 2000), one of the most well-known passages in Marx's *Capital* is the one in which he compares an architect to a bee, maintaining that 'what distinguishes the worst architect from the best of bees is this, that the architect raises his structure in imagina-tion before he erects it in reality' (Marx, 1977: 456). The predominance of architecture as metaphor in sociology undermines the hierarchical relationship between sociology and architecture implied by the use of the grammatical possessive in phrases such as the 'the sociology of architecture', thereby reit-erating the complexity of the relationship between sociology and architecture. This is instructive for the sociologist, since it demands an approach to architecture, and by extension, to other forms of art, which seeks not only to apply sociology to architecture, but also to understand the role of the aesthetic in the development of social theory. This necessitates extending Janet Wolff's (1983: 107) argument that, 'the sociology of art [...] needs a theory of the aesthetic,' and also entails reaching an understanding of the way in which architecture itself makes use of social theory.

Marx's use of the figure of the architect to signify the importance of humankind's potential for critical thought points towards a confidence in the architect, which can also be clearly discerned in both the theoretical and the practical work of many of those involved in the modern architectural move-ment in Berlin and beyond. Architects such as Paul Scheerbart, Bruno Taut, Peter Behrens, and, most famously, Le Corbusier, as well as architectural movements such as the German Werkbund and the Bauhaus demonstrated their confidence in their ability to alter political and social reality for the better. These architects were 'motivated by an idealistic desire to market ideas rather than goods through buildings whose appearance was intended to reach out to rather than float above the heads of the public as a whole' (James-Chakraborty, 2000: 6). Striving towards a unity of form and func-tion, the work of these architects was informed by a knowledge of theories of social space and social structures, and by a desire to provide the means through which people could achieve emancipation. A common thread uniting these architects was their belief that architecture was more than merely the backdrop against which social change takes place; in their view, architecture could also be an agent of social change. This is a view that is taken up by social theorists in the last decades of the twentieth century. In the introduction to their seminal collection, *Social Relations and Spatial Structures*, Gregory and Urry (1985: 3) argue that 'spatial structure is now seen not merely as an arena in which social life unfolds, but rather as a medium through which social relations are produced and reproduced.' Unlike the architects, and indeed the German sociologists explored earlier, however, Gregory and Urry do not focus on the role of the aesthetic in their study of the spatial production and reproduction of social relations.

As theories of social space and the city began to grapple with the relationship between spatial structures and social relations, however, architectural theory began to tone down the claims being made for architecture as the agent of social change. Siegfried Giedion (1967) diagnosed a certain confusion in architecture and sought to confront this by arguing that the role of architecture is to provide 'the interpretation of a way of life valid for our period.' The architect, Karsten Harries (1998: 4), takes this statement as the point of departure for his treatise, *The Ethical Function of Architecture*, in which he argues that the task of architecture is now 'to help articulate a common ethos.' It is not difficult to discern a change in attitude here, from the confidence of early twentieth-century architects, who saw architecture's role as the 'creation' of social change, through Giedion's insistence on 'interpretation' to Harries' focus on 'articulation'. Taking this shift into account, it is hardly surprising to find Neil Leach (1999: 122) arguing that architecture, like the other visual arts, merely functions as the backdrop for the political.

Architecture and the postmodern crisis

This shift in architectural thought is linked to the postmodern crisis. The loss of faith in grand narratives is mirrored by a loss of confidence in the omnipotence of the figure of the architect, both literally and as metaphor. Habermas (1997: 234) sees this loss of confidence as the direct result of the 'overburdened and instrumentalized architecture of the Modern Movement', adding that modern architecture's mistake was in allowing itself to become 'overburdened' (ibid.: 232). According to the philosopher of architecture, Massimo Cacciari (1993: 167) modern architecture is a 'technico-scientific project', the goal of which was the 'conquest of space'. In this response to Martin Heidegger's (1969) essay, 'Art and Space', Cacciari explains that he sees 'the conquest of space' as 'the liquidation of place as a collection of things, as a mutual belonging of things and dwelling' (167). The modern architectural project, which is concerned with planning, and therefore with possessing and dominating space, represents this act of emptying space of place, which Cacciari calls 'Ent-ortung' (166). Seen through Cacciari's eyes, the crisis of modern architecture is defined by its inability to counter 'Ent-ortung' and its consequences.

Habermas (1997) diagnoses three (aesthetic) strategies employed in an attempt to counter 'Ent-ortung' in recent architecture – 'postmodernism', 'neo-historicism' and 'alternative architecture'. Examples of all three directions can be seen at work in the architecture of 'New Berlin'. The first of these, 'postmodernism', defined by Habermas (1997: 235) as 'non-nostalgic stage-set architecture', is the architectural discourse that informs the steel and glass skyscrapers, the shopping arcades and the Mediathek erected on the historic Potsdamer Platz. Here, on swathes of land owned by global players such as Sony and Daimler-Chrysler, Berlin is being recreated as a 'global city'. This direction represents the (ironic) embrace of 'Ent-ortung' as the only possible defence against it, but it has been challenged by a very different discourse: 'critical reconstruction'. This is the name given to a direction in urban planning developed in Berlin in the 1980s that sets out to ensure that new buildings in the city are designed according to existing patterns and plans, so understanding and preserving Berlin's historic identity. This form of 'neo-historicism', which Habermas argues is closely linked to political neo-conservatism, can be seen above all in the Friedrichstadt and in individual buildings, such as the painstakingly rebuilt Hotel Adlon, situated on Unter den Linden not far from the Brandenburg Gate. The hotel, owned by the Cologne-based investors, Fundus, was described in a recent issue of the *Architectural Review* as a 'strange threat to the fabric of Berlin, [and an example of] the fungus of retro architecture' (Davey, 1999b: 25). The final way of countering 'Ent-ortung' described by Habermas is 'alternative architecture'. This is a direction linked to 'critical reconstruction' in its desire for 'the preservation of historically developed urban districts', but distinguished from it by its concern to address 'the problems of ecology' and to facilitate 'communal "participatory architecture"' (Habermas, 1997: 235). One well-known project which could fall in this category is the reconstruction of the 'Hackesche Höfe'. Like the Kunsthaus Tacheles, which stands at the opposite end of the Oranienburgerstrasse to the Hackesche Höfe, the early twentieth-century building had fallen into disrepair and was occupied by squatters in 1990. In contrast to the Kunsthaus Tacheles, however, reconstruction of the *Jugendstil* buildings was undertaken in a participatory framework (Gesellschaft Hackesche Höfe, 1993). Today, the Hackesche Höfe, with their expensive restaurants, exclusive shops, mainstream cinema and theatre space, have become a veritable tourist magnet.

In attempting to combat 'Ent-ortung', both 'neo-historicism' and 'alternative architecture' are forced to embrace a 'restorative nostalgia', which, according to Cacciari, is merely the flip-side of 'Ent-ortung'. If we can criticise the postmodern architecture of Potsdamer Platz for the way in which it empties space of place, by demolishing and concealing almost all traces of the site's history, then we must also be aware of the problems of 'critical reconstruction' and 'alternative architecture' which, at best, distort history, for they are based on a selective form of engagement with the past (Ladd, 1997; Flierl, 1998).[2] All three responses are, therefore, linked in their inadequacy. None is able to articulate a sense of place that would overcome the crisis in modern architecture. Yet in theory at least, the possibility of attaining some kind of solution has not been ruled out. Towards the end of *Architecture and Nihilism*, Cacciari reveals his philosophical counterpoint to the architectural double-bind of

either 'Ent-ortung' or nostalgia, which he terms 'the spirit of fulfilment'. This
is an aesthetic idea that, as Cacciari (1993: 209–10) puts it:

> implies neither the task of effecting solution nor that of effecting the end
> of all solution, but the idea of composition as a listening to the differ-
> ences, [it] knows that the shattered cannot ever again be relived; for this
> reason, it does not overcome it or subsume it but rather listens to it in its
> specific being-there, seeks it out in the invisibility of its being-for-death.

A model for architecture in the twenty-first century?

The first step towards the realisation of this creative imperative consists in
the disruption of totalization through the use of strategies based on differentiation, disunity and division. While the architectural rhetoric employed in
Berlin in the 1990s was largely founded on the dominant political ideal of
unification (Wise, 1998), a reading of Cacciari's philosophy of architecture
suggests that the interesting areas for further exploration may be those sites
which resisted the dominant call to unification, whether under the banner of
global capitalism or of 'critical reconstruction'. It is at this point that I want to
return to the two locations of culture introduced earlier in this chapter:
Libeskind's Jewish Museum and the Kunsthaus Tacheles.

While Huyssen (1997) is generally pessimistic about the creative potential
of architecture in the 'New Berlin', he does argue that it is possible for individual buildings, such as Libeskind's Jewish Museum, to provide resistance to
the dominant architectural and political discourses shaping the city. Indeed, it
can be argued that the main aesthetic idea articulated by the building is
disruption, which is achieved through the way in which it structures the
experience of space. As James-Chakraborty (2000: 120) points out, despite
the complexity and literary character of Libeskind's design, what differenti-
ates his architecture from that of canonical postmodernists such as Venturi
and Scott-Brown is that he is convinced that 'the experience of form [...] is
responsible for meaning in architecture.' The facade of the Jewish Museum
comprises a collection of zinc-clad zig-zags, themselves interrupted by the
irregular slashes in them that form the windows. While forming 'a very
effective response to the existing urban situation' (Heynen, 1999: 203), the
museum also disrupts the picture of the city as a totality, by creating a
building whose exterior is far removed from the strictures of 'critical reconstruction'. In other words, it is based on a dialectic of belonging and not
belonging, which reflects the narrative thrust of the Museum's first exhibition,
'Two Millenia of German-Jewish History'. In structuring the building's
interior, Libeskind continued to play with of an aesthetic of disruption,
using a skewed ground plan, a series of voids and materials such as concrete
to shape the way in which space is experienced. The primary response to
both the interior and the exterior of the building is that of disorientation
(James-Chakraborty 2000: 120). Casting herself both as part of the collec-
tivity experiencing space and also in the role of an informed commentator on

that experience, Heynen (1999: 208) notes that 'no direct image of utopia is offered us here, but the idea of utopia is preserved because we see clearly how great a distance separates our present reality from a utopian condition of reconciliation'.

Although the product of decomposition rather than careful composition, the Kunsthaus Tacheles also functions as a visible tear in Berlin's urban fabric. All around it, ruined and damaged buildings have been reconstructed, and the empty sites that had been a feature of this part of East Berlin, which had never been properly reconstructed after the bomb damage suffered during the Second World War, have been filled. In contrast, the Kunsthaus Tacheles has thus far resisted reconstruction to remain a combination of grafittied ruin and urban 'wasteland', that has been host to various events and home to a large number of 'alternative' artists over the past decade. Among the most famous works associated with the building are the giant mural on the gable-end of the ruin, which poses the question 'Where is Captain Nemo?', and a conceptual comment on German unification in the shape of an installation in the 'sculpture garden' involving a Trabi car (symbol of the old East Germany) burying into the ground, only to reappear as a Volkswagen (Rost et al., 1992). Tacheles, occupying the largest unreconstructed plot of land remaining in the centre of Berlin, exists as a visible and tactile challenge to the seamless representation of unification found elsewhere in Berlin's 'Neue Mitte'. It marks a clear break from both the monotonous blocks of the critically reconstructed Friedrichstrasse, which adjoins the site to the South-West, and the picturesque labyrinth of the Spandauer Vorstadt, to the North-East, and so the visitor coming to the Kunsthaus Tacheles for the first time from either the Spandauer Vorstadt or the Friedrichstrasse may well experience a sense of disquiet or disorientation. To echo Heynen's analysis of the impact of the Jewish Museum, this is a building that does not seek to offer an image of utopia, but that does serve to demonstrate the gap between reality and utopia.

Conclusion

At the outset of this chapter, it appeared as though Libeskind's Jewish Museum and the Kunsthaus Tacheles, although inscribed by similar scripts (the architecture of display), were buildings that would actually demand separate and different forms of analysis – a formal, architectural, approach to the Jewish Museum and a functional, sociological, approach to the Kunsthaus Tacheles. To do justice to these buildings in their dual function as aesthetic ideas and as locations in which aesthetic ideas are housed, displayed, created and stored, however, this chapter has argued that such binary oppositions must be overcome – without, however, losing sight of the considerable differences between the two architectural objects. The points of connection between the Jewish Museum and the Kunsthaus Tacheles have been found to lie in abstract ideas, such as the dialectic of permanence and transience, and the aesthetic of disruption that works through the sense of disorientation and discomfort that it engenders. These ideas have been revealed by subjecting the buildings to an analysis sensitive to sociology, architecture and the aesthetic, that seeks to recognise the integrity of all three discourses, while simultaneously being aware and taking advantage of the productive interplay between all three. In other words, in order to begin to understand what Cacciari means by an architecture informed by the 'spirit of fulfilment', it is not enough to set out to write the 'sociology of architecture'. Sociologists who wish to understand the critical potential of architecture in the twenty-first century must instead set themselves the task of combining sociology and architecture.

NOTES

1. The changing patterns of use of the building, which mirror socio-political changes in Berlin that took place over the course of the twentieth century, were documented in an exhibition presented in the Museum Mitte in 1999 and still available as a virtual exhibition at http://www.dhm.de/museen/berlin-mitte/nachk.htm (accessed 03.03.01).
2. One historical trace that has been preserved comprises the ruins of the former Hotel Esplanade, which have been reconstructed, encased in glass and now stand at the entrance to the Sony complex, after part of the old building, the 'Kaisersaal' was moved 75 metres using hydraulics (Enke et al., 1999: 62).

References

Adorno, Theodor W. (1967) 'Cultural Criticism and Society', in *Prisms*, London: Neville Spearman.

—— (1976) *Introduction to the Sociology of Music*, Seabury Press.

—— (1990) *The Culture Industry: Selected Essays on Mass Culture*, London: Routledge.

—— (1997 [1970]) *Aesthetic Theory*, eds G. Adorno & R. Tiedemann, trans. R. Hullot-Kentor, London: Athlone Press.

—— (1999) *Sound Figures*, Cambridge: Cambridge University Press.

Adorno, T.W. and Horkheimer, M. (1972) *Dialectic of Enlightenment*, New York: Herder and Herder.

Alberti, L.B. (1966) *On Painting*, trans. J.R. Spenser, London: Yale University Press.

Albrecht, Milton C. (1970) 'Art as an Institution' in Albrecht, Milton C. Barnett, James H., Griff, Mason (eds) *The Sociology of Art and Literature: A Reader*, London: Duckworth, pp. 1–28.

Alexander, Jeffrey C. (1988) 'Introduction: Durkheimian Sociology and Cultural Studies Today', in Jeffrey C. Alexander (ed.) *Durkheimian Sociology: Cultural Studies*, Cambridge: Cambridge Univeristy Press, pp. 1–21.

—— (1996) 'Cultural Sociology or Sociology of Culture? Towards a Strong Program', *Newsletter of the Sociology of Culture Section of the American Sociological Association*, Vol. 10, Nos 3–4, pp. 3–5.

Alexander, Jeffrey C. and Smith, Philip (1993) 'The Discourse of American Civil Society: A New Proposal for Cultural Studies', *Theory and Society*, Vol. 22, No. 2, pp. 151–207.

American Behavioral Scientist, Vol. 19, No. 2, July/August 1976. Special issue, 'The Production of Culture' (re-published 1976 by Sage under the same title, edited by Richard A. Peterson).

Anheier, Helmut K., Gerhards, Jurgen and Romo, Frank P. (1995) 'Forms of Capital and Social Structure in Cultural Fields: Examining Bourdieu's Social Topography', *American Journal of Sociology*, Vol. 100, No. 4, pp. 859–903.

Arblaster, A. (1992) *Viva la Liberta: Politics in Opera*, London: Verso.

Arnheim, R. (1933) *Film*, London: Faber & Faber.

Arnold, M. (1898 [1867]) 'Heine's Grave', in *Poetical Works of Matthew Arnold*, London: Macmillan, pp. 255–61.

Auerbach, E. (1968) *Mimesis: The Representation of Reality in Western Literature*, New Jersey: Princeton University Press.

Bakhtin, Mikhail (1984) *Rabelais and His World*, Bloomington: Indiana University Press.

Baldry, A.L. (1901) *Hubert von Herkomer: A Study and a Biography*, London: George Bell and Sons.

Barbu, Z. (1970) 'Sociological Perspectives in Art and Literature', in Jean Creedy (ed.) *The Social Context of Art*, London: Tavistock.

Barlow, Sean and Eyre, Banning (1995) *Afropop! An Illustrated Guide to Contemporary African Music*, Edison, NJ: Chartwell Books.

Barrett, M. (1992) *The Politics of Truth: From Marx to Foucault*, Cambridge: Polity.

Barrow, R. (2001) *Lawrence Alma-Tadema*, London: Phaidon.

Barthes, Roland (1993 [1957]) *Mythologies*, London: Vintage.

Battersby, Christine (1994) *Gender and Genius: Towards a Feminist Aesthetics*, London: Women's Press.

Baxandall, M. (1972) *Painting and Experience in Fifteenth-Century Italy: A Primer in the Social History of Pictorial Style*, Oxford and New York: Oxford University Press.

Becker, George (1978) *The Mad Genius Controversy: A Study in the Sociology of Deviance*, Beverley Hills: Sage.

Becker, Howard (1974) 'Art as Collective Action', *American Sociological Review*, Vol. 39, No. 6, pp. 767–76.

—— (1984) *Art Worlds*, Berkeley: University of California Press.

Benjamin, A. (1997) 'Eisenman and the Housing of Tradition', in N. Leach (ed.) *Rethinking Architecture*, London: Routledge.

Benjamin, Walter (1972) 'Probleme der Sprachsoziologie', in H. Tiedemann-Bartels (ed.) *Gesammelte Schriften*, Vol. 3, Frankfurt a.M.: Suhrkamp, pp. 452–80.

—— (1982) 'Das Passagenwerk', in R. Tiedemann (ed.) *Gesammelte Schriften*, Vol. 5, Frankfurt a.M.: Suhrkamp.

—— (1992) 'The Work of Art in the Age of Mechanical Reproduction', *Illuminations*, London: Fontana, pp. 211–44.

Bennett, Jonathon (1966) *Kant's Analytic*, Cambridge: Cambridge University Press.

Bensman, Joseph (1983) 'Introduction: The Phenomenology and Sociology of the Performing Arts', in J.B. Kamerman and R. Martorella (eds), *Performers and Performances*, South Hadley, MA: Bergin & Garvey Publishers.

Berger, J. (1972) *Ways of Seeing*, Harmondsworth: Penguin.

Berger, Peter and Luckmann, Thomas (1967) *The Social Construction of Reality: A Treatise in the Sociology of Knowledge*, Harmondsworth: Penguin.

Berlin, Isaiah (1976) *Vico and Herder: Two Studies in the History of Ideas*, London: The Hogarth Press.

—— (2000) *The Roots of Romanticism*, London: Pimlico.

Betterton, R. (1996) *An Intimate Distance*, New York: Routledge.

BFFS (2001) 'History of the BFFS', http://www.bffs.co.uk/history.htm.

Blaikie, Andrew and Hepworth, Mike (1997) 'Representations of Old Age in Painting and Photography', in A. Jamieson, S. Harper and C. Victor (eds) *Critical Approaches to Ageing and Later Life*, Buckingham: Open University Press.

Blanchard, S. and Harvey, S. (1983) 'The Post-war Independent Cinema – Structure and Organization', in J. Curran and V. Porter (eds) *British Cinema History*, London: Weidenfeld & Nicolson, pp. 226–41.

Bohlman, P. (2002a) 'World Music at the "End of History"', *Ethnomusicology*, Vol. 46, No. 1, pp. 1–31.

—— (2002b) *World Music: A Very Short Introduction*, Oxford: Oxford University Press.

Boime, Albert (1976) 'Entrepreneurial Patronage in 19th Century France', in E.C. Carter, R. Forster and J.N. Moody (eds) *Enterprise and Entrepreneurs in 19th and 20th Century France*, Baltimore: Johns Hopkins University Press.

Bokina, J. (1997) *Opera and Politics from Monteverdi to Henze*, New Haven: Yale University Press.

Bordo, Susan (1989) 'The Body and the Reproduction of Femininity: A Feminist Appropriation of Foucault', in A. Jaggar and S. Bordo (eds) *Gender/Body/Knowledge*, New Brunswick: Rutgers University Press.

Born, Georgina and Hesmondhalgh, David (2000) 'Introduction: On Difference, Representation and Appropriation in Music', in Georgina Born and David Hesmondhalgh (eds) *Western Music and Its Others: Difference, Representation and Appropriation in Music*, Berkeley: University of California Press, pp. 1–58.

Bourdieu, Pierre (1977 [1970]) *Reproduction in Education, Culture and Society*, trans. R. Nice, London/Beverley Hills: Sage Publications.

—— (1979 [1964]) *The Inheritors: French Students and Their Relation to Culture*, trans. R. Nice, Chicago: University of Chicago Press.

—— (1983) 'The Field of Cultural Production, or: The Economic World Reversed', *Poetics* 12 (4–5), pp. 311–56.

—— (1988) *Homo Academicus*, Cambridge: Polity.

—— (1990) *In Other Words*, Cambridge: Polity.

—— (1990 [1965]) *Photography: A Middlebrow Art*, trans. S. Whiteside, Cambridge: Polity Press (with L. Boltanski, R. Castel, J.C. Chamboredon).

—— (1991) *Language and Symbolic Power*, Cambridge: Polity.

—— (1991 [1969]) *The Love of Art: European Art Museums and Their Public*, trans. C. Beattie and N. Merriman, Cambridge: Polity Press (with A. Darbel and D. Schnapper).

—— (1992 [1979]) *Distinction: A Social Critique of the Judgement of Taste*, London: Routledge.

—— (1993a) *The Field of Cultural Production*, Cambridge: Polity.

—— (1993b) *Sociology in Question*, London: Sage.

—— (1996 [1992]) *The Rules of Art: Genesis and Structure of the Literary Field*, Cambridge: Polity.

Bourdieu, Pierre and Darbel, Alain (1991) *The Love of Art: European Art Museums and Their Public*, Cambridge: Polity.

Bourdieu, Pierre and Passeron, Jean-Claude (1979) *The Inheritors*, Chicago: University of Chicago Press.

—— (1990) *Reproduction in Education, Society and Culture*, London: Sage.

Bourdieu, Pierre and Wacquant, Loic (1996) *An Invitation to a Reflexive Sociology*, Cambridge: Polity.

Bowser, E. (1990) *History of the American Cinema*, Vol. II: *The Transformation of Cinema 1907–1915*, Berkeley, CA: University of California Press.

Broughton, Simon (2000) *World Music: 100 Essential CDs*, London: Rough Guides.

Broughton, Simon, Ellingham, Mark and Trillo, Richard (eds) (1999a) 'Introduction', in *World Music – The Rough Guide*, Vol. 1: *Africa, Europe and the Middle East*, London: Rough Guides, pp. ix–x.

—— (1999b) *World Music – The Rough Guide*, Vol. 2: *Latin and North America, Caribbean, India, Asia and Pacific*, London: Rough Guides.

Brumberg, Jacobs J. (1997) *The Body Project: An Intimate History of American Girls*, New York: Random House.

Budd, Mike, Entman, Robert M. and Steinman, Clay (1990) 'The Affirmative Character of U.S. Cultural Studies', *Critical Studies in Mass Communication*, No. 7, pp. 169–84.

Bull, Deborah (1999) *Dancing Away*, London: Methuen.

Bürger, P. (1984) *Theory of the Avant-Garde*, trans. M. Shaw, Manchester: Manchester University Press.

Burgin, Victor (1996) *In/Different Spaces: Place and Memory in Visual Culture*, Berkeley: University of California Press.

Burnett, Robert (1996) *The Global Jukebox: The International Music Industry*, London: Routledge.

Bussell, Darcey (with Judith Mackrell) (1998) *Life in Dance*, London: Arrow Books.

Butler, I. (1971) *'To encourage the art of the film': The Story of the British Film Institute*, London: Robert Hale.

Byrne, David (1999) 'I Hate World Music', *The New York Times*, 3 October, http://www.luakabop.com/david_byrne/cmp/worldmusic.html.

Bystryn, Marcia (1978) 'Art Galleries as Gatekeepers: The Case of the Abstract Expressionists', *Social Research*, 45, Summer, pp. 390–408.

Cacciari, M. (1993) *Architecture and Nihilism: On the Philosophy of Modern Architecture*, New Haven, London: Yale University Press.

Carson, F. (2000) 'Feminist Debate and Fine Art Practices', in F. Carson and C. Pajaczkowska (eds) *Feminist Visual Culture*, Edinburgh: Edinburgh University Press.

Cass, Joan (1993) *Dancing through History*, Englewood Cliffs, NJ: Prentice Hall.

Casteras, S.P. (1987) *Images of Victorian Womanhood in English Art*, London and Toronto: Associated University Presses.

Cherry, D. (1993) *Painting Women: Victorian Women Artists*, London and New York: Routledge.

Christopherson, Richard (1974) 'From Folk Art to Fine Art: A Transformation in the Meaning of Photographic Work', *Urban Life and Culture*, No. 3, pp. 123–57.

Clark, Kenneth (1970) 'Art and Society', in Milton C. Albrecht, James H. Barnett and Mason Griff (eds) *The Sociology of Art and Literature: A Reader*, London: Gerald Duckworth.

Clement, C. (1988) *Opera, or the Undoing of Women*, Minneapolis: University of Minnesota Press.

Clewing, U. (1993) 'Nichts für schwache Nerven. Das Tacheles – ein Berliner Gegenmodell', *Bauwelt*, Vol. 84, No. 44, pp. 2389–95.

Corse, Sarah M. and Griffin, Monica D. (1997) 'Cultural Valorization and African-American Literary History: Reconstructing the Canon', *Sociological Forum*, Vol. 12, No. 2, pp. 173–203.

Coser, Lewis (1978) 'Editor's Introduction', special issue, 'The Production of Culture', *Social Research*, Vol. 45, No. 2.

Cottingham, L. (1989) The feminine de-mystique. *Flash Art*, Summer, pp. 91–95.

Coward, Rosalind (1977) 'Class, "Culture" and the Social Formation', *Screen*, Vol. 18, No. 2 pp. 75–105.

Cowie, P. (1963) *International Film Guide 1964*, London: Tantivy Press.

Cowling, M. (1989) *The Artist as Anthropologist: The Representation of Type and Character in Victorian Art*, Cambridge: Cambridge University Press.

Crowther, Paul (1994) 'Sociological Imperialism and the Field of Cultural Production', *Theory, Culture and Society*, Vol. 11, No. 1, pp. 155–70.

Dahlhaus, C. (1989) *Nineteenth Century Music*, Berkeley, CA: University of California Press.

Danto, Arthur C. (1974) 'The Transfiguration of the Commonplace', *Aesthetics and Art Criticism*, Vol. 33, No. 2, pp. 139–48.

Davey, P. (1999a) 'Building Berlin', *The Architectural Review*, Vol. 205, No. 1223, pp. 28–30.

Davey, P. (1999b) 'Adlon Hotel. Unter den Linden, Berlin', *The Architectural Review*, p. 25.

Davidson, J. and Smith, M. (1999) 'Wittgenstein and Irigaray: Gender and Philosophy in a Language (Game) of Difference', *Hypatia*, Vol. 14, pp. 72–96.

Davis, Kathy (1995) *Reshaping the Female Body: The Dilemma of Cosmetic Surgery*, London: Routledge.

de Beauvoir, S. (1972 [1949]) *The Second Sex*, Harmondsworth: Penguin.

De Certeau, Michel (1988) *The Practice of Everyday Life*, Berkeley: University of California Press.

DeNora, Tia (1995) *Beethoven and the Construction of Genius: Musical Politics in Vienna 1792–1803*, Berkeley: University of California Press.

—— (1991) 'Musical Patronage and Social Change in Beethoven's Vienna', *American Journal of Sociology*, Vol. 97, No. 2, pp. 310–46.

DiMaggio, Paul (1986) 'Cultural Entrepreneurship in Nineteenth Century Boston: The Creation of an Organisational Base for High Culture in America', in Richard E. Collins, James Curran, Philip Schlesinger, Colin Sparks and Nicholas Garnham (eds) *Media, Culture and Society: A Critical Reader*, London: Sage.

—— (1992) 'Cultural Boundaries and Structural Change: The Extension of the High Culture Model to Theater, Opera and Dance, 1900–1940', in Michele Lamont and Marcel Fournier (eds) *Cultivating Differences: Symbolic Boundaries and the Making of Inequality*, Chicago: University of Chicago Press, pp. 21–57.

—— (1996) 'Are Art-Museum Visitors Different from Other People? The Relationship between Attendance and Social and Political Attitudes in the United States', *Poetics: Journal of Empirical Research on Literature, the Media ant the Arts*, Vol. 24, Nos 2–4. Special issue, 'Museum Research', pp. 161–80.

Docherty, D., Morrison, D. and Tracey, M. (1987) *The Last Picture Show?* London: BFI.

Donald, J., Friedberg, A. and Marcus, L. (eds) (1998) *Close Up 1927–1933: Cinema and Modernism*, London: Cassell.

Drell, Adrienne (1995) Chicago and the Joffrey, *Chicago Sun-Times*, 20 January.

Dubin, Steven (1999) *Displays of Power: Memory and Amnesia in the American Museum*, New York: New York University Press.

Duden, B. (1991) *The Woman Beneath the Skin: A Doctor's Patients in Eighteenth-Century Germany*, trans. Thomas Dunlop, Cambridge, MA: Harvard University Press.

Durkheim, Emile (1984 [1893]) *The Division of Labour in Society*, Basingstoke: Macmillan.

—— (2001 [1912]) *The Elementary Forms of the Religious Life*, Oxford: Oxford University Press.

Durkheim, Emile and Mauss, Marcel (1969 [1903]) *Primitive Classification*, London: Cohen and West.

Dusinberre, D. (1980) 'The Avant-Garde Attitude in the Thirties', in D. Macpherson (ed.) *Traditions of Independence: British Cinema in the Thirties*, London: BFI Publishing, pp. 34–50.

Duvignaud, Jean (1972) *The Sociology of Art*, New York: Harper and Row.

Elias, Norbert (1993) *Mozart: Portrait of a Genius*, Cambridge: Polity.

Elmie, B. (1993) 'The Domestication of Opera', *Cambridge Opera Journal*, Vol. 5, No. 2.

Enke, Roland, Alings, Reinhard, Schneider, Bernhard, Zohlen, Gerwin (1999) *Berlin: offene Stadt. Die Stadt als Ausstellung*, Berlin: Nicolai.

Erlmann, Veit (1993) 'The Politics and Aesthetics of Transnational Musics', *The World of Music*, Vol. 35, No. 2, pp. 3–15.

—— (1996) 'The Aesthetics of the Global Imagination: Reflections on World Music in the 1990s', *Public Culture*, Vol. 8.

Evans, J. (2000) 'Photography', in F. Carson and C. Pajaczkowska (eds) *Feminist Visual Culture*, Edinburgh: Edinburgh University Press.

Fairley, Jan (2001) 'The "Local" and the "Global" in Popular Music', in Simon Frith, Will Straw and John Street (eds) *The Cambridge Companion to Pop and Rock*, Cambridge: Cambridge University Press, pp. 272–89.

Feher, Ferenc (1987) 'Weber and the Rationalization of Music', *International Journal of Politics, Culture and Society*, No. 1, Winter, pp. 147–62.

Feld, Steven (1994) 'From Schizophonia to Schismogenesis: On the Discourses and Commodification Practices of "World Music" and "World at" ', in Charles Keil and Steven Feld, *Music Grooves: Essays and Dialogues*, Chicago: University of Chicago Press, pp. 238–46.

—— (2000) 'A Sweet Lullaby for World Music', *Public Culture*, Vol. 12, No. 1, pp. 145–71.

Film Society (1972) *The Film Society Programmes 1925–1939*, New York: Arno Press.

Finch, Janet (1993) 'Conceptualizing Gender' in Morgan, David and Stanley, Liz (eds) *Debates in Sociology*, Manchester: Manchester University Press.

Flax, J. (1986) 'Gender as a Problem in and for Feminist Theory', *American Studies*, Vol. 31, No. 2, pp. 193–213.

Flierl, B. (1998) *Berlin baut um – Wessen Stadt wird die Stadt?* Berlin: Verlag für Bauwesen.

Flint, K. (2000) *The Victorians and the Visual Imagination*, Cambridge: Cambridge University Press.

Frith, Simon (1989) 'Introduction', *World Music, Politics and Social Change*, Manchester: Manchester University Press.

—— (1998) 'Literary Studies as Cultural Studies – Whose Literature? Whose Culture?', *Critical Quarterly*, Vol. 43, No. 1, pp. 3–26.

—— (2000) 'The Discourse of World Music', in Georgina Born and David Hesmondhalgh (eds) *Western Music and Its Others: Difference, Representation and Appropriation in Music*, Berkeley: University of California Press, pp. 305–322.

Game, Anne (1991) *Undoing the Social: Towards a Deconstructive Sociology*, Buckingham: Open University Press.

Game, Ann (1996) *Undoing the Social: Towards a Deconstructive Sociology*, Milton Keynes: Open University Press.

Gane, Mike (1991) *Baudrillard: Critical and Fatal Theory*, London: Routledge, pp. 29–39.

Gans, Herbert J. (1974) *Popular Culture and High Culture: An Analysis and Elevation of Taste*, New York: Basic Books.

—— (1978 [1966]) 'Popular Culture in America: Social Problem in a Mass Society or Social Asset in a Pluralist Society', in Peter Davison, Rolf Meyersohn and Edward Shils (eds) *Literary Taste, Culture, and Mass Communication*, Vol. I, Teaneck, NJ: Chadwyck-Healey.

Gardinier, Alain (1991) ' "World Music' or Sounds of the Times', *The UNESCO Courier*, March, 37–39.

Gatens, Moira (1996) Imaginary Bodies: Ethics, Power and Corporeality, London: Routledge.

Gay, Peter (1998) *The Bourgeois Experience: Victoria to Freud*, Vol. V: *The Pleasure Wars*, New York: W.W. Norton.

Gesellschaft Hackesche Höfe (1993) *Die Hackeschen Höfe. Geschichte und Geschichten einer Lebenswelt in der Mitte Berlins*, Berlin: Argon Verlag.

Giedion, S. (1967) *Space, Time and Architecture: The Growth of a New Tradition*, Cambridge, MA: Harvard University Press.

Gillett, P. (1990) *The Victorian Painters' World*, Gloucester: Alan Sutton.

Gimpel, Jean (1969) *The Cult of Art: Against Art and Artists*, London: Weidenfeld and Nicolson.

Gladstone, Valerie (1995) 'Nureyev Auction Breaks Records', *Dance Magazine*, May, LXIX(5), 21.

Goethe, J.W.G. (1985 [1790]) *Torquato Tasso*, London: Angel Books.

Goldmann, Lucien (1964) *The Hidden God*, London: Routledge.

Gombrich, E. (1959) *Art and Illusion: A Study in the Psychology of Pictorial Representation*, Oxford: Phaidon Press.

Goodwin, Andrew and Gore, Joe (1990) 'World Beat and the Cultural Imperialism Debate', *Socialist Review*, Vol. 20, pp. 63–80.

Gordon, Avery (1997) *Ghostly Matters: Haunting and the Sociological Imagination*, Minneapolis: University of Minnesota Press.

Gordon, C.M. (1988) *British Paintings of Subjects from the English Novel 1740–1870*, 2 vols, New York & London: Garland Publishing Inc.

Grana, Cesar (1964) *Bohemian and Bourgeois: French Society and the French Man of Letters in the 19th Century*, New York: Basic Books.

Gray, Herman (1996) 'Is Cultural Studies Inflated? The Cultural Economy of Cultural Studies in The United States', in Cary Nelson and Dilip Parameshwar Gaonkar (eds) *Disciplinarity and Dissent in Cultural Studies*, London: Routledge, pp. 203–16.

Greenberg, Clement (1986 [1939]) 'Avant-garde and Kitsch', in John O'Brian (ed.) *Clement Greenberg: The Collected Essays and Criticism*, Vol. I: *Perceptions and Judgements 1939–1944*, Chicago: University of Chicago Press.

Gregory, D. and Urry, J. (1985) *Social Relations and Spatial Structures*, Basingstoke: Macmillan.

Grossberg, Lawrence, Nelson, Cary and Treichler, Paula (eds) (1992) *Cultural Studies*, London: Routledge.

Grosz, E. (1994) *Volatile Bodies: Toward a Corporeal Feminism*, Bloomington: Indiana University Press.

Grosz, E. (2001) *Architecture from the Outside (Writing Architecture)*, Cambridge, MA: MIT Press.

Grout, D.J. (1988) *A Short History of Opera*, third edition, Columbia University Press.

Guilbault, Jocelyne (1993) *Zouk: World Music in the West Indies*, Chicago: University of Chicago Press.

—— (1996) 'Beyond the "World Music" Label: An Ethnography of Transnational Musical Practices', http://www2.rz.hu-berlin.de/fpm/texte/guilbau.htm.

—— (1997) 'Interpreting World Music: A Challenge in Theory and Practice', *Popular Music*, Vol. 16, No. 1, pp. 31–44.

—— (2001) 'World Music', in Simon Frith, Will Straw and John Street (eds) *The Cambridge Companion to Pop and Rock*, Cambridge: Cambridge University Press, pp. 176–92.

Habermas, Jurgen (1985) *The Philosophical Discourse of Modernity*, Cambridge: Polity Press.

—— (1997) 'Modern and Postmodern Architecture', in N. Leach (ed.) *Rethinking Architecture*, London: Routledge, pp. 227–35.

Hall, Stuart (1980) 'Cultural Studies and the Centre: Some Problematics and Problems', in D. Hobson, S. Hall, A. Lowe and P. Willis (eds) *Culture, Media, Language*, London: Hutchinson, pp. 15–47.

—— (1990) 'The Emergence of Cultural Studies and the Crisis of the Humanities', *October*, 53, pp. 11–23.

—— (1992) 'Cultural Studies and Its Theoretical Legacies', in L. Grossberg, C. Nelson and P. Treichler (eds) *Cultural Studies*, London: Routledge, pp. 277–86.

Hanna, Judith Lybbe (1988) *Dance, Sex and Gender*, Chicago: University of Chicago Press.

Haraway, Donna (ed.) (1989) 'Teddy Bear Patriarchy: Taxidermy in the Garden of Eden, New York City, 1908–1936', in *Primate Visions: Gender, Race, and Nature in the World of Modern Science*, New York: Routledge, pp. 26–58.

Hardy, F. (1938) 'Censorship and Film Societies', in C. Davy (ed.) *Footnotes to the Film*, London: Lovat Dickson Ltd, pp. 264–78.

Harries, K. (1998) *The Ethical Function of Architecture*, Cambridge, MA: MIT Press.

Harris, A.S. and Nead, L. (1978) *Women Artists: 1550–1950*. New York: Knopf.

Haskell, Francis (1963) *Patrons and Painters: A Study in the Relations between Italian Art and Society in the Age of the Baroque*, New York: Alfred A. Knopf.

Hatch, Martin (1989) 'Popular Music in Indonesia', in Simon Frith (ed.) *World Music, Politics and Social Change*, Manchester: Manchester University Press.

Hauser, Arnold (1982) *The Sociology of Art*, London: Routledge and Kegan Paul.

—— (1985 [1958]) *The Philosophy of Art History*, Evanston: Northwestern University Press.

—— (1991) *The Social History of Art*, 4 vols, London: Routledge.

Heelas, Paul (1996) *The New Age Movement*, Oxford: Blackwell.

Hegel, G.W.F. (1975a) *Aesthetics: Lectures on Fine Art*, Vol. I, Oxford: Clarendon Press.

—— (1975b) *Aesthetics: Lectures on Fine Art*, Vol. II, Oxford: Clarendon Press.

Heidegger, M. (1969) *Die Kunst und der Raum*, St Gallen: Erker.

Henery (2004) 'At Last A Weekend to Shout About', *The Times* (London), p. 1.

Henning, Edward B. (1960) 'Patronage and Style in the Arts: A Suggestion Concerning Their Relations', *Journal of Aesthetics and Art Criticism*, Vol. XVIII, April, pp. 464–71.

Hepworth, Mike (1995) 'Images of Old Age', in J. Coupland and J. Nussbaum (eds), *Handbook of Communication and Ageing Research*, New York: Erlbaum.

—— (2000) *Stories of Ageing*, Buckingham: Open University Press.

Herder, Johann Gottfried (1800) *Outlines of a Philosophy of the History of Man*, London: Johnson.

Hesmondhalgh, David (1998) 'Globalisation and Cultural Imperialism: A Case Study of the Muic Industry', in Ray Kiely and Phil Marfleet (eds) *Globalisation and the Third World*, London: Routledge.

—— (2000) 'International Times: Fusions, Exoticism, and Antiracism in Electronic Dance Music', in Georgina Born and David Hesmondhalgh (eds) *Western Music and Its Others: Difference, Representation and Appropriation in Music*, Berkeley: University of California Press, pp. 280–304.

Heynen, H. (1999) *Architecture and Modernity*, Cambridge, MA: MIT Press.

Hichberger, J. (1989) 'Old Soldiers', in R. Samuel (ed.) *Patriotism: The Making and Unmaking of British National Identity*, London and New York: Routledge.

Hill, J. (2000) 'The Rise and Fall of British Art Cinema: A Short History of the 1980s and 1990s', *Aura: Film Studies Journal*, Vol. 6, No. 3, pp. 18–32.

Holmes, Mary (2000) 'When Is the Personal Political? The President's Penis and Other Stories', *Sociology*, Vol. 34, No. 2, pp. 305–21.

Holt, Elizabeth Gilmore (1981) *The Art of All Nations: 1850–1873; The Emerging Role of Exhibitions and Critics*, Princeton: Princeton University Press.

Horkheimer, Max (1972) 'Art and Mass Culture', *Critical Theory: Selected Essays*, New York: Herder and Herder.

Horner, Bruce and Swiss, Thomas (2003) *Key Concepts in Popular Music and Culture*, Oxford: Blackwell.

Hume, David (1985 [1757]) 'Of the Standard of Taste', Eugene F. Miller (ed.) in *Essays: Moral, Political and Literary*, Indianapolis: Liberty Fund.

Huyssen, A. (1997) 'The Voids of Berlin', *Critical Inquiry*, Vol. 24, No. 1, pp. 57–81.

Iggers, Georg G. (1968) *The German Conception of History: The National Tradition of Historical Thought from Herder to the present*, Middletown: Wesleyan University Press 1968.

Illich, Ivan (1986) 'Body History', *Lancet*, Vol. 11, pp. 1325–27.

Inglis, David and Hughson, John (2003) *Confronting Culture: Sociological Vistas*, Cambridge: Polity.

Irigaray, L. (1985) *Speculum of the Other Woman*, Ithaca: Cornell University Press.

Ivins, W.M. Jr (1964) *Art and Geometry: A Study in Space Intuitions*, New York: Dover.

Jacobs, L. (1968 [1939]) *The Rise of the American Film: A Critical History*, New York: Teachers College Press.

Jalland, P. (1996) *Death in the Victorian Family*, Oxford: Oxford University Press.

James-Chakraborty, K. (2000) *German Architecture for a Mass Audience*, London and New York: Routledge.

Jameson, Fredric (1997) 'The Cultural Logic of Late Capitalism', in N. Leach (ed.) *Rethinking Architecture*, London: Routledge, pp. 238–47.

Jowers, Peter (1993) 'Beating New Tracks: WOMAD and the British World Music Movement', in Simon Miller (ed.) *The Last Post: Music After Modernism*, Manchester: Manchester University Press.

Kadushin, Charles (1976) 'Networks and circles in the Production of Culture', in Richard A. Peterson (ed.) *The Production of Culture*, Beverly Hills: Sage.

Kant, Immanuel (1992 [1790]) *Critique of Judgement*, Oxford: Oxford University Press.

—— (1999 [1787]) *Critique of Pure Reason*, Cambridge: Cambridge University Press.

Karatani, K. (1995) *Architecture as Metaphor: Language, Number, Money*, Cambridge, MA: MIT Press.

Kerman, J. (1985) *Musicology*, London: Fontana Books.

Korner, Stephan (1955) *Kant*, Harmondsworth: Pelican.

Kracauer, Siegfried (1995) 'Farewell to the Linden Arcade', *The Mass Ornament*, Cambridge, MA: Harvard University Press.

Kramer, Judith R. (1970) 'The Social Role of the Literary Critic', in Milton C. Albrecht, James H. Barnett and Mason Griff (eds) *The Sociology of Art and Literature: A Reader*, London: Gerald Duckworth.

Kraus, Richard Curt (1989) *Pianos and Politics in China: Middle-Class Ambitions and the Struggle Over Western Music*, Oxford: Oxford University Press.

Kristeva, Julia (1982) *Powers of Horror: An Essay on Abjection*, trans. L.S. Roudiez, New York: Columbia University Press.

Kuper, Adam (1999) *Culture: The Anthropologists' Account*, Cambridge, MA: Harvard University Press.

Ladd, B. (1997) *The Ghosts of Berlin*, Chicago: University of Chicago Press.

Lambourne, L. (1999) *Victorian Painting*, London: Phaidon Press.

Lamont, Michele (1992) 'Crisis or No Crisis: Culture and Theory in Sociology – The Humanities and Elsewhere', *Newsletter of the Sociology of Culture Section of the American Sociological Association*, Vol. 6, No. 3, Spring, pp. 8–9.

Lane, Jeremy (1999) *Pierre Bourdieu*, London: Pluto.

Lang, Gladys Engel and Lang, Kurt (1988) 'Recognition and Renown: The Survival of Artistic Reputations', *American Journal of Sociology*, Vol. 94, July, pp. 79–109.

Laurenson, Diana T. and Swingewood, Alan (1972) *The Sociology of Literature*, London: Paladin.

Leach, N. (ed.) (1997) *Rethinking Architecture*, London: Routledge.

—— (1999) *Architecture and Revolution: Contemporary Perspectives on Central and Eastern Europe*, London: Routledge.

Levine, Lawrence W. (1988) *Highbrow, Lowbrow: The Emergence of a Cultural Hierarchy in America*, Cambridge: Harvard University Press.

Leymarie, Isabelle (1991) 'Musiques Du Monde: Le Grande Méttssage', *Le Courrier de l'UNESCO*, March, p. 11.

Libeskind, D. (1992) *Erweiterung des Berlin Museums mit Abteilung Jüdisches Museum*, Berlin: Ernst & Sohn.

Lindenberger, H. (1984) *Opera: The Extravagant Art*, Ithaca, NY: Cornell University Press.

—— (1998) *Opera in History: From Monteverdi to Cage*, Palo Alto, CA: Stanford University Press.

Lindsay, V. (2000 [1915]) *The Art of the Moving Picture*, New York: Modern Library.

Ling, Jan (2003) 'Is "World Music" the "Classic Music" of Our Time?', *Popular Music*, Vol. 22, No. 2, May, pp. 235–40.

Lipsitz, George (1994) *Dangerous Crossroads: Popular Music, Postmodernism and the Poetics of Place*, London: Verso.

Long, Elizabeth (ed.) (1997) *From Sociology to Cultural Studies: New Perspectives*, Oxford: Blackwell.

Loos, A. (1982) 'Architektur', *Trotzdem*, Vienna: Prachner.

Loosely, David L. (2003) *Popular Music in Contemporary France: Authenticity, Politics, Debate*, Oxford: Berg.

Lopes, Paul (2002) *The Rise of a Jazz Art World*, New York: Cambridge University Press.

Low, R. (1971) *The History of the British Film 1918–1929*, London: George Allen & Unwin.

Low, R. (1985) *The History of the British Film 1929–1939: Film Making in 1930s Britain*, London: George Allen & Unwin.

Lowenthal, Leo (1957) *Literature and the Image of Man*, Boston: The Beacon Press.

Lowenthal, Leo (1961) *Literature, Popular Culture and Society*, Englewood Cliffs, NJ: Prentice Hall.

Luhmann, Niklas (2000) *Art as a Social System*, Stanford: Stanford University Press.

Lukacs, Georg (1971 [1923]) *History and Class Consciousness*, London: Merlin.

Macleod, D.S. (1996) *Art and the Victorian Middle Class: Money and the Making of Cultural Identity*, Cambridge: Cambridge University Press.

Mannheim, Karl (1956) *Essays on the Sociology of Culture*, London: Routledge.

—— (1985 [1936]) *Ideology and Utopia*, Orlando: Harcourt Brace Jovanovich.

Maquet, Jacques (1979) *Introduction to Aesthetic Anthropology*, Malibu: Undena Publications.

Marks, J.G. (1896) *The Life and Letters f Frederick Walker ARA*, London: Macmillan and Co Ltd.

Martindale, Andrew (1978) 'The Sociology of Female Artists', *Studies in Symbolic Interaction*, Vol. 3, No. 1, pp. 289–318.

Marx, Karl (1977 [1859]) *A Contribution to the Critique of Political Economy*, Moscow: Progress Publishers.

Marx, K. (1977) *Karl Marx. Selected Writings*, Oxford: Oxford University Press.

McArthur, C. (2001) 'Two Steps Forward, One Step Back: Cultural Struggle in the British Film Institute', *Journal of Popular British Cinema*, Vol. 4, pp. 112–27.

McCall, Michal M. and Howard S. Becker (1990) 'Introduction', in H.S. Becker and M.M. McCall (eds) *Symbolic Interaction and Cultural Studies*, Chicago: University of Chicago Press, pp. 1–15.

McClary, S. (1989) 'Constructions of Gender in Monteverdi's Dramatic Music', *Cambridge Opera Journal*, Vol. 1, No. 3, pp. 203–23.

McGuigan, Jim (1992) *Cultural Populism*, London: Routledge.

McKerrow, M. (1982) *The Faeds: A Biography*, Edinburgh: Canongate.

McLennan, Gregor (1998a) 'Sociology and Cultural Studies: Rhetorics of Disciplinary Identity', *History of the Human Sciences*, Vol. 11, No. 3, pp. 1–17.

—— (1998b) '*Fin de Sociologie*? The Dilemmas of Multidimentional Social Theory', *New Left Review* 230, pp. 58–90.

McRobbie, Angela (1990) 'Women in the Arts into the 1990s', *Alba*, September, pp. 4–12.

Meintjes, Louise (1994) 'Paul Simon's *Graceland*, South Africa and the Mediation of Musical Meaning', *Ethnomusicology*, Vol. 34, No. 1, Winter, pp. 37–73.

Meyer, Karl E. (1979) *The Art Museum: Power, Money, Ethics*, New York: William Morrow and Co.

Mitchell, Tony (1993) 'World Music and the Popular Music Industry: An Australian View', *Ethnomusicology*, Vol. 37, No. 3, pp. 309–37.

Montagu, I. (1970) *The Youngest Son: Autobiographical Sketches*, London: Lawrence & Wishart.

—— (1972) 'Interview: Ivor Montagu', *Screen*, Vol. 13, No. 3, pp. 71–112.

—— (1980 [1932]) 'The Film Society, London', *Cinema Quarterly* 1 (1), reprinted in D. Macpherson (ed.) *Traditions of Independence: British Cinema in the Thirties*. London: BFI Publishing, pp. 105–108.

Morris, E. (1994) *Victorian and Edwardian paintings in the Lady Lever Art Gallery (British Artists Born after 1810 Excluding the Early Pre-Raphaelites)*, London: HMSO.

Morris, E. and Roberts, E. (1998) *The Liverpool Academy and Other Exhibitions of Contemporary Art in Liverpool 1774–1867*, Liverpool: Liverpool University Press and National Museums and Galleries on Merseyside.

Morrison, J. (1989) *Rural Nostalgia: Painting in Scotland c.1860–1880*, University of St Andrews, Unpublished PhD thesis.

Moxey, Keith (1991) 'Semiotics and The Social History of Art', *New Literary History*, Vol. 22, No. 4, pp. 985–99.

Mulvey, Laura (1975) 'Visual Pleasure and Narrative Cinema', *Screen*, Vol. 16, No. 3, pp. 6–18.

Nead, L. (1992) *The Female Nude: Art, Obsenity and Sexuality*, London: Routledge.

Neale, S. (1981) 'Art Cinema as Institution', *Screen*, Vol. 22, No. 1, pp. 11–39.

Nelson, Cary (1991) 'Always Already Cultural Studies: Two Conferences and a Manifesto', *Journal of the Midwest Modern Language Association*, Vol. 14, No. 1, pp. 24–38.

Nettl, Bruno (1985) *The Western Impact on World Music: Change, Adaptation and Survival*, New York: Schirmer/Macmillan.

Newall, C. (1987) *Victorian Watercolours*, Oxford: Phaidon.

Newman, D. (2000) *Sociology: Exploring the Architecture of Everyday Life*, Pine Forge: Sage Publications Inc.

Nietzsche, Friedrich (1967) 'The Genealogy of Morals', *Genealogy of Morals and Ecce Homo*, New York: Random House.

Nochlin, Linda (1973) 'Why Have There Been No Great Women Artists?', in Thomas B. Hess and Elizabeth C. Baker (eds) *Art and Sexual Politics: Women's Liberation, Women Artists, and Art History*, New York: Macmillan.

Ostrower, Francie (1995) *Why the Wealthy Give*, Princeton, NJ: Princeton University Press.

Oudshoorn, N. (1994) *Beyond the Natural Body: The Archaeology of Sex Hormones*, New York, London: Routledge.

Pacini, Deborah Hernandez (1993) 'A View From the South: Spanish Caribbean Perspectives on World Beat', *The World of Music*, Vol. 35, pp. 48–69.

Pahlen, Kurt (1949) *Music of the World: A History*, New York: Crown Publishers.

Panofsky, Erwin (1951) *Gothic Architecture and Scholasticism*, Latrobe, Penn.: The Archabbey Press.

Parker, Rozsike and Pollock, Griselda (1981) *Old Mistresses: Women, Art and Ideology*, London: Pandora.

Perna, Vincenzo (1996) 'Latin Lovers: Salsa Musicians and Their Audience in London', in Paul Rutten (ed.) *Music, Culture and Society in Europe*, Part II, Brussels: European Music Office, pp. 104–15.

Peterson, Richard A. (1972) 'A Process Model of the Folk, Populr, and Fine Art Phases of Jazz', in C. Nanry (ed.) *American Music: From Storyville to Woodstock*, New Brunswick, NJ: Rutgers University Press.

—— (1994) 'Culture Studies through the Production Perspective: Progress and Prospects', in D. Crane (ed.) *The Sociology of Culture: Emerging Theoretical Perspectives*, Oxford: Blackwell, pp. 163–89.

Peterson, Richard A. and Kern, Roger M. (1996) 'Changing Highbrow Taste: From Snob to Omnivore', *American Sociological Review*, Vol. 61, No. 5, pp. 900–907.

Pevsner, Nicholas (1940) *Academies of Art: Past and Present*, Cambridge: Cambridge University Press.

—— (1945) *An Outline of European Architecture*, London: Pelican.

Pfister, John (1996) 'The Americanization of Cultural Studies', in J. Storey (ed.) *What is Cultural Studies?* London: Arnold, pp. 287–99.

Plattner, Stuart (1996) *High Art Down Home*, Chicago: University of Chicago Press.

Poggioli, Renato (1971) *The Theory of the Avant-Garde*, Cambridge: Harvard University Press.

Pointon, Marcia (1986) *Mulready*, London: Victoria and Albert Museum.

Pollock, Griselda (1988) *Vision and Difference: Femininity, Feminism and the Histories of Art*, London: Routledge.

Price, Sally (1989) *Primitive Art in Civilized Places*, Chicago: Chicago University Press.

Reitlinger, Gerald (1961) *The Economics of Taste: The Rise and Fall of Picture Prices 1760–1960*, London: Barrie and Rockcliff.

Rennell, T. (2000) *Last Days of Glory: The Death of Queen Victoria*, London: Penguin.

Rice, T. (2000) 'World Music in Europe', in T. Rice, J. Proter and C. Goertzen (eds) *The Garland Encyclopedia of Music*, Vol. 8, 'Europe,' New York: Garland Reference Library of the Humanities, pp. 224–30.

Robertson, Allen and Hutera, Donald (1990) *The Dance Handbook*, Boston: G.K. Hall & Co.

Robertson, Roland (1992) *Globalization: Social Theory and Global Culture*, London: Sage.

—— (1995) 'Glocalization: Time-Space, Homogeneity, Heterogeneity', in Mike Featherstone and Scott Lash (eds) *Global Modernities*, London: Sage.

Robinson, Deanna Campbell, Buck, Elizabeth B. and Cuthbert, Marlene (1991) *Music at the Margins: Popular Music and Global Cultural Diversity*, Nebury Park, CA: age.

Robinson, P. (1985) *Opera and Ideas*, Ithaca, NY: Cornell University Press.

Rose, G. (1993) *Feminism and Geography: The Limits of Geographical Knowledge*, Cambridge: Polity Press.

Rose, G. (2000) 'Practising Photography: An Archive, a Study, Some Photographs and a Researcher', *Journal of Historical Geography*, Vol. 26, No. 4, pp. 555–71.

Rost, A., Havemeiste, Heinz and Grics Annette (1992) *Tacheles: Alltag im Chaos*, Berlin: Elefantenpress.

Rostand, E. (1991) *Opera in Seventeenth Century Venice*, Berkeley, CA: University of California Press.

Rosand, Ellen (1992) *Opera in Seventeenth Century Venice: The Creation of a Genre*, Berkeley: University of California Press.

Rotha, P. (1930) *The Film Till Now*, London: Cape.

Rothehbuhler, Eric (1988) 'The Liminal Fight: Mass Strikes as Ritual and Interpretation', in J.C. Alexander (ed.) *Durkheimian Sociology: Cultural Studies*, Cambridge: Cambridge University Press, pp. 66–90.

Rousseau, Jean-Jacques (1933) *Confessions*, Book II, Boston: The Bibliophilist Society.

Rutten, Paul (1996) 'Global Sounds and Local Brews', in Paul Rutten (ed.) *Music, Culture and Society in Europe*, Part II, Brussels: European Music Office, pp. 64–76.

Ruzek, S. (1978) *The Women's Health Movement*, New York: Praeger.

Ryan, T. (1980) 'Film and Political Organisations in Britain 1929–39', in D. Macpherson (ed.) *Traditions of Independence: British Cinema in the Thirties*, London: BFI Publishing, pp. 51–69.

—— (1983) ' "The New Road to Progress": The Use and Production of Films by the Labour Movement, 1929–39', in J. Curran and V. Porter (eds) *British Cinema History*, London: Weidenfeld & Nicolson, pp. 113–28.

Said, Edward (1993) *Culture and Imperialism*, London: Chatto and Windus.

Samson, J. (1986) 'The Film Society, 1925–1939', in C. Barr (ed.) *All Our Yesterdays: 90 Years of British Cinema*, London: BFI Publishing, pp. 306–13.

Sandström, Pär (1993) 'Operan/Kungliga Teatern: En Publikstudie', unpublished report, Stockholm.

Sarris, Andrew (1968) *The American Cinema: Directors and Directions 1929–1968*, New York: E.P. Dutton.

Saxon Mills, J. (1923) *Life and Letters of Sir Hubert Herkomer*, London: Hutchinson & Co.

Scaff, L. (1995) 'Social Theory, Rationalism and the Architecture of the City: Fin-de-siecle Thematics', *Theory, Culture and Society*, Vol. 12, No. 2, pp. 63–85.

Schudson, Michael (1997) 'Cultural Studies and the Social Construction of "Social Construction": Notes from "Teddy Bear Patriarchy" ', in E. Long (ed.) *From Sociology to Cultural Studies: New Perspectives*, Oxford: Blackwell, pp. 379–98.

Seidman, Steven (1994) *Contested Knowledge: Social Theory in the Postmodern Era*, Oxford: Blackwell.

—— (1997) 'Relativizing Sociology: The Challenge of Cultural Studies', in E. Long (ed.) *From Sociology to Cultural Studies: New Perspectives*, Oxford: Blackwell, pp. 37–61.

Sherwood, Steven Jay, Philip Smith and Jeffrey Alexander (1993) 'The British Are Coming…Again! The Hidden Agenda of "Cultural Studies" ', *Contemporary Sociology*, Vol. 22, No. 3, pp. 370–75.

Shilling, Chris (1993) *The Body and Social Theory*, London: Sage.

Shiner, Larry (2001) *The Invention of Art: A Cultural History*, Chicago: Chicago University Press.

Shires, L.M. (ed.) (1992) *Rewriting The Victorians: Theory, History and The Politics of Gender*, New York and London: Routledge.

Showalter, Elaine (1985) 'Feminist Criticism in the Wilderness', in Elaine Showalter (ed.) *The New Feminist Criticism: Essays on Women, Literature, and Theory*, New York: Pantheon, pp. 243–70.

Shrum, Wesley (1991) 'Critics and Publics: Cultural Mediation in Highbrow and Popular Performing Arts', *American Journal of Sociology*, Vol. 97, No. 2, pp. 347–75.

Shuker, Roy (1998) *Key Concepts in Popular Music*, London: Routledge.

Silverstone, Roger (1994) 'The Power of the Ordinary: On Cultural Studies and the Sociology of Culture', *Sociology*, Vol. 28, No. 4, pp. 991–1001.

Simmel, Georg (1997) 'The Berlin Trade Exhibition', in D. Frisby and M. Featherstone (eds) *Simmel on Culture*, London: Sage.

Slobin, Mark (1994) 'Music in Diaspora: The View From Euro-America', *Diaspora*, Vol. 3, Part 3, pp. 243–51.

—— (2003) 'The Destiny of "Diaspora" in Ethnomusicology', in Martin Clayton, Trevor Herbert and Richard Middleton (eds) *The Cultural Study of Music: A Critical Introduction*, London: Routledge, pp. 284–96.

Smith, Dorothy E. (1987) *The Everyday World as Problematic*, Boston: Northeastern University Press.

—— (1990) *Texts, Facts and Femininity*, London: Routledge.

Smythe, D.W., Parker, B.L. and Lewis, C.A. (1953) 'Portrait of an Art-Theater Audience', *Quarterly of Film, Radio and Television*, Vol. 8, No. 1, pp. 28–50.

Social Research (1978) Vol. 45, No. 2 (Summer). Special issue, 'The Production of Culture'.

Sociological Theory (1991) Vol. 9, No. 2 (Fall). 'Symposium on Postmodernism'.

Sorell, Walter (1981) *Dance in Its Time*, New York: Columbia University Press.

Spencer, Herbert (1961 [1897]) 'The Factors of Social Phenomena', in Talcott Parsons, Shils, Edward, Naegele, K.D. and Pitts, Jesse R. (eds) *Theories of Society*, Vol. II, Glencoe: Free Press.

Spottiswoode, R. (1935) *A Grammar of the Film: An Analysis of Film Technique*, London: Faber and Faber.

Stael, Madame de (Anne-Louise-Germaine) (1803) *A Treatise on Ancient and Modern Literature: Illustrated by striking references to the principal events and characters that have distinguished the French Revolution*, London: Cawthorn.

Stanley, Liz (1999) 'Debating Feminist Theory: More Questions than Answers?', *Women's Studies Journal*, Vol. 15, pp. 87–106.

Stokes, Martin (2003) 'Globalization and the Politics of World Music', in Martin Clayton Trevor Herbert, Richard Middleton (eds) *The Cultural Study of Music: A Critical Introduction*, London: Routledge, pp. 297–308.

Strauss, Anselm (1970) 'The Art School and Its Students: A Study and an Interpretation', in Milton C. Albrecht, James H. Barnett and Mason Griff (eds) *The Sociology of Art and Literature: A Reader*, London: Gerald Duckworth.

Strong, Phil (1979) 'Sociological Imperialism and the Profession of Medicine', *Social Science and Medicine*, Vol. 13A, pp. 199–215.

Stuart, Otis (1995) *Perpetual Motion*, New York: Simon & Schuster.

Sutcliffe, T. (1996) *Believing in Opera*, London: Faber.

Sydie, R.A. (1989) 'Humanism, Patronage, and the Question of Women's Artistic Genius in the Italian Renaissance', *Journal of Historical Sociology*, Vol. 2, No. 3, pp. 175–205.

Synott, Anthony (1993) *The Body Social: Symbolism, Self and Society*, London: Routledge.

Sztompka, Piotr (1993) *The Sociology of Social Change*, Oxford: Blackwell.

Tambling, J. (1996) *Opera and the Culture of Fascism*, Manchester: Manchester University Press.

Taylor, J.R. and Brooke, B. (1969) *The Art Dealers*, New York: Charles Scribner's Sons.

Taylor, Timothy (1997) *Global Pop: World Music, World Markets*, London: Routledge.

Theory and Society (1992) Vol. 21, No. 4 (August). Special issue, 'A Forum on Postmodernism'.

Thompson, E.P. (1978) 'The Peculiarities of the English', *The Poverty of Theory*, London: Merlin.

Tickner, L. (1978) 'The Body Politic. Female Sexuality and Women Artists since 1970', *Art History*, Vol. 1, No. 2, pp. 236–51.

Tomlinson, John (1997) *Cultural Imperialism: A Critical Introduction*, London: Pinter.

Tuchman, Gaye (1989) *Edging Women Out: Victorian Novelists, Publishers and Social Change*, New Haven: Yale University Press.

Tudor, Andrew (1999) *Decoding Culture*, London: Sage.

Turner, Bryan (1996) *For Weber: Essays on the Sociology of Fate*, London: Sage.

Urry, John (2000) *Sociology Beyond Societies*, London: Routledge.

Venturi, Robert, Scott Brown, Denise and Izenour, Steven (1992) *Learning from Las Vegas* (revised edition), Cambridge, MA: MIT Press.

Vice, S. (1998) 'Psychoanalytic Theory', in S. Jackson and J. Jones (eds) *Contemporary Feminist Theorists*, Edinburgh: Edinburgh University Press.

Vico, Giambattista (1999 [1744]) *The New Science*, Harmondsworth: Penguin.

Volkov, Solomon (1986) *Balanchine's Tchaikovsky*, New York: Anchor Books.

Wahjudi, C. (1999) *Metroloops: Berliner Kulturentwürfe*, Bremen: Ullstein.

Walby, Sylvia (1995) 'Is Citizenship Gendered?', *Sociology*, Vol. 28, No. 2, pp. 379–95.

Warde, Alan, Martins, Lydia and Olsen, Wendy (1999) 'Consumption and the Problem of Variety: Cultural Omnivorousness, Social Distinction and Dining Out', *Sociology*, Vol. 33, No. 1, February, pp. 105–27.

Watt, Ian (1985 [1957]) *The Rise of the Novel: Studies in Defoe, Richardson and Fielding*, Harmondsworth: Penguin.

Weber, Max (1958) *The Rational and Social Foundations of Music*, Southern Illinois University Press,.

Weber, W. (1977) 'Mass Culture and the Reshaping of European Musical Taste, 1770–1870', *International Review of the Aesthetics and Sociology of Music*, Vol. 8, No. 1, pp. 5–21.

Weiskel, Thomas (1976) *The Romantic Sublime: Studies in the Structure and Psychology of Transcendence*, Baltimore: Johns Hopkins University Press.

White, Harrison C. and White, Cynthia (1965) *Canvases and Careers: Institutional Change in the French Painting World*, New York: Wiley.

Willcox, T. (1990) Soviet Films, Censorship and the British Government: A Matter of Public Interest', *Historical Journal of Film, Radio and Television*, Vol. 10, No. 3, pp. 275–92.

Williams, Raymond (1977) *Marxism and Literature*, Oxford: Oxford University Press.

—— (1981) *Culture*, London and Glasgow: Fontana.

Williams, S. and Bendelow, G. (1998) *The Lived Body: Sociological Themes, Embodied Issues*, London: Routledge.

Willis, Paul, Jones, S. Canaan, J. and Hurd, G. (1990) *Common Culture*, Milton Keynes: Open University Press.

Wiora, Walter (1965) *The Four Ages of Music*, New York: Norton.

Wise, M.Z. (1998) *Capital Dilemma. Germany's Search for a New Architecture of Democracy*, New York: Princeton Architectural Press.

Witkin, Robert W. (1993) 'From the "Touch" of the Ancients to the "Sight" of the Moderns: Social Structure and the Semiotics of Aesthetic Form', in Scholhammer, Georg and Kravagna, Christian (eds), *Real Text: Reflections on the Periphery of the Subject*, Klagenfurt: Verlag Ritter, pp. 89–134.

Witkin, Robert (1995) *Art and Social Structure*, Cambridge: Polity Press.

Wolff, Janet (1981) *The Social Production of Art*, Basingstoke: Macmillan.

—— (1983) *Aesthetics and the Sociology of Art*, first edition, London: George Allen and Unwin.

—— (1990) *Feminine Sentences: Essays on Women and Culture*, Cambridge: Polity Press.

—— (1993) *Aesthetics and the Sociology of Art*, second edition, Basingstoke: Macmillan.

Wolff, Janet and Seed, John (eds) (1988) *The Culture of Capital: Art, Power and the Nineteenth Century Middle Class*, Manchester: Manchester University Press.

Wood, C. (1978) *The Dictionary of Victorian Painters*, second edition, Woodbridge: Antique Collectors' Club.

—— (1988) *Paradise Lost: Paintings of English Country Life and Landscape 1850–1914*, London: Barrie and Jenkins.

Woodley, Karin (1985) 'The Inner Sanctum', *Artrage*, No. 9/10, pp. 89–101.

Wulff, Helena (1998) *Ballet Across Borders*, Oxford: Berg.

—— (2000) 'Access to a Closed World: Methods for a Multi-Locale Study on Ballet as a Career', in V. Amit (ed.) *Constructing the Field*, London: Routledge.

—— (2002) 'Aesthetics at the Ballet: Looking at "National" Style, Body, and Clothing in the London Dance World', in N. Rapport (ed.) *British Subjects*, Oxford: Berg.

—— (2003) 'Steps on Screen: Technoscapes, Visualization and Globalization in Dance', in C. Garsten and H. Wulff (eds), *New Technologies at Work*, Oxford: Berg.

Yeldham, C. (1984) *Women Artists in Nineteenth-Century France and England*, New York & London: Garland Publishing Inc.

Young, Iris Marion (1990) 'Throwing like a Girl: A Phenomenology of Feminine Body Comportment, Motility and Spatiality', in Young, Iris Marion, *Throwing like a Girl and other essays in Feminist Philosophy and Social Theory*, Bloomington: Indiana University Press.

Zolberg, Vera (1983) 'Changing Patterns of Patronage in the Arts', in Jack B. Kamerman and Rosanne Martorella (eds) *Performers and Performances: The Sociology of Artistic Work*, New York: Praeger.

—— (1992) 'Barrier or Leveller? The Case of the Art Museum', in Michele Lamont and Marcel Fournier (eds) *Cultivating Differences: Symbolic boundaries and the Making of Inequality*, Chicago: University of Chicago Press, pp. 187–209.

Index